A. B. SIMPSON

A. B. SIMPSON

HIS MESSAGE AND IMPACT
on the
THIRD GREAT AWAKENING

Michael G. Yount

Foreword by Garth M. Rosell

WIPF & STOCK · Eugene, Oregon

A. B. SIMPSON
His Message and Impact on the Third Great Awakening

Copyright © 2016 Michael G. Yount. All rights reserved. Except for brief quotations in critical publications or reviews, no part of this book may be reproduced in any manner without prior written permission from the publisher. Write: Permissions, Wipf and Stock Publishers, 199 W. 8th Ave., Suite 3, Eugene, OR 97401.

Wipf & Stock
An Imprint of Wipf and Stock Publishers
199 W. 8th Ave., Suite 3
Eugene, OR 97401

www.wipfandstock.com

PAPERBACK ISBN: 978-1-4982-8280-2
HARDCOVER ISBN: 978-1-4982-8282-6
EBOOK ISBN: 978-1-4982-8281-9

Manufactured in the U.S.A.   10/24/16

To my wife, Sue Yount, thank you for your love
and encouragement throughout our life.

CONTENTS

Foreword by Garth M. Rosell | ix
Acknowledgements | xi
Introduction | xiii

Chronology of the Life and Ministry of Albert Benjamin Simpson | xv
Chronology of "The Great Century" (1792–1919) | xix

- I   The Great Century | 1
- II   A. B. Simpson: The Forgotten Man in Renewal | 23
- III   Simpson's Place in Evangelism | 54
- IV   Simpson's Impact on the Holiness Movement | 66
- V   Simpson's Influence on the Healing Movement | 92
- VI   Simpson's Involvement in the Premillennial Movement | 107
- VII   Simpson's Contributions to Urban and Worldwide Evangelization | 120
- VIII   Simpson's Message and Its Ramifications on the Church Today | 154

Appendix | 173

Bibliography | 191

Index | 199

FOREWORD

"Fame," the wise old adage reminds us, "is fleeting," and one generation's heroes are often largely forgotten by the next. Some, of course, deserve to be forgotten, while others need to be remembered as inspirational examples of uncommon wisdom, outstanding leadership, and good old-fashioned common sense. Albert Benjamin Simpson, the distinguished founder of the Christian and Missionary Alliance, clearly belongs among those who are eminently worth remembering. Pastor, theologian, author, evangelist, educator, hymn-writer, and poet, A. B. Simpson, as he was known by thousands of his contemporary admirers, provides today's global Christian church with a clear and much-needed voice.

Thankfully, we now have a wonderful new tool for rediscovering and exploring the life and ministry of this truly amazing servant of God. Michael Yount's well-researched and beautifully written new book provides exactly what we have needed to begin this adventure, and the gifted editors at Wipf & Stock Publishers are to be congratulated in making it available in this exciting new volume. Indeed, Simpson's own insatiable hunger to reach a needy world with the life-giving gospel of Jesus Christ; his abiding concern for the poor, the unwanted, the infirmed, the neglected, and the homeless; and his passionate commitment to the proclamation of Christ as Savior, Sanctifier, Healer, and Coming King are as needed in our own day as they were in his.

Born on Prince Edward Island in 1843, Simpson was raised in a Christian home and converted under the ministry of H. Grattan Guinness in 1859. After graduating from Toronto's Knox College in 1865, he was ordained by the Presbyterian Church in Canada and subsequently served as the pastor of Knox Presbyterian Church (Ontario), Chestnut Street Presbyterian Church (Louisville), Thirteenth Street Presbyterian Church (New York City), and the New York Tabernacle (New York City). Deeply touched by the physical and spiritual needs of the thousands of immigrants who were arriving daily in New York City during the final decades of the nineteenth century, Simpson searched for more effective means of addressing their physical needs, of providing much-needed educational resources, and of sharing with them the joyous good news of new life in Jesus Christ. The "Christian church," as Simpson phrased it in *A Larger Christian Life* (1890), "can be at once the mother and home of every form of help and blessing which Jesus came to give to lost and suffering men, the birthplace and the home of souls, the fountain of healing and cleansing, the sheltering home for the orphan and distressed, the school for the culture and training of God's children, the armory where they are equipped for the battle of the Lord and the army which fights those battles in His name."[1]

For anyone who hungers for a more authentic faith, a deeper commitment to the spread of the glorious gospel, a more profound experience of life in Christ, and a more active engagement with a needy world, this book is for you! It will engage your mind, warm your heart, and broaden your vision of all that Christian life can be.

Garth M. Rosell
Senior Research Professor of Church History
Gordon-Conwell Theological Seminary
Hamilton, Massachusetts

---

1. Simpson, *Larger Christian Life*, 278–79.

ACKNOWLEDGEMENTS

So many people have helped make writing this book possible. These are just a few of the people who directly contributed to the writing of this book, but there were many along the way who encouraged me to keep at it. A special thanks goes to them. Any the success this book may see is because of those people who have helped make it possible. Special thanks must go to the people at Phillipsburg Alliance Church who gave me the time to work on this project. Ultimately, it is God who deserves all the credit and glory; it was he who got this work done. I can only take credit for its shortcomings.

First, I want to thank Garth Rosell, who as my advisor on my dissertation read and directed this work. He really was the one who helped develop the idea for the book. Also, a special thanks to Robert Mayer, the librarian at Gordon-Conwell Theological Seminary at the Charlotte campus, who also aided in this project. This text began as a part of my Doctor of Ministry project and eventually evolved into this current book.

A special thanks goes to Donna Wineberg, who read and typed this entire manuscript. It took a tremendous amount of work and a special ability to interpret my handwriting. My colleague Randall Nelson edited the writing and came up with many helpful suggestions in getting the book in readable form.

A special thanks goes out to all those who agreed to be interviewed for this book. They were a tremendous help in seeing the impact of Simpson on the Christian and Missionary Alliance today, and they helped make this book possible as well. A special thanks to Daniel Evearitt, David Fessenden, Mark Hanes Sr., Barry Jordan, Peter Nanfelt, John Soper, Ron Walborn, and the late Larry Zulauf as well as the late George Reitz.

Most of all, I want to thank my wife, Sue, who painstakingly read the original manuscript in handwritten form. She edited and corrected it. It

Acknowledgements

took many hours, and she did a wonderful job and deserves much of the credit for the finished work.

On behalf of those who labored in this work, it is my hope you will be blessed by the reading of it.

Michael Yount
March 5, 2016
Phillipsburg, NJ

INTRODUCTION

I have had an interest in Albert Benjamin Simpson for over thirty years. It began shortly after I became a Christian. The person who shared the gospel with me and discipled me took me to a Christian and Missionary Alliance Church. It was there that I first heard of A. B. Simpson, the founder of the Christian and Missionary Alliance denomination. It was at the First Alliance Church in Columbus, Ohio, that I first heard of the Fourfold Gospel and the distinctive biblical message that characterized Simpson's preaching. It was while I was at this same church that I began to read some of Simpson's works such as *The Four-Fold Gospel*[1] and *A Larger Christian Life*. It was there that I read two biographies of Simpson's life: *Wingspread* by A. W. Tozer and *A. B. Simpson: His Life and Work* by A. E. Thompson. Both books helped generate a personal interest in A. B. Simpson that has continued to the present.

Years later, I became an Alliance pastor. Going through the ordination process, I was again exposed to Simpson and his message of the Fourfold Gospel, although in much greater detail. During my time as a pastor in the Alliance, my interest in Simpson steadily increased. Over time, I endeavored to learn more from Simpson's works, but my interest did not come to full fruition until I was a student at Princeton Theological Seminary. While working on my Master's of Theology in Church History, a professor of American Church History told me that there had yet to be a definitive work written on A. B. Simpson and his impact on the church. As I began my doctoral study program at Gordon-Conwell Theological Seminary in the program's "Revival and Renewal: Renewing the Congregational Life"

---

1. Simpson, *Four-Fold Gospel*. The original title of Simpson's *The Four-Fold Gospel* had a hyphen between the words "Four" and "Fold." The hyphen was dropped and the term came to be spelled "Fourfold." Newer reprints of this work use the corrected spelling.

Introduction

track, I had the opportunity to write a thesis on A. B. Simpson as part of my studies.

The question must be asked, "What is revival?" Walter Kaiser defines it as "the restoration of something to its true nature and purpose. In as much as all of us were made to glorify God, revival simply fulfills his desire that we might know him in the fullness of his spirit and declare his praise to the ends of the earth."[2] Keith Hardman goes further to elaborate on revival. He states,

> The words revival or awakening may be defined as the restoration of God's people after a period of indifference and decline. There are two main thrusts: (1) The conversion or salvation of a number of unbelievers, and (2) the re-establishment of biblical truth so that the church is built up and empowered for the work of God in a lost and dying world.[3]

As I examined the Third Great Awakening, I discovered the great impact that Simpson had on the Awakening. Simpson's life and ministry were intricately interwoven with the Awakening, but I found that very little had been written to demonstrate this fact. This explains the rationale for why this book, *A. B. Simpson: His Message and Impact on the Third Great Awakening*, needed to be written. The question I asked was "What impact did Simpson have on the Third Great Awakening, and how has this impact influenced the modern church and the denomination he founded, the Christian and Missionary Alliance?" This is the question I will attempt to answer in this book.

Simpson's life as a minister and leader corresponded to the period of the Third Great Awakening and, as a result, he would play an important role in that Awakening. Before exploring the life of A. B. Simpson, we need to consider the historical period and environmental milieu he ministered in. In chapter 1, titled "The Great Century," we will look at what was going on in the Christian church during this important period.

---

2. Kaiser, *Revive Us Again*, ix.
3. Hardman, *Seasons of Refreshing*, 16.

CHRONOLOGY OF THE LIFE AND MINISTRY OF ALBERT BENJAMIN SIMPSON

1843—Albert Benjamin Simpson was born on December 15, 1843 in Bayview, Prince Edward Island, Canada.

1857—Simpson's nervous breakdown and first religious crisis.

1861—On January 19, Simpson makes a solemn covenant to God. He totally dedicates himself to God.[1]

1861—In October, Simpson enters Knox College, a seminary of the Presbyterian Church of Canada in Toronto.

1865—In April, Simpson graduates from Knox College.

1865—On August 15, Simpson receives a call to be a pastor of Knox Presbyterian Church in Hamilton, Canada.

1865—On September 12, Simpson is ordained for the ministry in the Presbyterian Church of Canada.

1865—Simpson marries Margaret Henry on September 13 in Toronto, Canada.

1873—Simpson preaches at the Evangelical Alliance Conference in October in New York City.

1873—Simpson resigns from Knox Presbyterian Church in Hamilton to take a call from the Chestnut Street Presbyterian Church in Louisville, Kentucky.

---

1. See Thompson, *A. B. Simpson*. Simpson's covenant is given in its entirety, and he wrote two rededications on it: one on September 1, 1863, and a second on April 18, 1878.

Chronology of the Life and Ministry of Albert Benjamin Simpson

1874—Simpson begins his ministry as pastor of the Chestnut Street Presbyterian Church in January.

1874—Simpson has a crisis experience of being filled with the Holy Spirit after attending the Christian Worker's Conference sponsored by the Moody Evangelistic Association.

1874—Simpson launches a united crusade with the churches in Louisville together with Major Daniel Whittle and P. P. Bliss. This was the beginning of a religious awakening in Louisville.

1877—Simpson receives his missionary vision in a dream of seeing the world without Christ.

1879—Simpson resigns from Chestnut Street Presbyterian Church on November 6, 1879.

1879—Simpson begins his ministry on December 9 at the Thirteenth Street Presbyterian Church in New York City.

1880—Simpson launches the first illustrated missionary magazine, *Gospel to All Lands*.

1881—Simpson experiences divine healing in late July or early August at Old Orchard, Maine. He had heard a message on divine healing from Dr. Charles Cullis.

1881—Simpson resigns on November 6 from the Thirteenth Street Presbyterian Church. The next day he resigned from the Presbyterian ministry.

1881—On November 20, Simpson holds his first meeting with seven people at Caledonian Hall on Eighth Avenue and Thirteenth Street in New York City.

1882—Simpson starts the New York Gospel Tabernacle with thirty-five members on February 10 in New York City.

1882—Simpson begins another missionary journal, *The Word, the Work, and the World*.

1883—Simpson starts the Berachah Home for Healing.

1883—On October 1, 1882, Simpson and the Gospel Tabernacle open the Missionary Training College, one of the first Bible Colleges in North America.

Chronology of the Life and Ministry of Albert Benjamin Simpson

1884—Simpson holds his first "deeper life" and missionary convention at the Gospel Tabernacle.

1889—The Gospel Tabernacle erects its first permanent building complex on the east side of Eighth Avenue and Forty-fourth Street in New York City.

1889—In the summer at Old Orchard, Maine, the Christian Alliance and the Evangelical Missionary Alliance are organized.

1897—The Christian Alliance and the Evangelical Missionary Alliance merge in April to form the Christian and Missionary Alliance.

1897—The Missionary Training Institute moves to Nyack, New York. Simpson also moves his residence to Nyack.

1917—The Christian and Missionary Alliance has 292 missionaries and 270 Alliance evangelists and superintendents in the United States and Canada.

1919—Simpson dies on October 25 at Nyack, New York.

CHRONOLOGY OF "THE GREAT CENTURY" (1792—1919)

1792—William Carey publishes "An Enquiry into the Obligation of Churches to Use Means for the Conversion of the Heathen."

1793—William Carey goes to India as a missionary.

1800—The Second Great Awakening begins at Yale University in the East and Cane Ridge in Kentucky in the West.

1807—Robert Morrison goes to China as a missionary.

1810—Robert Moffet goes to South Africa as a missionary.

1810—American Board of Commissioners for Foreign Missions is founded (First American Missions Board).

1816—American Bible Society is founded.

1821—Charles Finney is converted and begins his ministry.

1840—Phoebe Palmer begins her Holiness ministry.

1843—A. B. Simpson is born.

1858—William Boardman publishes "The Higher Christian Life."

1857—Businessman's Prayer Meeting begins in New York City, which initiates the Third Great Awakening.

1859—Darwin publishes *On the Origin of the Species*.

1861-1865—American Civil War.

1865—Hudson Taylor founds the China Inland Mission.

1865—The Salvation Army is founded in London by William Booth.

Chronology of "The Great Century" (1792–1919)

1867—John Inskeep founds the National Camp Meeting Association for the Promotion of Holiness.

1873-1875—Moody and Sankey host evangelistic meetings in Great Britain.

1875—The Keswick Convention is founded in Great Britain.

1880—The Salvation Army comes to the United States.

1882—A. B. Simpson founds the Gospel Tabernacle in New York City.

1886—D. L. Moody founds the Student Volunteer Movement.

1897—The Christian and Missionary Alliance comes into existence.

1897—Charles Sheldon publishes *In His Steps*.

1904—Welsh Revival.

1906—Azusa Street Revival.

1914-1918—Word War I.

1917—Walter Raushenbusch publishes "A Theology for the Social Gospel."

1919—A. B. Simpson dies in Nyack, New York.

I

THE GREAT CENTURY

Introduction

The church historian Kenneth Scott Latourette called the period of the church from AD 1800 to 1914 "The Great Century of the Church." He referred to it this way because of the worldwide expansion of the church during this period. He writes, "In geographic extent, the movements issuing from it, and in its effect upon the race, the nineteenth century Christianity had a far larger place in human history than at any previous time."[1] There were a number of factors that led to the expansion of the church, and we will be looking at them in this chapter.

The main focus of the book will be Albert Benjamin Simpson and the role he played in the Third Great Awakening.

This was a time of great changes in the church, possibly the most changes since the birth of the church in the first century. It was a time of excitement, growth, and great outreach by the church. During this period, men such as Asahel Nettleton, Charles Finney, and D. L. Moody led thousands to Christ and brought them into the church. Moody preached to more people in his lifetime than anyone else until Billy Graham began his ministry after World War II. Finney and Moody's impact was felt in North America and in Great Britain. It was D. L. Moody and Ira Sankey

---

1. Latourette, *History of the Expansion of Christianity*, 1.

who helped spread the revival to the British Isles. After ministering in the British Isles, they came to the United States to minister.

The Great Century was a period of missionary outreach. It began with a British cobbler-turned-minister, William Carey. Carey went to India in 1793 and generated interest in missions work literally to the ends of the earth. In the first half of the nineteenth century, the focus of missions was on the coastal regions of Asia and Africa. The missionaries would follow the colonial powers as they settled in these countries. Later in the nineteenth century, Hudson Taylor, a missionary to China, left the safety of the colonial-controlled areas and went to the interior of the country, away from his countrymen. Others followed Hudson Taylor's example to reach the interior of Africa and Asia. Missionary boards arose to send out missionaries into these unreached areas.[2] Moody also impacted this worldwide missionary movement by starting the Student Volunteer Missionary Movement, which raised up numerous college students to go into the mission field in the later half of the nineteenth century.

In the eighteenth century, John and Charles Wesley were integral in what would come to be known as the First Great Awakening in Great Britain, at which time they also founded the Methodist Church. The Wesleys taught the importance of holiness and the necessity of a second work of grace for sanctification. This emphasis on holiness spread throughout the British Isles and came to America through the ministry of Francis Asbury. Salvation and sanctification were preached together throughout the United States. The message was spread by the Methodist circuit riders who preached the gospel to enthusiastic audiences. This enthusiasm was a reaction against the cold orthodoxy found in many of the denominations at the time in the United States. The holiness movement spread from the Methodist Church to other Christian churches until it became one of the major forces in British and American Christianity in the nineteenth century.

The nineteenth century was also a period of new ideas that came into conflict with Christianity. It was a time when the Bible was under attack by Bible scholars and theologians in Germany. Men such as Julius Wellhausen and F. C. Baur were teaching that the Scriptures were simply like any other book written by man. They taught that the Scripture was not inspired by God, destroying the average churchgoer's confidence in the Word of God. Many Bible students would study in Germany and would find their faith shaken by this higher criticism. It was during this time that Charles Darwin

---

2. Foster, *Streams of Living Water*, 299.

took the world by storm with the publication of his book *On the Origin of the Species* in 1859. He introduced the theory of evolution, which challenged all Christendom. It called into question the divine origin of man. This affected not only Great Britain, but also Europe and the United States. In America, the majority of the church fought against the idea of evolution. Although the higher critical method was becoming popular in Britain, a large part of the church that rejected its claims.

During this period, large number of immigrants flooded the United States. The Industrial Revolution was taking place in both Great Britain and America. The cities in both nations became filled with factories. People moved to the cities to work in the factories and lived in squalid conditions. In the United States, poor immigrants from Europe flooded the urban areas looking for work. Overpopulation in these areas caused ghetto-like conditions. The church attempted to reach out with the gospel and to improve living conditions. In England, William Booth tried to reach the poor through the Salvation Army he founded. The Salvation Army preached the gospel and tried to meet people's physical needs with food and job training. In the United States, men such as Washington Gladden and Walter Rauschenbusch introduced the Social Gospel, which was concerned with improving the living conditions of the working man and the poor. This Social Gospel claimed to be concerned with the whole person, but it focused primarily on people's physical wellbeing. The Social Gospel movement began to weaken after World War I.

The Evangelists

The two most influential evangelists in the nineteenth century, both of whom were integral to the Second Great Awakening that commenced in 1800 and to the Third Great Awakening that began in 1857, were Charles Finney and D. L. Moody. A third evangelist who also played an important role, although not to quite the extent of Finney and Moody, was Asahal Nettleton. Nettleton was involved in the Second Great Awakening and had a tremendous impact on the Northeastern part of the United States. Charles Finney was involved in the Second Great Awakening, and his ministry extended into the Third Great Awakening. Although Finney had vast influence in the United States, his impact was somewhat less in Great Britain. D. L. Moody's ministry began during the Third Great Awakening and lasted until the end of the nineteenth century. Moody had a significant impact on both the British Isles and the United States. Moody helped to spread the gospel throughout the English-speaking world. He was considered the greatest evangelist in the Great Century.

Asahel Nettleton was a congregational pastor and evangelist who went to different churches and held crusades. He helped spread the Awakening throughout New York and Connecticut. Nettleton always worked with local churches and pastors and was very constrained in his approach and his methods. He would preach in churches and speak to the congregation about the need for salvation. He would then pray with them. His meetings were described in the following way: "In his meetings, the atmosphere was quiet, dignified and solemn. He always involved local pastors in his awakening work, and emphasized the need to teach and nurture any who were convicted."[3] Nettleton was a bachelor who lived a simple lifestyle and never asked for money, nor did he accumulate any property.[4] During Nettleton's ministry in the early 1800s, he saw close to thirty thousand conversions.[5]

Charles Finney was a New York lawyer who became the greatest evangelist in the first part of the nineteenth century. Finney was converted in 1821 and began to preach the gospel almost immediately.[6] He became a full-time Presbyterian evangelist sponsored by the Female Missionary Society of the Western District.[7] Finney drew on the skills he developed as a lawyer in his evangelism methods.[8] His ministry blossomed in 1830 and 1831 in Rochester, New York, where he held an evangelism campaign. Later he preached and held meetings all over the state of New York and throughout New England.[9] During his ministry, Finney saw over one hundred thousand people come to Christ.[10] This was an immense number of people at the time. As a result of his ministry efforts, Charles Finney became one of the most well known men in the United States and Great Britain.

Finney also introduced to the church what were called the "New Methods." Finney received criticism about these New Methods from fellow evangelists such as Asahel Nettleton and Lyman Beecher, who were both

---

3. Nettleton, "Did You Know?" 30.
4. Ibid.
5. Ibid.
6. Towns and Porter, *Ten Greatest Revivals Ever*, 98.
7. Foster, *Streams of Living Water*, 326.
8. Ibid.
9. Cairns, *Christianity Through the Centuries*, 471.
10. Towns and Porter, *Ten Greatest Revivals Ever*, 98.

prominent evangelists in their own right. What were these New Methods? For one, Finney introduced the "anxious seat," which was a bench in the front of the church or hall where someone who was "under conviction" could come and receive Christ. This popularized the idea of public invitations at evangelical meetings.[11] Finney also held protracted meetings that were longer than normal. He prayed for people by name and held women's prayer meetings.[12] Finney was well ahead of his time with these evangelism methods, but this did not always make him popular among his contemporaries. Elmer Towns and Douglas Porter called Finney "the Father of modern revivalism" and generally considered him to be the prototype of American evangelists.[13]

Finney left his revival ministry in 1835 and became the pastor of the Broadway Tabernacle Church, which was a Congregational church in New York City. He resigned in 1837 to become the pastor of a Congregational church in the small town of Oberlin, Ohio, and during this time he also taught at Oberlin College.[14] Later, Finney would become president of the college. At the time, Oberlin was a center in the holiness movement as well as the abolition movement, and Oberlin College was the first college to admit African American students and women students. Finney would become a leader in all of these movements.

Finney was also involved with the rise of urban evangelism in the 1850s. It was at this time that the Third Great Awakening broke out in New York City in 1858. Finney's ministry overlapped both Awakenings, and he would have a direct influence on D. L. Moody's ministry. Moody adopted Finney's focus on urban evangelism and would go on to popularize it in the Third Great Awakening during the second half of the nineteenth century.[15]

Dwight Lyman Moody emerged as the most important spokesman for the Awakening and is widely considered to be the greatest evangelist of the latter half of the nineteenth century. Moody impacted not only the United States, but also Great Britain. Unlike Finney and Nettleton, who were both pastors, Moody was a layman—a businessman from Chicago. He had been involved in starting Sunday schools, the YMCA, and a church in Chicago. Yet he was never ordained. Moody felt he would have a greater impact as a

---

11. Ibid., 102.
12. Cairns, *Christianity Through the Centuries*, 431.
13. Towns and Porter, *Ten Greatest Revivals Ever*, 102.
14. Latourette, *Christianity in a Revolutionary Age*, 29.
15. Cairns, *Christianity Through the Centuries*, 432.

layperson. Moody's style of evangelism appealed to the common man, and average Americans were attracted to this evangelist.

In 1873, D. L. Moody took his song leader, Ira Sankey, to Great Britain for a simple preaching tour. Although only a few meetings were scheduled, more speaking engagements were arranged soon after people began hearing Moody preach. This evangelism tour changed Moody and Sankey, and God used them to change Britain.[16] Moody was God's instrument to spread the Awakening throughout the land. Moody and Sankey remained in Great Britain for two years, and vast numbers of people came to the Savior. During the four-and-a-half months Moody was in London, an estimated million-and-a-half people came to hear him speak.[17] Moody impacted all levels of society from the average man all the way to the most influential leader in British society.[18] Moody met Prime Minister William Gladstone, and even Queen Victoria came to hear him speak.[19]

When Moody returned to the United States, his popularity had skyrocketed, and he was asked to preach all over America. He held crusades throughout most of the cities in the United States.[20] Moody focused his efforts on larger cities, believing that they would have a greater influence on the nation than villages in rural areas.[21] Moody was also able to reach people from all levels of society in the United States. As Latourette comments, "he was a layman and remained such to the end of his days. He had only a smattering of formal education; but by reason of his transparent sincerity, informality, and good sense, he had a striking influence on university students and graduates."[22]

Moody and Sankey returned to Great Britain in 1881 and stayed through 1884, and again their meetings were overflowing. Moody continued to spread the revival. In 1891, Moody made his final trip to Britain and spent most of his ministry focused on Scotland.[23] When Moody came back to the United States, he was engulfed with speaking engagements and continued to minister until his death in 1899.

16. Noll, *History of Christianity in the United States*, 288.
17. Pollock, *D. L. Moody*, 189.
18. Ibid., 169
19. Ibid., 176.
20. Noll et al., *Eerdman's Handbook of Christianity*, 293.
21. Latourette, *Christianity in a Revolutionary Age*, 32.
22. Ibid., 33.
23. Ibid., 32.

Moody also had a great influence on the holiness movement. He would have holiness speakers come to his Northfield Bible Conferences to speak on the importance of sanctification. People like A. B. Simpson, A. J. Gordon, F. B. Meyer, and a host of others would speak on the importance of being filled with the Holy Spirit. He also helped found the Student Volunteer Missionary Movement, which encouraged college students to go into the mission field in the latter part of the nineteenth century. This was one of the keys to the missionary movement during the Great Awakening.

Missionary Outreach

One of the reasons for the unusual growth in Christianity in the nineteenth century was the Protestant missionary movement. Missions was rediscovered by the Protestant Church during this period. Although the Roman Catholic Church had put an emphasis on missions through the centuries, the Protestant Church had for the most part neglected foreign missions (except for the Moravian Church in the eighteenth century). At the end of the eighteenth century, William Carey brought missions to the forefront for the Protestant Church. This began in 1792 with the publication of Carey's book titled *An Enquiry into the Obligation of Christians to Use Means for the Conversion of the Heathens*, which was actually the shortened title.[24]

The missions movement resulted from the First Great Awakening. It was influenced by the leaders of the Awakening: men such as Jonathan Edwards, George Whitfield, and the Wesley brothers. Many of the early missionaries—including Henry Martyn, who followed William Carey to India—had been influenced by David Brainerd.[25] Brainerd had been a missionary to the American Indians in the 1740s in New Jersey and Pennsylvania, but he died of tuberculosis at an early age. Jonathan Edwards published Brainerd's journal, which would go on to impact Christianity on both sides of the Atlantic, especially with regards to missions. John Wesley recommended it to his Methodist societies. Brainerd's journal became an inspiration to all those who were interested in missions.

Earle Cairns states that the missionary excitement was the result of revivalism among the pietists, Methodists, and evangelicals in the Anglican Church. They wanted to see others experience the joy of conversion they

---

24. Tucker, *From Jerusalem to Irian Jaya*, 115.
25. Ibid., 133.

had experienced.[26] During the period from 1792 to about 1830, all kinds of benevolent and missionary societies were founded in England and North America. This trend was initiated by evangelical fervor from the First Great Awakening and continued as a result of the Second Great Awakening that began in 1800 in America.[27]

Missionaries traditionally followed governments as they set up colonies. Great Britain was the main colonizing force in the world, but other nations were also busy colonizing the world. Much of the time these colonial governments did not welcome missionaries with open arms; they fought to keep them out. William Carey went to India in 1793 and was employed as a foreman in an indigo factory, since missionaries were not permitted entry at that time.[28] Carey was able to become a full-time missionary only after the East India Company was forced to open India up to missionary work after 1813.[29] Carey stayed and worked in India for forty years.[30] Other missionaries such as Henry Martyn followed Cary to India. Another English missionary, Robert Morrison, opened China for missions work in 1807 at the Portuguese colony of Macao in South China. Robert Moffat, another missionary who hailed from Britain, went to South Africa to begin mission work on that continent in 1815.[31] Moffat's son-in-law went on to achieve much greater fame than he had. His son-in-law was David Livingston, the famous missionary and explorer of Africa's interior. Missionaries were being sent out to all parts of the globe.

In America, several important societies were founded as the result of the Second Great Awakening. The American Board of Commissioners for Foreign Missions was the result of a covenant made by a group of students who were meeting for prayer out in a farmer's field. When a thunderstorm broke out, they went to meet under a haystack, where they agreed to devote themselves to foreign missions.[32] Adoniram and Ann Judson were one of the first missionary couples the American Board of Commissioners for Foreign Missions sent out to serve as missionaries, but on the ship to Burma, they became Baptists and left their original mission board. A Baptist Board

26. Cairns, *Christianity Through the Centuries*, 409.
27. Ibid.
28. Tucker, *From Jerusalem to Irian Jaya*, 117.
29. Cairns, *Christianity Through the Centuries*, 407.
30. Tucker, *From Jerusalem to Irian Jaya*, 119.
31. Ibid., 141.
32. Gonzalez, *Story of Christianity*, 245.

The Great Century

of Missions was founded in the United States to support them.[33] Adoniram Judson continued to work in Burma until his death in 1850.

For the most part, missionaries during this period worked under the shadow of colonial power structures. Most missionaries would not venture out from the protection of the established colonial government. They were not reaching the interiors of the countries they were working in. This changed with the emergence of a new missionary, Hudson Taylor, who established the China Inland Mission as a new missionary organization. This was the first of what would become known as the "Faith Missions."

Hudson Taylor was from England and went to China as a missionary in 1853. Taylor was a missionary with the Chinese Evangelization Society, which was an independent missionary organization.[34] Taylor adopted Chinese dress and lived among the Chinese, which was totally revolutionary at the time. Missionaries traditionally wore Western clothes and stayed within their missionary compounds, which meant that missionaries to China were staying in the large cities on the coast rather than penetrating the interior of China.

In 1865, Taylor founded the China Inland Mission with the goal of reaching the interior of China—to go where no missionaries were going. The China Inland Mission made no appeals for funds and relied on God for all of its needs. It was an interdenominational missionary organization that took men and women from all denominations as missionaries. Missionaries did not have to be ordained; they could be laypeople who felt called to the mission field.

The China Inland Mission became the first, and the model of, "faith missions." Faith Missions were interdenominational and relied on individuals and churches to supply their funds. They also would take the layperson as a missionary and were run by independent boards. A number of them came into existence after the Third Great Awakening. Their focus was to reach the interior of the countries that lay beyond the coastal regions, which at that time was the main focus of missions.[35] Taylor and his CIM (China Inland Mission) were profoundly affected by the Third Great Awakening. Many of his missionaries were converted during the initial Awakening and later from D. L. Moody's crusades.

---

33. Tucker, *From Jerusalem to Irian Jaya*, 123.
34. Steer, "Pushing Inward," 12.
35. Noll et al., *Eerdman's Handbook to Christianity*, 301.

Taylor was also influenced by the holiness movement, which was key to his mission and the life of the China Inland Mission. After the Third Great Awakening, a number of faith missions emerged, such as the Sudan Interior Mission, the Africa Inland Mission, the Scandinavian Alliance Mission (which later became The Evangelical Alliance Mission also known as TEAM), the Christian and Missionary Alliance founded by A. B. Simpson, and the Inland South American Mission. The faith mission movement flourished in the second half of the nineteenth century and put out the lion's share of the missionaries serving around the world. Most of these independent mission boards were part of the holiness movement that was integral to the Faith Missions message.

During the second half of the nineteenth century, another missionary movement emerged in the Student Volunteer Missionary Movement. The Student Volunteer Missionary Movement was born in 1886 at the Mount Herman conference grounds in Massachusetts, where it grew out of D. L. Moody's Northfield Conferences.[36] The Student Volunteer Missionary Movement's goal was to send out college students as foreign missionaries. Their motto was "The evangelization of the world in this generation." Many students signed a pledge to become foreign missionaries "if God permits."[37] During the time the Student Volunteer Missionary Movement was in existence, over 20,500 students were sent to the mission field.[38] John Mott, who was a leader for the Student Volunteer Missionary Movement, became the foremost missionary statesman in the first half of the twentieth century.[39]

Other great mission leaders who came out of this movement included Robert Speer, a Presbyterian lay missionary leader in the first half of the twentieth century who focused his efforts on students.[40] The Student Volunteer Missionary Movement reached its peak before World War I and was in decline by the late 1920s. Modernism and liberalism began to negatively affect it.[41] Many students lost interest when they were taught universalism in the mainline churches. After all, what was the point of being missionaries if everyone would be saved eventually?[42] Gradually, the Student Volunteer

---

36. Ibid., 295.
37. Ibid.
38. Tucker, *From Jerusalem to Irian Jaya*, 261.
39. Foster, *Streams of Living Water*, 365.
40. Noll, *Eerdman's Handbook to Christianity*, 301.
41. Tucker, *From Jerusalem to Irian Jaya*, 261.
42. Ibid.

Missionary Movement died. By 1940, only a few hundred delegates attended their convention.[43]

Sherwood Eddy, a leader in the movement and a missionary with the YMCA, serves as an example of this change in theology over the years. He went from being a very conservative evangelist to being more liberal in his theological outlook. He ended up aligning himself with liberal theologians such as Kirby Page and Reinhold Niebuhr.[44] As a result of moving away from its evangelical roots and its emphasis on holiness, the Student Volunteer Missionary Movement came to an end.

Holiness Movement

John Wesley emphasized the necessity of individual salvation and the importance of sanctification in the believer's life. Sanctification always followed salvation. Wesley believed all believers come to a point in their lives where it became necessary to surrender complete control of their lives to Christ. This point was called by various names, such as a "second work of grace," "perfect love," "heart purity," or "Christian perfection."[45]

Gregory Schneider describes the experience of the "second work of grace" in the following manner:

> It was a distinctive Methodist doctrine that sanctification, while something that grew gradually in the believer, was also an instantaneous second experience of grace. It could be dated and located like the new birth. This second religious crisis filled the soul with the pure love of God such that the impulse to sin was expelled from the heart and life . . .[46]

This message was preached throughout all the Methodist societies in England and then crossed the Atlantic to the United States, where it was preached at throughout America's Methodist camp meetings. Sanctification, along with conversion, became the primary components of the Methodist message.

The message of sanctification was picked up by non-Methodist evangelicals such as Asa Mahan, the famous evangelist and president of

---

43. Noll, *Eerdman's Handbook to Christianity*, 295.
44. Nutt, "G. Sherwood Eddy and the Attitudes of Protestants," 518.
45. Schneider, "Conflict of Associations."
46. Ibid.

Oberlin College. It was also spread by Charles Finney, who disseminated the message outside Methodist circles. Mahon and Finney taught that this "second work of grace" could be taken by faith, just as salvation was. It was an instantaneous process, and it was not necessary to struggle with sin as the Methodists had taught.[47] Both Mahon and Finney denied that there were any necessary preparations for salvation or sanctification; all that was necessary was to believe. The Methodists believed conversion and sanctification might involve a long spiritual struggle and that it was necessary to have a time of waiting for the "witness of the spirit." For many Methodists, what Mahon and Finney were teaching was considered too simple and dependent on individual will rather than on the Holy Spirit.[48]

A Methodist layperson by the name of Phoebe Palmer also helped to spread the message of sanctification. She began in 1840 by hosting Bible studies in her home, where she taught the doctrine of sanctification.[49] Palmer taught a more simplified version of Wesley's "second work of grace." Her method was called "altar theology," and she taught that believers could achieve sanctification by following three simple steps: consecration, faith, and testimony. The Christian just had to dedicate everything to God, believe God's promises, and then receive the gift of salvation.[50]

Palmer expanded her ministry and spoke in more than three hundred camp meetings and revival services. She played an important role in the beginning of the Third Great Awakening.[51] In 1859, she went to England to minister and became integral in the spread of the Third Great Awakening in the British Isles.[52] During Phoebe Palmer's life, she spoke to over one hundred thousand people about salvation and sanctification.[53] Charles White wrote, "This emphasis on attainable sanctification made her the mother of the Holiness Movement."[54]

The holiness movement's message continued to spread beyond Methodist circles. William Boardman, a Presbyterian and an executive director of the YMCA, helped spread the message of holiness. His 1858 book, *The*

---

47. Tait, "Cleansing Wave," 22.
48. Ibid., 23.
49. White, "Holiness Fire-Starting," 19.
50. Ibid.
51. Ibid.
52. Ibid.
53. Ibid., 16.
54. Ibid., 19.

Higher Christian Life, had a tremendous impact on the evangelical church. Boardman was considered to be the most successful evangelist between the time of Charles Finney's and D. L. Moody's ministries.[55] In fact, Boardman's book had a great influence on A. B. Simpson's sanctification experience. Another couple who preached sanctification was Hannah Whitehall Smith together with her husband, Robert. Hannah Smith wrote the book *The Christian's Secret of a Happy Life* in 1875. This book was about how believers could live victorious Christian lives by being filled with the Holy Spirit. Both Boardman and the Smiths would play a key role in the holiness movement in England as well as in the United States.[56] The Smiths inspired the Keswick movement in Great Britain, which stressed the importance of sanctification in a non-Wesleyan sense.[57] The non-Wesleyan view of sanctification then beginning to spread into the mainstream churches was a key factor in the spreading of the Third Great Awakening.

The emphasis on sanctification was now finding its way into Presbyterian, Baptist, and Congregational churches.[58] Boardman and Hannah Whitehall Smith were popularizing a different version of sanctification. Their belief differed from the Wesleyan's view in that they taught that innate sin is a permanent condition until people get to heaven. It cannot be eradicated, but it can be subjugated. This subjugation, they taught, happens when a person surrenders complete control of his or her life to the Holy Spirit. This crisis experience was often called the "Baptism of the Holy Spirit."

This phrase would later be used by the pentecostal movement to define that point when the believer would be filled by the Holy Spirit—an experience that was evidenced by speaking in tongues.[59]

Grant Wacker, describing the baptism of the Spirit, says that "its primary purpose is not to purify the heart, but to empower the will, the will to act—to witness, sacrifice and serve."[60] After the time of the American Civil War and during the Third Great Awakening, this view of sanctification became even more popular than the Wesleyan view of sanctification. It was popularized by A. B. Simpson, A. J. Gordon, A. T. Pierson, R. A. Torrey, and

---

55. Tait, "Cleansing Wave," 24.
56. Noll, *History of Christianity in the United States*, 380.
57. Tait, "Cleansing Wave," 24.
58. Noll et al., *Eerdman's Handbook to Christianity in America*, 334.
59. Ibid.
60. Ibid.

D. L. Moody. In fact, D. L. Moody was a primary promoter of the holiness movement in both the United States and Britain in non-Methodist circles.[61]

Moody interpreted the "Baptism of the Holy Spirit" primarily in terms of power and service rather than freedom from sin. This became the primary focus of the American Keswick holiness teaching. This also became the main emphasis of the Bible college movement, which was taught and practiced at schools such as Gordon College, Columbia Bible College, Nyack College, and Dallas Theological Seminary. These schools helped popularize the teaching of sanctification that became known as the "Higher Christian Life."[62]

Grant Wacker writes, "Ultimately, their [reformed view of holiness] was institutionalized in the Christian and Missionary Alliance."[63] The Christian and Missionary Alliance became the vehicle to spread this view of holiness. The Keswick form of the "Baptism of the Holy Spirit" was part of the evangelism message preached by evangelists and Bible teachers in the second half of the nineteenth century. This view of holiness spread throughout many non-Methodist denominations across both the United States and in Great Britain.

The Wesleyan view of holiness was part of the Methodist Church from its inception. By the mid-nineteenth century, however, changes were taking place in the church. The Methodist Church was the largest denomination in America at that time. Methodism had stressed conversion and sanctification, but as the church became more firmly established and more mainstream, a change of perspective took place. As Methodists achieved more public respectability, the term "holiness" became a problem in the denomination.[64] Methodists who were involved in the holiness movement fought to keep holiness as a primary focus, but they were losing ground. Their opponents to the "second work of grace" wanted to make sanctification synonymous with what happened at conversion. It began at conversion and continued throughout the Christian's life.[65] This conflict began in the 1830s and gained strength in the mid-nineteenth century. As the church became more settled, moved away from circuit preaching, and began to enjoy the benefits of more educated clergy, Methodists began to de-emphasize

---

61. Ibid., 335.
62. Ibid.
63. Tait, "Cleansing Wave," 24.
64. Schneider, "Conflict of Associations," 269.
65. Ibid., 270.

the "second work of grace." Churches were becoming more urban and increasingly wanted to fit into the community and to stay away from the emotionalism that was often associated with holiness.[66]

In 1867, John Inskeep and a group of Methodist ministers established the National Camp-Meeting Association for the Promotion of Christian Holiness. Describing this new effort, Wacker writes, "Within a decade, the National Association had directly sponsored or indirectly fostered an extensive network of national, regional and local holiness associations, periodicals, missions, schools, camps, conferences and weekly prayer meetings."[67] It seemed for a time the holiness movement would sweep the entire Methodist Church, both south and north. But serious opposition developed, and those in the holiness movement began to lose ground. This opposition was from the more liberal segment of the Methodist Church. During the period between 1880 and 1905, over one hundred thousand people left the Methodist Church to start or join other denominations.[68] They left because they wanted a more evangelical church. A few of the denominations begun during this exodus were the Church of the Nazarene founded by Phineas F. Breeze, a former Methodist minister; the Church of God located in Anderson, Indiana; and the Pilgrim Holiness Church.[69]

The nineteenth century was a period of new ideas. There were new ideas on the inspiration of the Scripture and what it meant. There were also new ideas on man's origins, as expounded by Charles Darwin. These ideas were to have a significant influence on the church.

Intellectual Threats

There were two intellectual upheavals facing nineteenth-century Christianity. Both theories were disseminated in American universities. One was the theory of evolution. The other was the higher criticism approach to the Bible. These two philosophies rocked not only the scientific and academic world, but also the Christian world. In 1859, Charles Darwin's book *On the Origin of the Species* introduced his theory of evolution to the world. This theory presented a major challenge to the church because it undermined

---

66. Noll et al., *Eerdman's Handbook of Christianity in America*, 333.
67. Ibid., 33.
68. Ibid.
69. Ibid.

the Christian perspective of creation.[70] Bruce Shelly states the challenge in the following manner: "If there was no overseer, eye of providence in creation; if in fact there was no creation at all but merely an evolution from simple to more complex forms of matter and energy, what was left of traditional Christian belief in a creating and sustaining God? If Darwin was right, how could the Bible be true?"[71] The theory of evolution called the traditional Christian view that God created the universe into question. Until then, Christians had almost universally accepted that God had created everything by simply a word. Protestant and Catholic theologians had argued that all was created "ex-nihilo," or "out of nothing," all down through the centuries. The argument of divine design pointed to the Creator.[72] Protestant education in America had taught that the design of the universe proved the existence of God. The argument of design was the mainstay in American higher education.[73]

The theory of evolution was being applied to the sciences, humanities, and even religion. British philosophers Herbert Spencer and Thomas Huxley were saying that evolutionary theories could provide the basis for a person's whole philosophy of life.[74] The evolutionary theory was impacting universities in Europe, and it soon began to affect colleges and universities in America. Some of the seminaries in America were teaching evolution along with higher critical views of the Bible. This trend caused some Christians to wonder whether the Bible could be trusted at all.[75]

In nineteenth-century European universities, the Bible was being challenged by liberal biblical scholars. They were teaching that the Scriptures were no different than any other type of ancient literature such as the *Iliad* or the *Odyssey*. They taught that the Bible evolved like any other work of literature and was just a product of human religious imagination. German theologians had been attacking the reliability of the Scriptures before the American Civil War. After the Civil War, this view of Scripture began to filter into the United States. Such views challenged the very bedrock of nineteenth-century Christianity.

---

70. Shelly, *Church History in Plain Language*, 391.
71. Ibid.
72. Noll, *History of Christianity in the United States*, 366.
73. Ibid., 366–67.
74. Ibid., 367.
75. Noll et al., *Eerdman's Handbook to Christianity in America*, 285.

More and more American colleges and seminary professors were studying in Germany, where they were taught the higher critical view of the Scripture, which would in turn became dominant throughout some of the major denominations in America.[76] Consider for a moment that the typical church-attendee during this time was being taught that the book of Exodus was not by Moses but was instead a myth. One could only imagine the turmoil this caused.[77] The higher critical method's approach to looking at the Scriptures became a battleground in the second half of the nineteenth century. The leaders in the Third Great Awakening counter-attacked higher critical view of the Scriptures, which resulted in the publication of twelve paperback books called *The Fundamentals*. This project was financed by two wealthy southern California businessmen, Lyman and Matthew Stewart.[78] Three million copies of these books were distributed—seemingly to every theological student, pastor, and missionary in America.[79] These books included articles by over sixty-four authors that defended the Christian faith, rejecting the "higher critical view" of the Bible and liberal Christianity.[80]

There was a group that accepted both higher critical views and evolution. They adapted them and incorporated them in their faith. They saw this new knowledge as a blessing from God and embraced it. They became what is known as the modernists, or Liberals, in today's Christianity. Out of this group would come many of the leaders of what would become known as the Social Gospel movement.[81]

The Social Gospel

The years after 1850 proved to be a time of rapid industrialization in the cities of Great Britain. People were moving from rural areas to work in urban factories. Oftentimes they lived in slums and squalor and worked long hours for pitifully small wages. Christians in England became concerned about the condition of the poor and wanted to help those living in such terrible conditions. The same pattern was happening in the United States, where rapid industrialization fueled a massive immigration to the cities.

76. Shelly, *Church History in Plain Language*, 391.
77. Ibid., 392.
78. Noll et al., *Eerdman's Handbook to Christianity in America*, 331.
79. Shelly, *Church History in Plain Language*, 433.
80. Ibid.
81. Ibid., 392.

Within the church, Christians took two distinct approaches to reaching out to people in such difficult settings. Those churches that were part of the holiness movement, with its focus on individual salvation, tried to reach those suffering around them through various social outreach programs. One of the most successful efforts was the formation of the Salvation Army, which began in England in 1865. The other reactionary effort by the church was known as the Social Gospel movement, and its focus was on meeting people's physical needs, with comparatively less emphasis on the spiritual needs.

The Salvation Army was founded by William Booth to reach the poor with the gospel while also helping to meet their physical needs. Booth had been a Methodist minister in London and saw that he had to do something to help the poor in the slums in East London.[82] His "street preaching" in London would ultimately have a great effect. In just eleven years, he established thirty-two outreach centers to evangelize and meet the social needs of the people. Booth organized churches like an army, and the Salvation Army's leaders were given ranks. They dressed in uniforms and were organized in military units.[83]

By 1888, Booth had established one thousand units, or corps. In England, the movement was growing like wildfire. In 1890, he published the book *In Darkest England and the Way Out*, which helped to show the church the great need of the day's poor. It also showed how Christians could help.[84] Booth's daughter Evangeline came to the United States to lead the Salvation Army in America, where the Salvation Army continued the same type of ministry they had led in England. They focused on evangelism along with providing food, shelter, medical help, vocational training, elementary schooling, prisoner visitation, and legal help. By 1904, the Salvation Army had over nine hundred outreach centers, or corps, in the United States.[85] The Salvation Army had a tremendous impact in helping the needy both in England and in the United States throughout the nineteenth century, and it continues to do the same today.

In addition to the response from the holiness movement, another attempt to reach the ignored urban masses became known as the Social Gospel movement. This movement was an attempt by the more liberal part

---

82. Noll, *History of Christianity in the United States*, 304.
83. Ibid.
84. Shelly, *Church History in Plain Language*, 411.
85. Noll, *History of Christianity in the United States*, 304.

of the church to reach people in the cities. Mark Noll comments on the origin of the Social Gospel movement by writing, "This strong link in the American revival tradition between personal holiness and social reform contributed to the seriousness of the movement, as did a newer concern for the scientific study of social problems that accompanied the rise in the American university of social problems after the Civil War."[86]

David Bebbington states, "The most characteristic doctrine of the social gospelers, that the Kingdom of God was to be realized by social improvement, was derived primarily from the German liberal theologian Albrecht Ritsehl."[87] Indeed, the higher critical view of the Scripture was accepted by most who were then preaching the Social Gospel, while those who accepted the Bible as the Word of God tended to think the Social Gospel was corrupting the message of the Bible. The Social Gospelers based their doctrines on liberal views such as the God's Fatherhood of all people, whether Christians or not. They also taught that all people were going to heaven whether they accepted Christ as their Lord and Savior or not. The Social Gospelers turned their focus from individual salvation to improving economic life in order to help set up the kingdom of God on earth.[88] Their focus was on the economic good of humankind, with a lesser emphasis on the salvation.

The Social Gospelers' concern for improving economic conditions and ideas on how to achieve this goal would often come from outside the Christian tradition, especially from social scientists and others who saw the same need. Some of the leaders with the most innovative ideas were from Britain, such as Thomas Chalmers of Scotland and F. D. Maurice of England. They formulated new Christian responses and answers to the problems of industrialization. Both leaders impacted Americans who were interested in Christian reform.[89]

Those who espoused the Social Gospel embraced a wide range of political and economic ideas. The Social Gospelers ranged from fairly conservative to very liberal in their Christian and economic views. All those who were in the Social Gospel movement were concerned with the suffering of others. They espoused reforms such as eliminating child labor, the need for a day of rest, shorter workdays, and controlling industry to protect

86. Ibid.
87. Bebbington, *Dominance of Evangelicalism*, 247.
88. Cairns, *Christianity Through the Centuries*, 438.
89. Noll, *History of Christianity in the United States*, 305.

workers.[90] Their focus was on social justice for all the downtrodden. Most in the movement were pastors or seminary professors who had accepted the higher critical view of the Scriptures and the evolutionary perspectives influencing the sciences. They did not form any organizations but preferred instead to incorporate their goals into their particular denominations and seminaries. They also pushed their agendas through the appropriate public and political agencies.[91] As Bruce Shelly comments,

> The Crux of The Social Gospel was the belief that God's saving work includes corporate structures as well as personal lives. If it is true that social good and evil are collective in nature, not simply the total of good and evil individuals, then Christians are obliged to work for the reconstruction of the social order. It is part of their religious responsibility.[92]

One of the most prominent leaders of the Social Gospel movement was Washington Gladden, the pastor of the First Congregation Church in Columbus, Ohio. The leading theologian and academic proponent of the Social Gospel was Walter Rauschenbusch, a professor of church history of Rochester Seminary in Rochester, New York. A third proponent of the Social Gospel was the author Charles Sheldon, whose book *In His Steps* became immensely popular in the late nineteenth century. All three played an important role in popularizing the Social Gospel.

As a pastor, Washington Gladden had a great care for the poor and for exploited workers. Gladden, in his church in Columbus, had both factory workers and the owners of the factories sitting in pews right across from each other. His concern for the workers in those factories was immensely practical because he saw them every Sunday. His goal was to impose the brotherhood of man on both groups.[93] He wrote a number of books exposing the dangers of the powerful industrialist and the conditions of the workingman.[94] His commitment to justice would lead him to fight for labor rights and to apply the "golden rule" of the New Testament to industrial organization.[95] Gladden became the primary spokesman from the pastoral perspective for the Social Gospel.

---

90. Noll et al., *Eerdman's Handbook to Christianity in America*, 319.
91. Shelly, *Church History in Plain Language*, 413.
92. Ibid.
93. Ibid.
94. Noll et al., *Eerdman's Handbook to Christianity*, 319.
95. Noll, *History of Christianity in the United States*, 305.

The Great Century

Walter Rauschenbusch was a German Baptist pastor who ministered for ten years in New York City's Hell's Kitchen. His church was very close to that of A. B. Simpson, who ministered at the Gospel Tabernacle in the same area. After ten years in New York City, Rauschenbusch left to become a professor of church history at Rochester Seminary. It was there that he published his seminal works on the Social Gospel. He became the prime spokesman and leader of the movement. Rauschenbusch published *Christianity and Social Crisis* in 1907, *For God and the People: Prayers of the Social Awakening* in 1910, *Christianity, the Social Order* in 1912, and finally in 1917 his magnum opus, *A Theology for the Social Gospel*.[96] Raushenbusch taught a prophetic idea of justice and emphasized idea of building the kingdom of God through the power of Jesus Christ.[97] The Social Gospel also became associated with Christianity's liberal trends. While Gladden helped popularize the higher criticism of the Bible, Rauschenbusch taught that some of the miracles in the Scriptures never took place.[98] For the most part, the Social Gospel was looked on with distrust among those Christians who were part of the Third Great Awakening.

A final spokesman who helped popularize the Social Gospel was Charles Sheldon. Sheldon was a Congregational pastor in Topeka, Kansas. Sheldon hoped, through the influence of *In His Steps*, to see God's kingdom realized on earth through evangelism and social action.[99] Sheldon's book poses the question "What would happen to a community if everyone asked themselves 'What would Jesus do?' and then proceed to do it."[100] Sheldon felt that answering this question would revolutionize society. This book sold millions of copies and is still popular today. The original text was never copyrighted, so it has been published by a number of different publishers, which helped its rise in popularity. In fact, one sees the acronym WWJD (What would Jesus do?) that originated from the book even to this today. Although Sheldon's book played an important role in the spread of these ideas, the Social Gospel itself became less and less popular after the Great Depression and has since fallen into obscurity.

---

96. Ibid., 306.
97. Ibid.
98. Ibid., 307.
99. Ibid., 411.
100. Ibid.

Conclusion

In this chapter, we have looked at the factors that impacted Christianity in the nineteenth century. All these factors played a role in Christianity in the Great Century. In the following chapters, the life of A. B. Simpson will be examined along with the role he played in the Third Great Awakening.

II

A. B. SIMPSON
THE FORGOTTEN MAN IN RENEWAL

Historical Background: The Third Great Awakening

The most important factors impacting the growth of the church during the Great Century were the Second and Third Great Awakenings, which began in the United States and spread worldwide.

A great majority of the nineteenth century was influenced by these two spiritual awakenings. William McLoughlin, a revivalist historian, states that the Second Great Awakening began in 1800 and lasted until 1830.[1] The Second Great Awakening began simultaneously in the eastern and western United States. The revival in the west began at the Cane Ridge meetinghouse in central Kentucky and spread throughout the western frontier. Paul K. Conkin writes, "It arguably remains the most important religious gathering in all of American history, both for what it symbolized and for the effects that flowed from it."[2] Conkin may be exaggerating the importance of Cane Ridge, but the meeting undoubtedly played a very important part in America's religious history, and its role as an impetus in the Second Great Awakening in the west cannot be ignored.

In the east, the revival broke out in New England at Yale University under the leadership of Timothy Dwight, who was then the president of

---

1. McLoughlin, *Revivals, Awakenings and Reform*, 10.
2. Conkin, *Cane Ridge: America's Pentecost*, 3.

the university. It was Dwight's inspired preaching and ministry that spiritually awoke the student body at Yale University. It is interesting to note that Dwight was the grandson of Jonathan Edwards, who had been an integral player at the start of the Great Awakening in North America that began in the eighteenth century. Keith Hardman writes, "Timothy Dwight was not only the central figure in the college revivals that radiated from Yale and other New England schools; but through his writings and his leadership, he established the desire for awakenings as a permanent feature of American Protestantism from 1800 until the beginning of the Civil War."[3]

Revivals in both the eastern and western United States blended together to become the Second Great Awakening. It would then be Charles Finney, the evangelist from western New York, who would carry out the second phase of the Second Great Awakening and spread the revival throughout the United States.[4] Gradually, the Awakening began to fade. By 1840, religious life in the United States was at low ebb. It would continue to decline until the Third Great Awakening began in 1857.[5]

Most church historians agree that the Third Great Awakening began in 1857. There is, however, debate on how long the Third Great Awakening lasted. Paulus Scharpft states, "The prayer movement of 1857–1859 began a worldwide revival that lasted more than fifty years and reached its climax in the work of Dwight L. Moody."[6] J. Edwin Orr calls this Third Great Awakening "The Second Evangelical Awakening" and traces its beginnings to 1857. Orr argues this nineteenth-century Evangelical Awakening lasted until World War I—a period covering roughly fifty years—and states that it was comparable to the Great Awakening in the eighteenth century.[7]

During the year of 1857, many factors contributed to the start of the Third Great Awakening. Hardman traces the beginning of the Third Great Awakening to the ministry of Dr. Walter Palmer and his wife Phoebe, both of whom were instrumental in the holiness movement in the United States. This was especially true of Mrs. Palmer, who was often the main speaker at their meetings. After 1850, the Palmers devoted about half of each year to revival and camp meetings in Canada and the eastern United States.[8] As the

---

3. Hardman, "Return of the Spirit," 28.
4. Ibid., 29.
5. Ibid., 32.
6. Scharpff, *History of Evangelism*, 173.
7. Orr, *Second Evangelical Awakening*, 121.
8. Hardman, *Seasons of Refreshing*, 173.

Palmers were speaking at the McNabb Street Wesleyan Methodist Church in Hamilton, Ontario, in the fall of 1857, a revival broke out and more than six hundred people were converted. According to most revival historians, this was the beginning of the Third Great Awakening.[9]

In July of 1857, a quiet businessman by the name of Jeremiah Lanphier began work as an urban missionary for the North Dutch Reformed Church in New York City. At noon on September 23, 1857, Lanphier opened the church doors for a noonday prayer meeting.[10] Two days after the prayer meeting began, the Bank of Pennsylvania failed in Philadelphia. This panicked the American business community.[11] On October 10, the New York Stock Market crashed, putting many people out of business.[12] Hardman writes, "The financial panic, it seems, was the catalyst that propelled the Awakening. Within six months, 10,000 people were gathering daily for prayer in numerous places throughout New York."[13] Other cities also developed prayer meetings, and these meetings were usually led by lay people. The revival then spread throughout the United States and Canada.[14] In 1859, the revival spread across the Atlantic to Great Britain.

In the United States, the revival continued to impact both the Union and Confederate armies during the Civil War. Thousands of soldiers were converted during the war between the states. How many soldiers were converted? Gardiner Shattuck estimates that between 100,000 and 200,000 men were converted in the Union Army, while in the Confederate Army, which was much smaller, almost 100,000 were converted.[15] Shattuck states, "Since these numbers include only conversions and do not represent the number of soldiers actually swept up in the revivals—a yet more substantial figure—the impact of revivals during the Civil War surely was tremendous."[16] The Third Great Awakening would continue until World War I.

Orr divides the Third Great Awakening into three phases. The first phase was the initial outpouring of the Holy Spirit during the noonday prayer meetings. This outpouring spread out from New York City to cover

---

9. Ibid.
10. Ibid., 174.
11. Hardman, "Time for Prayer," 33.
12. Ibid.
13. Ibid.
14. Ibid.
15. Shattuck, "Revivals in the Camp," 30.
16. Ibid., 33.

much of the United States and Canada, then later spread to the United Kingdom and Europe. Orr writes,

> The first phase began in the revival of religion which followed an outpouring of the Holy Spirit, first clearly manifested in the remarkable movement of prayer with its attendant conviction of sin. In the general sense, leaderless, this phase of the revival became the means of winning hundreds of thousands to the Christian way of life. Its peak passed, but the Christian communities were by then operating upon a higher level of spiritual effectiveness.[17]

Many historians label this final phase as the Third Great Awakening, although in fact it was merely the first of the three-part phase that, taken together, would become the Third Great Awakening.

Orr goes on to say that the second phase of the Awakening was the development of evangelism. He states,

> Dwight L. Moody, whose Christian service actually began during the first phase of the Awakening, after 1873, became a force in Britain as well as America. Moody extended the scope and the methods of the same Awakening, for he introduced little that was new... Moody was without question the greatest single product of the revival. But he was not alone in his heyday of usefulness from 1873 to 1899. Those years were outstanding in the history of the expansion of English-speaking Christianity.[18]

This was the period in which a great many evangelists preached throughout the United States in both urban and rural areas. The focus during this period, however, became increasingly urban. The leaders in the urban evangelical outreach helped to keep the Third Great Awakening alive.

The third phase of the Great Awakening began around the turn of the twentieth century and coincided with the Welsh Revival in 1905. Orr comments,

> The third phase of the Awakening began shortly after the turn of the century. Like the first, it manifested another outpouring of the Spirit of prayer with its accompanying conviction of sin. Its effects were seen in sharpest focus in the Welsh Revival of 1905 under hortatory preaching of evangelist Evan Roberts. It also had an evangelistic phase in the worldwide ministry of Reuben Torrey and Wilbur Chapman, who, with their team-mate, Charles M.

17. Orr, *Second Evangelical Awakening*, 121.
18. Ibid.

Alexander, led great evangelistic campaigns in Australasia, Britain and North America. The third phase closed before the outbreak of the First World War.[19]

The Third Great Awakening had a tremendous effect on the world. In fact, this Awakening's enduring impact on behalf of Christ is still felt today. Considering all three of these phases makes the great magnitude of the Third Great Awakening's influence upon the nineteenth and the early twentieth-century world clear.

Simpson's Neglect Today

During this period, there were many Christian leaders who were initially involved in the Third Great Awakening. One Christian leader who was instrumental in the Awakening and who seems to have been neglected by most religious historians—even many of the more evangelical Christian historians—is A. B. Simpson, the founder and first president of the Christian and Missionary Alliance denomination. He was a leader in the Awakening and built his ministry upon both evangelistic outreach in the urban setting of the United States as well as an international mission emphasis. He was one of the leaders in the holiness movement and the related healing movement. He was well known at the time in evangelical circles and played an important role in the Third Great Awakening.

Why, then, has Simpson been forgotten by most religious historians and writers on revival? In *A Religious History of the American People*,[20] which is one of the more popular books on the history of the American church, author Sydney E. Ahlstrom fails to mention A. B. Simpson even once in 1,096 pages except in a single footnote. In his classic work, *Revivals, Awakenings and Religion*, William McLoughlin also neglects to write one word about Simpson or his impact on the period. The same is true of McLoughlin's book *Modern Revivalism: Charles Grandison Finney to Billy Graham*, in which Simpson is not addressed. In his classic work, *They Gathered at the River*, Bernard Weisberger also makes no mention of Simpson. In William Sweet's book *Revivalism in America*, there is also no reference to Simpson. Daniel Cohen does not include Simpson in his book

---

19. Ibid., 122.
20. Ahlstrom, *Religious History of the American People.*, 812 n. 5.

The Spirit of the Lord: Revivalism in America.[21] Ernest Sandeen writes about the founding of Bible colleges in North America in his book *The Roots of Fundamentalism*, but he fails to recognize Simpson in the text. Although Simpson founded one of the first Bible schools in North America, the only mention Sandeen makes of Simpson is in a footnote at the bottom of a page.

When evangelical scholars do mention Simpson, it is usually with reference to his contribution to the mission movement in the nineteenth century. An exception is J. Edwin Orr, who gives Simpson his proper place and recognizes his importance. Most secular scholars have ignored the impact Simpson had on the church in the nineteenth century as well. Even within the Christian and Missionary Alliance, the society Simpson founded, it is pastor and author A. W. Tozer who is better known among the laity than Simpson. Simpson is truly the forgotten man.

Why this neglect? Why has Simpson been so nearly forgotten? Most of the historians who have written about revival and the Third Great Awakening have focused on D. L. Moody and his associates. The reason for this is obvious, since these figures had the greatest impact on the period. No one had more impact on spreading the revival than Moody. All scholars who look at the Third Great Awakening recognize that it was Moody who was responsible for spreading the Awakening worldwide. Later it would be R. A. Torrey and Wilbur Chapman, both of whom were Moody's associates, who would continue to spread the revival after Moody's death in 1899.

Chapman eventually took a young man under his wing who would become the setup man for Chapman's crusade work. When Chapman retired from crusades, he recommended this young man for a revival in Iowa. The young man's name was Billy Sunday.[22] Sunday would become the greatest evangelist in the early part of the twentieth century. Sunday was at the height of his popularity when World War I broke out. After the war, his fame and popularity diminished.

In looking at the Third Great Awakening, it becomes clear that Moody's influence was integral, whether it was directly through him, through associates such as Torrey and Chapman, or indirectly through leaders like Sunday. These men are widely recognized as the most important figures of this period. Moody and his associates were all interdenominational and not aligned with any one church. They were well known in all church circles.

---

21. Cohen, *Spirit of the Lord*, 149.
22. Ibid.

Perhaps, if they had been connected to one denomination, they might have been kept from becoming so well known.

Simpson's Popularity

Simpson may have been forgotten by modern historians, but he was well known at the time among his contemporaries for his influence and impact on the church. A. E. Thompson comments about Moody and Simpson by writing, "One day when Dwight L. Moody was in New York, he said to his friend, Dr. A. T. Pierson, 'Pierson, I have just been down to hear A. B. Simpson preach. No one gets at my heart like this man.'"[23] F. B. Meyer, the great English preacher and author of devotional literature, said this about Simpson: "He leaves a trail of light which will linger long as an inspiration and appeal."[24] C. I. Scofield, the original editor of the Scofield Reference Bible, said, "It has been my privilege to know with some measure of intimacy the greatest preachers and men of God of the present time. Among those, and with no disparagement to any, I found Dr. A. B. Simpson the foremost in power to reach the depths of the human soul. And his message was so bathed in love that it was always redolent of the personality of him whom having not seen we love."[25]

Thompson, in his biography on Simpson, quotes T. Dewitt Talmage, a contemporary of Simpson's. On Talmage's impression of Simpson, Thompson writes, "Dr. T. Dewitt Talmage said that he had recently attended a meeting in a New York City church with a dingy auditorium and a very ordinary looking crowd of people, with nothing aesthetic or emotional in the service; but before the minister had been preaching three minutes he felt that his head and shoulders had been lifted into heaven."[26] Edward Shaw, who was a little boy in Simpson's first church in Hamilton, Ontario, related this story to Thompson:

> Waiting for a train in a little village in Massachusetts, I got into conversations with a flagman. There was no mistaking that he was Irish. 'Did you ever hear a man named Simpson?' said he. 'Yes,' I said, 'I have known him many years.' 'And how do you like him?' he asked. 'Very much,' said I. 'He is a great preacher!' 'Son,' he said,

23. Thompson, *A. B. Simpson*, 200.
24. Ibid.,199.
25. Ibid.
26. Ibid., 200.

'I could sit on the point of a picket fence twenty-four hours and listen to that man.'[27]

Simpson was certainly well known by his contemporaries.

Simpson's writings were also quite popular in his time. He published a weekly deeper life and missionary periodical called *The Word, the Work, and the World*. It was the first illustrated missionary magazine. At the close of the nineteenth century, paperback books were becoming quite popular. Moody was the first religious author to take advantage of them, and Simpson soon followed suit. Simpson published a number of these paperback books.[28] He initially published four books, and Simpson wrote in June 1899 that "tens of thousands of copies of these four paperbacks had been sold in the last few years."[29] These books were popular among the Christian reading public. One of the books Simpson published was *The Life of Prayer*. This book had a profound effect on Jonathan Goforth, who played an important part in the revival that took place in Manchuria, China, at the end of the nineteenth century and early twentieth century. Goforth wrote,

> I have read and reread Dr. Simpson's book, *The Life of Prayer*, with the deepest interest and profit. No one can give this little book a careful reading without realizing that the author has lived in the secret of his Master's presence. Every page makes it evident that here is a man who has prayed through. Down through the Christian centuries few men have had greater prayer results. Great would be the spiritual quickening if every Christian mastered this classic on the prayer life.[30]

Simpson's preaching and writings helped spread his message, which he called "the Fourfold Gospel." In fact, one of the first books Simpson published was called *The Four-Fold Gospel*, and it explains this important message.[31] What was the Fourfold Gospel? It was the preaching of Jesus Christ as Savior, Sanctifier, Healer, and Coming King. In the incorporation papers of the Christian and Missionary Alliance it is stated, "For the Christian Alliance its particular business was to bear united testimony to:

1. Salvation through Christ.

---

27. Ibid., 202.
28. Hartzfeld and Nienkirchen, *Birth of a Vision*, 298.
29. Ibid.
30. Simpson, *Life of Prayer*, 7.
31. Hartzfeld and Nienkirchen, *Birth of a Vision*, 298.

2. Sanctification through Christ for all who fully yield themselves to him.
3. Healing through the name of Jesus for those who believe and obey him.
4. Christ's personal and pre-millennial coming."[32]

Indeed, the message of the Alliance was Simpson's own message, and this was the Fourfold Gospel.

Many leaders in the Christian church during this period were influenced by Simpson. He was considered a leader in both the holiness and healing movements as well as in urban evangelical and missionary developments at the end of the nineteenth century. As Orr comments on Simpson's impact on this period of time,

> In 1886, A. B. Simpson organized a summer convention at Old Orchard, Maine, out of which came the Christian and Missionary Alliance, at first interdenominational. Simpson laid emphasis upon Sanctification and Healing, but his primary motivation was the preaching of the gospel to all nations before the coming again of Jesus Christ. When he died in 1919, the Alliance was worldwide.[33]

Orr also explains that although Simpson's Christian and Missionary Alliance was at first an interdenominational organization, the Alliance "later itself became a denomination as missionary-minded as the Moravians."[34]

Simpson also made a tremendous impact on urban evangelism. Joel Carpenter states that Simpson, along with D. L. Moody and A. J. Gordon, was integral in prodding complacent churches into new evangelistic outreach.[35] Simpson was involved in the holiness movement, and his message helped spread the deeper life view of sanctification.[36]

The Reason for Neglect

If Simpson was so important, why has he been largely forgotten? As stated earlier, one major reason is that Moody and his associates have gotten most

---

32. Ibid., 2.
33. Orr, *Light of the Nations*, 204.
34. Ibid., 273.
35. Carpenter, *Revive Us Again*, 78.
36. Orr, *Light of the Nations*, 206.

of the press. In addition, Simpson was not a traveling evangelist but chose instead to stay in a settled pulpit, which lessened his exposure. He founded a denomination—the Christian and Missionary Alliance—and ministered predominately within Alliance circles, though he did minister outside at times. All of his books have been published by a publishing arm of the Christian and Missionary Alliance, so most of his writings have stayed within the reading of Alliance readers. Simpson was also a very humble man and did not build himself up. He was happy if others got the credit and praise.

The author of this book was once asked by a seminary professor why nothing had been written on Simpson. He concluded that Simpson is one of the most neglected men in the modern church. This has also been true in the wider branches of church history and academic circles. Simpson is mentioned here and there, but usually just in passing. Most of what has been written about Simpson has been confined to authors within the Christian and Missionary Alliance circles or those who have close ties with it. Those books have not been widely disseminated among the academic community and the general reading public.

So who was Albert Benjamin Simpson? The following section will trace his life and work to highlight the ministry of this often-overlooked evangelical leader.

The Life of Albert Benjamin Simpson

Albert Benjamin Simpson was born on December 15, 1843, in Bayview on Canada's Prince Edward Island. Both his father, James, and his mother, Jane, were from Scottish backgrounds and traced their ancestry back to the Reformers in Scotland.[37] As a baby, Albert was baptized and dedicated in prayer to missionary service by the Presbyterian missionary John Geddie.[38] Geddie was the first missionary from Canada to go overseas and was known as the Apostle to Aneityum in the South Sea Islands.[39] On furlough twenty-one years later, Geddie would remind Simpson of that prayer of dedication.[40]

---

37. Thompson, *A. B. Simpson*, 2.
38. Niklaus et al., *All for Jesus*, 20.
39. Stoesz, *Understanding My Church*, 102.
40. Niklaus et al., *All for Jesus*, 20.

Young Albert was born into a religious family. His father was an elder in the Presbyterian Church and would lead the family in daily devotions. On the Sabbath, he would teach the children the Westminster Shorter Catechism. Simpson's mother was also religious and sensitive. Young Albert inherited his love for poetry and literature, as well as his sensitive nature, from her. When Simpson described his upbringing later in life, he said, "We were brought up according to the strictest Puritan formula."[41] Even though Albert was brought up in the faith from infancy, he would not meet Christ as his Lord and Savior until his teenage years.

Albert's father was a shipbuilder on Prince Edward Island. Due to a financial depression, he was forced to sell his business, and the family moved to Western Ontario. There they bought a farm, and James Simpson became a farmer.[42] Albert grew up helping with chores on the farm. He had dreamt ever since the age of ten that he would become a minister. Albert kept this dream completely to himself despite this intense desire. His father decided that Howard, Albert's older brother, would go into the ministry and that Albert would stay on the farm to work.[43] After a difficult struggle with his father's decision, Albert went to his father to reveal his desire and asked his permission to go into the ministry. He describes this encounter with his father this way:

> I can still feel the lump that rose in my throat as I stammered out my acquiescence. Thus I ventured with broken words and stammering tongue to plead that they would consent to my getting an education if I could work it out without asking anything from them but their approval and blessing. I had a little scheme of my own to teach school and earn the money for my education. But even this I did not dare divulge, for I was a lad, less than fourteen. I remember the quiet trembling tones with which my father received my request and said, 'God bless you my boy!'[44]

Albert was given permission to pursue the ministry, but he would not get any financial help from his parents for this goal. He would be on his own.

---

41. Thompson, *A. B. Simpson*, 9.
42. Niklaus et al., *All for Jesus*, 19.
43. Stoesz, *Understanding My Church*, 102.
44. Thompson, *A. B. Simpson*, 14.

At age fifteen, Albert suffered a physical collapse. At the time, the doctor labeled it nervous exhaustion. Today one might call it a nervous breakdown. In describing his illness, Simpson says,

> A physician told me that I must not look at a book for a whole year for my nervous system had collapsed, and I was in the greatest danger. There followed a period of mental and physical agony that no language can describe. I was possessed with the idea that at a certain hour I was to die; and every day as that hour drew near, I became prostrated with dreadful nervousness, watching in agonized suspense till the hour passed and wondering that I was still alive.[45]

During this time, Simpson began reading Walter Marshall's *The Gospel Mystery of Sanctification* and came to the full assurance of his salvation.[46] He soon recovered from his illness and went on to graduate from high school at the age of sixteen. After graduation, Albert taught school for two years to save money for college so he could prepare for the ministry.[47]

In those days, the first step before entering college for the Presbyterian ministry in Canada was to go before the local presbytery. Simpson and his brother Howard both went before the Presbytery of London, Ontario, and both were accepted for the ministry. Howard Simpson would wait a year before starting college, while Albert started immediately.[48] In the fall of 1861, two months before Albert's eighteenth birthday, he enrolled as a student at Knox College in Toronto, Canada, to prepare for the Presbyterian ministry.[49] While at Knox College, Simpson supplied his services to local churches to help earn money for school.[50] Although Simpson was a good student, he excelled at preaching.[51] J. M. Mitchell, an upperclassman at Knox, described Simpson's preaching this way: "I did my work faithfully and acceptably, but was quite thrown into the shade by my junior, for already his pulpit gifts were notable."[52] Before Simpson graduated from Knox College in the spring of 1865, he was serving as a supply preacher at

45. Ibid.
46. Stoesz, *Understanding My Church*, 102.
47. Ibid., 103.
48. Tozer, *Wingspread*, 30.
49. Ibid., 33
50. Stoesz, *Understanding My Church*, 103.
51. Niklaus et al., *All for Jesus*, 26.
52. Ibid., 26–27.

Knox Church in Hamilton, Ontario. Knox Church was considered one of the most important and prestigious churches in all of Canada.[53] Only the best preachers in Canada were invited to preach there.

Simpson graduated from Knox College in April of 1865. Knox Church immediately extended an invitation to young Simpson to be their pastor. Simpson was only twenty-one years old when he was called to pastor one of the most important Presbyterian churches in Canada.[54] Tozer gives a description of Simpson's first week at the church. He writes:

> But A. B. Simpson was not the average man. So on September 11 he delivered his maiden sermon as the new pastor of Knox Church, Hamilton. The next day in the afternoon he appeared before some of the local luminaries and was solemnly ordained to the ministry by prayer and the laying on of hands. That same night he caught a train for Toronto, and the next day he was married! There followed a short honeymoon trip down the St. Lawrence, a swift journey back across the country to Hamilton and a rousing reception for the bride and groom given at the manse by the members of Knox Church.[55]

Simpson and his new wife, Margaret, served at Knox Church for eight years and had a successful and popular ministry there. During this time, they added over 750 new members to the church.[56] While at Knox Church, Simpson suffered from the cold, harsh Canadian winters that were beginning to take their toll on him.[57] Knox Church would always hold a special place in the couple's hearts, and later on they were asked to come back for special occasions.[58]

While pastoring at Knox Church, Simpson became acquainted with the Evangelical Alliance. This organization was a worldwide fellowship of evangelical Christians working for closer unity and cooperation that would show the world the oneness of the body of Jesus Christ.[59] The Evangelical Alliance sponsored a convention in New York City in 1873 that Simpson attended as a delegate. While in New York City, Simpson preached a message

---

53. Ibid., 27.
54. Ibid.
55. Tozer, *Wingspread*, 39.
56. Ibid., 44.
57. Ibid.
58. Niklaus et al., *All for Jesus*, 30.
59. Ibid., 29.

on a Sunday morning at the Thirteenth Street Presbyterian Church. It was there that convention delegates from Chestnut Street Presbyterian Church in Louisville, Kentucky, first heard Simpson preach. They extended a call to him to be their pastor, which he accepted.[60] Nearly six years later, Simpson left the church in Kentucky when the Thirteenth Street Presbyterian Church in New York called him to be their pastor.[61]

Simpson resigned from Knox Church to begin his ministry in Kentucky in January of 1874. At this time, Louisville was still a divided city following the wake of the Civil War. Kentucky had been a border state, and loyalties were still sharply split. What better way to unite a church than to bring a Canadian pastor who would be neutral?[62] This is exactly what Simpson did. During Simpson's ministry at Louisville, he organized a citywide crusade. He and other pastors invited Major D. W. Whittle, an important evangelist, along with gifted soloist P. P. Bliss, to lead the crusade. During this crusade, hundreds were converted throughout the city.[63] After Whittle and Bliss left, Simpson continued with the evangelistic crusades on Sunday evenings. His church built a tabernacle to try to reach the unevangelized masses in Louisville. It was during this time that Simpson experienced a deeper understanding of sanctification. It was also in Louisville that God gave Simpson a vision for a worldwide outreach.[64] Simpson had a desire to be involved in the center of missionary activity, and he had already begun formulating the idea of publishing an illustrated missionary magazine.[65]

When Simpson received a call from the Thirteenth Street Presbyterian Church, he saw it as an opportunity to expand his vision to reach the world—both those in his own church and in other denominations. Thompson, a personal friend of Simpson and his biographer as well, wrote, "In New York he would be at the missionary center of his own denomination and others, and plans were formulating for a personal ministry on behalf of Christian millions."[66] Simpson accepted the call and began his ministry at Thirteenth Street Presbyterian Church on December 9, 1879.[67] Mem-

60. Ibid., 28.
61. Ibid., 29.
62. Tozer, *Wingspread*, 55.
63. Ibid., 58.
64. Ibid., 61.
65. Stoesz, *Understanding My Church*, 105.
66. Thompson, *A. B. Simpson*, 83.
67. Niklaus et al., *All for Jesus*, 35.

bership at Thirteenth Street Presbyterian Church began increasing almost immediately after Simpson began his ministry there, since many who attended were being converted.

It was during these two years of ministry at Thirteenth Street that Simpson experienced a divine healing that would change his ministry. Although things were progressing well at the church, conflict arose between Simpson and the leadership of the church. The congregation and its leaders had a different vision of who it was that they wanted to reach and bring into the church for the Savior than Simpson did. Church leaders wanted only those of similar social and economic status in their church. They did not want to allow those from the lower classes to attend their fellowship. Simpson had been doing street evangelism that had won more than one hundred converts from a poor Italian quarter of the city. When he came to bring these converts into the church session, the leaders asked him to find a church for them that would be more in line with the newcomers' social and economic class. It was felt that these converts would be more "comfortable" with people of their own status.[68] Simpson realized that at this church, he could never fulfill his vision of reaching the lost masses. Writing about the experience, Simpson states,

> For two years I spent a happy ministry with this noble people, but found after a thorough and honest trial it would be difficult for them to adjust themselves to the radical and aggressive measures to which God was leading me. What they wanted was a conventional parish for respectable Christians. What their young pastor wanted was a multitude of publicans and sinners. Therefore, after two years of most congenial and cordial fellowship with these dear people, and without a strain of any kind, I frankly told them that God was calling me to a different work, and I asked them and the Presbytery of New York to release me for the purpose of preaching the Gospel to the masses.[69]

Simpson resigned from the church on November 6, 1881, and he preached his last message at the midweek service. His sermon was from Luke 4:18: "The Spirit of the Lord is upon me, because he hath anointed me to preach the Gospel to the poor."[70]

---

68. Thompson, *A. B. Simpson*, 68.
69. Ibid., 84–85.
70. Ibid., 85.

A. B. Simpson

The Beginning of the Christian and Missionary Alliance

Simpson asked the people from his church to stay rather than to follow him in his new outreach. Most followed his advice. He announced in the New York newspapers that he would begin Sunday afternoon services in Caledonia Hall near Eighth Avenue. At the first meeting, seven people showed up.[71] In February of 1882, the group organized a church. There were thirty-five original members. They called the church the New York Gospel Tabernacle.[72] Over the next year, the church would meet in such diverse locations as the Academy of Music, Steinway Hall, Grand Opera Hall, a tent, an armory that had been refurbished into a theater, a massive church building, and the Hippodrome that would later become Madison Square Garden.[73] The church finally built a permanent building on the corner of Eighth Avenue and West Forty-fourth Street, which was jut one block from Times Square. It was dedicated in May of 1889.[74] The Gospel Tabernacle soon grew to well over one thousand members.[75]

From the beginning, many new ministries were born from the Gospel Tabernacle Church. The New York Missionary Training College was founded in October of 1882. This would later evolve into Nyack College. The Training College was one of the first Bible colleges in the country.[76] During this time, Simpson began a publishing house that began printing the magazine *The Word, the Work, and the World*, a missionary and deeper life periodical. In 1883, Simpson opened a home in the city to help those in need of spiritual and physical healing. This would become known as the Berachah Home and would later move to Nyack.[77] Several rescue missions were also opened, and an orphanage was begun on Long Island.[78] The Gospel Tabernacle became a hub of activity reaching out to the lost masses throughout New York City and to the outermost parts of the world.

In 1887, Simpson began the Christian Alliance. The Christian Alliance was to be a group of evangelical Christians in various churches who

---

71. Stoesz, *Understanding My Church*, 107.
72. Ibid.
73. Ibid..
74. Tozer, *Wingspread*, 91.
75. Stoesz, *Understanding My Church*, 109.
76. Ibid.
77. Ibid.
78. Ibid.

believed in the Fourfold Gospel. They would meet together to fellowship, to pray, and to encourage one another. They would aggressively proclaim these great truths to all those around them.[79] This group of believers was organized into several small groups called "branches." Simpson emphasized that this was not a church body. He stated, "It is not an ecclesiastical body in any sense, but simply a fraternal union of consecrated believers in connection with the various evangelical churches. It does not organize distinct churches or require its members to leave their present church connections."[80] Anyone could join by signing a simple pledge that was an outline of the gospel and belief in the Fourfold Gospel.[81] Simpson formed the Evangelical Missionary Alliance in 1887, shortly after the Christian Alliance. It was to be an association within the Christian Alliance that was to support missions and missionaries. The Evangelical Missionary Alliance was to serve as the missionary outreach of the Christian Alliance.[82]

Tozer defines the goals of the Evangelical Missionary Alliance in simple terms. He writes, "It was an undenominational society for the rapid evangelization of the most neglected sections of the foreign mission field, using laymen and laywomen as well as regular ministers to carry on its work."[83] The name was changed two years later to the International Missionary Alliance.[84] Simpson was the leader of both of these societies. Ten years later, in 1897, these societies combined to form one society called the Christian and Missionary Alliance.[85] This was the forerunner of the present denomination. Simpson was elected president of this new society the same year and would continue to lead the Christian and Missionary Alliance until his death in 1919.

With each passing year, the Alliance continued to grow. By 1917, shortly before Simpson's death, the Alliance had 292 missionaries overseas and 270 Alliance evangelists and superintendents in the United States and Canada.[86] John Sawin comments, "By 1917, after an entire generation of

---

79. Thompson, *A. B. Simpson*, 128–29.
80. Ibid., 129.
81. Ibid., 129–30.
82. Niklaus et al., *All for Jesus*, 76.
83. Tozer, *Wingspread*, 84.
84. Ibid., 100.
85. Ibid., 100–101.
86. Niklaus et al., *All for Jesus*, 132.

activity, the Alliance was looking more and more like a missionary denomination instead of a missionary movement."[87]

While talking to a visitor from Jamaica on his porch at his home at Nyack, Simpson passed into the presence of God. This was on October 28, 1919. On hearing of Simpson's death, Henry Frost, President of the China Inland Missions, made this comment: "Dr. Simpson belonged to the whole Church of Christ. His ministries overflowed boundaries and went out into every place."[88] Simpson died shortly after the Third Great Awakening ended.

In the next section, we will look at Simpson's message and how he personally experienced the Fourfold Gospel before he preached it to the world.

Simpson's Message: The Fourfold Gospel

The Fourfold Gospel, which was the message of A. B. Simpson, also became the message of the Christian and Missionary Alliance. What is the Fourfold Gospel? As David Fessenden explains, "Simpson's formula [the Fourfold Gospel] placed the emphasis on Christ, but also stressed the benefits to the individual believer from a relationship with Him (Christ our Savior, our Sanctifier, our Healer and our Coming King). Moreover, the use of the term 'gospel' implies the necessity to proclaim it as the church's primary message, while the four 'folds' of the phrase outline the content of the message."[89] Each of the folds of the Fourfold Gospel speaks of the roles that Christ plays in a believer's life. It is a Christ-centered message.[90] It was a message being

---

87. Ibid.

88. Ibid., 141.

89. Fessenden, "Present Truths," 3.

90. Hartzfeld and Nienkirchen, *Birth of a Vision*, 4. Simpson explained the message of the Fourfold Gospel as follows: He writes:

> 1. Christ is our complete Savior from guilt . . . from inbred sin, from sickness . . . for time and for eternity. 2. Christian holiness is . . . Christ life, perfection in Christ abiding in a perfect Christ. 3. Christian holiness is a free gift of God through Jesus Christ . . . received by faith and retained by abiding in Him . . . We do not grow into it, but we go into it and grow out from it into all the fullness of stature of Christ. 4. Healing is the purchase of Christ's atonement and the gift of Christ indwelling and resurrection life. Through the indwelling Christ, we are supernaturally quickened, sustained and enabled to rise above the power of disease, to overcome infirmity and to fulfill all of the work to which He calls us until our life work is complete and we rise to the higher life of immortal resurrection. 5. The age we live in points to a speedy consummation. The Holy Scriptures meet this expectation with the personal and pre-millennial coming of the Lord Jesus Christ to set up His Kingdom on earth (ibid.).

proclaimed and preached by many in the late nineteenth and early twentieth centuries. The term "Fourfold Gospel"—which sums up an emphasis on Jesus as Savior, Sanctifier, Healer, and Coming King—was coined by Simpson. It became the watchword of the Alliance and many other movements. While speaking at the opening of a convention in 1890 at the Gospel Tabernacle, Simpson remarked that the term "the Fourfold Gospel" came to him by inspiration.[91] William MacArthur, who was an associate and friend of Simpson's, comments on the Fourfold Gospel's impact on Simpson: "The facts of the Fourfold Gospel became like fire in his bones."[92] Simpson saw the Fourfold Gospel as a whole as well as the sum of its components. It was necessary to preach and emphasize all the folds of the Fourfold Gospel because they were deeply interrelated.[93] Simpson wrote:

> Christ as our Savior is not enough. The new convert must be led forward into the baptism of the Holy Spirit. Every Christian needs the inspiration and support of a deeper life and an abiding union with the Lord Jesus Christ. Divine healing alone will surely lead you into fanaticism and distortion. It must spring in its truest meaning from a deep spiritual intimacy with the Lord Jesus.[94]

The message of the Fourfold Gospel is simply that one needs to accept Christ as one's Savior, Sanctifier, Healer, and Coming King. Sawin, an Alliance historian, understood Simpson to believe that the Fourfold Gospel was the key to unlocking people's hearts so that they would accept the burden of reaching the world for Christ.[95] This was the emphasis of Simpson's ministry, and the Christian and Missionary Alliance continued this message in its local and worldwide outreach.

For Simpson, the Scripture was always primary; whatever he believed or taught had to be based on the Bible. Simpson turned first to the Scriptures to answer the questions that came up in his life and ministry. After he was convinced a notion was biblical, he would then seek to have it confirmed by his own experience. All the ideas that Simpson preached had to be taught by the Scripture and confirmed in the Scripture. Simpson also looked to the history of the church to validate his experience. Simpson had been educated with a classical seminary education and was familiar

91. Ibid.
92. Hartzfeld and Nienkirchen, *Birth of a Vision*, 3.
93. Ibid., 4–5.
94. Ibid., 6.
95. Ibid., 4–5.

with both church history and theology. He wrote about how the medieval treatise *True Peace*, a book that dealt with listening to God, impacted his life and changed his ministry.[96] This shows Simpson's familiarity with this period of the church.[97] Simpson did not preach anything he had not experienced personally. Experience was important to him, but the Bible reigned supreme as the best judge of experience. This is one of the reasons why Simpson was such an effective preacher of such powerful messages.

Frederic Senft, in the introduction to Simpson's *The Four-Fold Gospel*, wrote,

> The title of this little volume, *The Four-Fold Gospel*, has been a familiar phrase to thousands of God's children during the past 40 years. Not that the truths contained in the statement were unknown before, but the grouping of them in form was given to Dr. A. B. Simpson after he had happily experienced the fullness of the Fourfold Gospel in his own life.[98]

Without this truth, all that Simpson accomplished would have been in vain and his ministry never would have had the impact it did.[99] Walter Turnbull, an early leader in the Alliance, wrote in the foreword to the first volume of Simpson's *The Holy Spirit* that "Sunday after Sunday Dr. Simpson poured out his heart in Scriptural teaching and earnest exhortation, aiming constantly to lead his auditors to definite acceptance of the fullness of the Spirit. His own life flamed with the reality of the message his lips proclaimed."[100]

Simpson shares in his writings that there were three crises he went through to discover the first three folds of the Fourfold Gospel. While Simpson was speaking in 1885 at the International Convention on Holiness and Divine Healing at Bethshan, London, he shared the following testimony with the delegates:

> Some twenty-seven years ago, I floundered for ten months in the waters of despondency, and I got out of there just by believing in

---

96. Simpson, *Holy Spirit*, 1:160–62.

97. Hartzfeld and Nienkirchen, *Birth of a Vision*, 166. Dwayne Ratzliff, in his chapter titled "An Old Medieval Message: A Turning Point in the Life of A. B. Simpson," writes of the impact of the treatise *True Peace* and other literature that had an impact on Simpson's spiritual life and ministry.

98. Simpson, *Four-Fold Gospel*, 4.

99. Ibid., 5.

100. Simpson, *Holy Spirit*, 1:3.

Jesus as my Saviour. About twelve years ago I got into another deep experience of conviction, and I got out of that by believing in Jesus as my Sanctifier. After years of teaching and waiting on Him, the Lord Jesus Christ showed me four years ago that it was his blessed will to be my complete Savior for body as well as soul.[101]

The following section shows how those three crises actually came about and how they changed Simpson's life.

Simpson's Three Crises

A. B. Simpson grew up in a Christian home. Both his parents were devout Christians who attempted to bring up their children in the ways of God. His parents were Presbyterians and brought the children up under Reformed and Puritan principles of the faith. Young Simpson had memorized the Westminster Shorter Catechism by the time he reached the age of twelve.[102] Simpson, looking back at his strict religious upbringing, saw its value as preparation for his ministry. He reminisces:

> Looking back on these early influences I cannot say I wholly regret the somewhat stern mould in which my life was shaped. It taught me a spirit of reverence and wholesome discipline for which I have often had cause to thank God, the absence of which is perhaps the greatest loss of the rising generation today. It threw over my youthful spirit a natural horror of evil things which often safeguarded me afterwards when as a young man amid the temptations of the world.[103]

Simpson valued the doctrine he was taught as a child and even the lessons he found boring as a child. He remembers:

> The religious knowledge, which was crammed into my mind even without my understanding it, furnished me with forms of doctrine and statements of truth which afterwards became illuminated by the Holy Spirit and realized in my own experience, and thus became ultimately the precious vessels for holding the treasures of divine knowledge.[104]

---

101. Simpson, *Four-Fold Gospel*, 3.
102. Stoesz, *Sanctification*, 11.
103. Thompson, *A. B. Simpson*, 11.
104. Ibid.

Simpson saw God's hand on his life even before his conversion. He recognized God's divine protection in saving him from death at least three times in his unregenerate state.[105]

Although raised in a spiritual environment, Simpson had no idea how he could know God in a personal way. God seemed far off and austere to Simpson, and there appeared to be no way he could ever please God. Martin Luther's struggle to know God and his resulting realization that he could do nothing to make himself acceptable to God closely paralleled young Simpson's own struggle with God. It was during this time that Simpson had a nervous breakdown and sank into a deep despondency. Simpson commented that up until and during this crisis, no one had shared with him the simple gospel message. He remarks, "It now seems strange that there was no voice there to tell me the simple way of believing in the promise and accepting the salvation fully provided and freely offered."[106] It was during this time that Simpson met Christ as his Savior.

During those months of darkness and despondency, Simpson happened to be in the library of his former minister and teacher when he stumbled on an old and musty book.[107] The book was Walter Marshall's *Gospel Mystery of Sanctification*. Tozer describes Simpson flipping through the pages. He writes:

> . . . suddenly his eyes were fixed on a passage that stood out like fire from the rest: "the first good work you will ever perform is to believe on the Lord Jesus Christ. Until you do this, all your works, prayers, tears and good resolutions are vain. To believe on the Lord Jesus Christ is to believe that he saves you according to his Word, that he receives and saves you here and now for he has said: 'Him that cometh to me I will in no wise cast out.'"[108]

This was enough for young Simpson; he got down on his knees and received Christ as Savior.[109] After Simpson's conversion, he recovered physically and was ready to serve God as his child rather than as an outsider.

The second crisis that influenced the next fold of the Fourfold Gospel happened during Simpson's pastorate at the Chestnut Street Presbyterian Church in Louisville, Kentucky. He ministered there from 1874 to 1879

---

105. Ibid., 12.
106. Ibid., 16.
107. Ibid.
108. Tozer, *Wingspread*, 24–25.
109. Ibid.

during the turbulent years after the Civil War. This was a time of struggle for Simpson. While in Louisville, Simpson sensed his lack of personal holiness and failure of power for service.[110] Simpson later describes this struggle while referring to himself in the third person.[111] Recounting his despondency, Simpson writes of himself, "He struggled long and vainly with his own intense nature, his strong self will, his peculiar temptations, and his spiritual life had been constant humiliation. He had talked to the people about the deeper things of the spirit but there was a hollow ring, and his heart was breaking to know the Lord Jesus as a living reality."[112]

Upon hearing of a Christian Worker's Conference sponsored by the Moody Evangelistic Association in Chicago, Simpson decided to attend. He went to a pre-conference testimony service, and there God spoke to him.[113] Simpson later describes what happened: "I came here expecting Mr. Moody to help me. But last night I saw Jesus, and I got such a look at Jesus that I am never going to need anything [else] as long as I live."[114] After experiencing this, Simpson came to the conviction that he must go directly to Jesus.[115]

Without attending the conference, Simpson took the train back to Louisville and arrived early in the morning. He talked to no one and went directly to his study, where he locked himself inside.[116] Simpson went directly to God on this issue. While in his library, he took out W. E. Boardman's *The Higher Christian Life* and started to read through the book. He began to see Christ was indeed the Sanctifier. The Christian life was not meant to be understood as Christians trying to live their lives independently, but rather as a personal surrendering to Christ to allow Christ to live his life through humankind. Samuel Stoesz writes: "Christ had not saved him merely from future peril and then left him to fight the battle of life, but the Christ who had justified him was waiting to sanctify him through the Holy Spirit. Christ had come to enter his spirit and to substitute his strength, holiness, joy, love, faith and power for a helplessness and emptiness that had troubled him."[117]

---

110. McGraw, "A. B. Simpson as a Missions Advocate," 3.
111. Gilbertson, *Baptism of the Holy Spirit*, 36.
112. Ibid.
113. Stoesz, *Sanctification*, 21.
114. Hartzfeld and Nienkirchen, *Birth of a Vision*, 113.
115. Ibid.
116. Ibid.
117. Stoesz, *Sanctification*, 60.

Following this crisis experience, Simpson's personal life and ministry underwent tremendous change. This new infilling of the Holy Spirit inspired Simpson to unite the quarreling Louisville churches in order to conduct a city-wide crusade in 1875.[118] The Louisville ministers invited Major Daniel Whittle and Phillip P. Bliss to lead the meetings. Both men were involved with Moody and his ministry. Whittle, besides preaching a salvation message, also proclaimed the necessity of being filled with the Holy Spirit.[119] This message only confirmed what Simpson had discovered about Christ the Sanctifier in his study. During the crusade, five thousand people were converted, and these conversions had a tremendous impact on Louisville. As a result of their meetings, revival came to the Louisville churches.[120] Simpson was moved by the effectiveness of mass evangelism. He was also impressed by the spiritual power in Whittle's ministry.[121] Simpson's ministry would never be the same, as he would make evangelism his priority for the remainder of his life.[122] Although it was in Kentucky that Simpson came to understand Jesus as Sanctifier, it was in New York City that he would discover Christ as Healer, the third fold of the Fourfold Gospel.

Simpson considered his healing as the third greatest crisis of his life, surpassed only by his salvation and the infilling of the Holy Spirit.[123] For most of his life, Simpson had very poor health. Even as a young pastor at Knox Church in Hamilton, Canada, Simpson would carry around a bottle of ammonia in his pocket to take for his heart. If he went up even a slight elevation or climbed a flight of stairs, his heart would race until he felt he could not breathe. His health gradually deteriorated until his condition became very serious. By the time he began his pastorate in New York City, there were serious questions as to whether he could continue to minister or, for that matter, how long he might live. Simpson describes his condition by writing:

> A few months before I took Christ as my Healer, a prominent physician in New York insisted on speaking to me about my health. He told me that I had not constitutional strength to last more than

---

118. Gilbertson, *Baptism of the Holy Spirit*, 37.
119. Ibid.
120. Ibid.
121. Ibid.
122. Ibid.
123. Niklaus et al., *All for Jesus*, 43.

a few months. He required my taking immediate measures for the preservation of my life and usefulness.[124]

The future looked bleak for Simpson and his ministry.

The feeble pastor took the advice of his physician, and in the summer of 1881 he went to Saratoga Springs to recuperate and to try to regain his health. On a Sunday afternoon there, he heard an African American singing group called the Jubilee Singers. They were leading the music at an evangelistic service.[125] Simpson describes his mood as follows: "I had been deeply depressed. All things in life looked dark and withered. Suddenly I heard a chorus: My Jesus is the Lord of lords: No man can work like him!"[126] The Lord spoke to Simpson through a song. He said it was like a voice from heaven and seemed to possess his being. This knowledge that Jesus could do all things enveloped his soul. He comments: "I took Jesus to be my Lord of lords and to work in my behalf. I know not how much it all meant. But I took him in the dark and went from that rustic old-fashioned service remembering nothing else, but strongly lifted up forevermore."[127] This was the preparation that Simpson needed to later take in Christ as Healer.

A few weeks later, in late July or early August, Simpson and his family went on vacation in Old Orchard, Maine. At the time it was one of the most popular seashore resorts and religious convention grounds in the country.[128] While there, Simpson lived on the seashore and occasionally went to the meetings on the conference grounds. He reminisces, "Up to that time, I had not committed myself in any full sense to the truth or experience of divine healing."[129] However, Simpson had been interested in divine healing before his experience at Old Orchard, Maine. Several years before, he had been called by a member of his church to come pray for her son as he lay dying. Simpson prayed for the son, and he was miraculously healed. For a while, Simpson trusted Christ as his Healer, but he abandoned this position when a devout Christian physician told him it was presumptuous.[130]

---

124. Simpson, *Gospel of Healing*, 121.
125. Ibid., 122.
126. Ibid.
127. Ibid.
128. Niklaus et al., *All for Jesus*, 40.
129. Simpson, *Gospel of Healing*, 123.
130. Ibid., 124.

Simpson confesses, "I abandoned my position of simple dependence on God alone and floundered and stumbled for years."[131]

While Simpson was at Old Orchard, Charles Cullis was conducting meetings on divine healing on the conference grounds. Cullis, a Boston physician and former director of a tuberculosis hospital, was a devout Episcopalian layman. He not only treated his patients medically, he also prayed for them. Cullis saw some remarkable healings. This drove him to the Scriptures and convinced him of the truth of divine healing. He became convinced that God wanted him to carry on a healing ministry while continuing his medical practice.[132] Simpson wandered into one of Cullis' meetings in which people were sharing how they had been miraculously healed by simply trusting Christ for their healing as they trusted him for their salvation.[133] Simpson comments:

> These testimonies drove me to my Bible. I determined that I must settle the matter one way or the other. I am glad I did not go to man. At Jesus' feet, alone, with my Bible open and with no one to help or guide me I became convinced that this was part of Christ's glorious gospel for a sinful and suffering world—the purchase of his blessed cross for all who would believe and receive his Word.[134]

He went out into the woods and made a pledge to God that he would never doubt the truth again and that he would preach Christ the Healer as a regular part of the gospel message.[135]

It was not long after Simpson took Christ as his Divine Healer that his faith was tested. A few days after his experience at Old Orchard, he was asked to preach at a Congregational church several miles north of Intervale, New Hampshire.[136] Simpson felt impressed by God to preach a message on divine healing, but instead he preached what he labeled a "good sermon." He immediately felt convicted, and that night at the service that was being held in his hotel he gave this testimony on how God had healed him.[137] He never shrank back from preaching on divine healing again.

---

131. Ibid.
132. Niklaus et al., *All for Jesus*, 40.
133. Simpson, *Gospel of Healing*, 124.
134. Ibid.
135. Ibid., 125.
136. Niklaus et al., *All for Jesus*, 41.
137. Simpson, *Gospel of Healing*, 127.

He was tested again a few days later. A small group had invited Simpson to hike up Mount Kearsarge, a 3,000-foot mountain in New Hampshire. Simpson recalls what went through his mind after the invitation: "Did I not remember the dread of heights that had always overshadowed me? Did I not recall the terror with which I had resolved in Switzerland and Italy never attempt high places again? Did I not know how ordinary stairs exhausted me and distressed my poor heart?"[138] Simpson trusted that God had healed him and could give him the strength, and he ascended Mount Kearsarge. He would never be the same again. Simpson's health was restored, and he was a new man physically. Simpson writes of his newfound strength and vigor: "A few months after my healing, God called me into the special pastoral, evangelistic and literary work that has since engaged my time and energy. I may truthfully say it has involved four times more labor than have any period of my life. And yet it has been a continual delight."[139]

The final test for Simpson came when his three-year-old daughter Margaret came down with diphtheria. Simpson's wife wanted to call the doctor. They had already lost a son of the same age from the same disease.[140] Simpson instead anointed her with oil and prayed for her. He lay down with her that night, and the following day little Margaret was fine.[141] These three tests confirmed to Simpson that Christ is indeed the believer's Healer.

Simpson was faithful in preaching on divine healing, which alienated him from some of his Christian friends who could not go along with the third fold of the Fourfold Gospel. Simpson writes: "My old friends seemed to leave me, and for months I seemed to be alone—separated from hundreds and thousands of ministers and people I had loved and worked with all of my life. I felt I did not know them now and they did not know me as before."[142]

Simpson taught that although healing was important, it was subservient to the first two folds of the Fourfold Gospel: Christ as Savior and Christ as Sanctifier. He explains: "It is most important that it [healing] should be ever held in the true place in relation to the other parts of the Gospel. It is not the whole Gospel, or perhaps the chief part of it, but it is a part, and in

---

138. Ibid., 129.
139. Ibid., 140.
140. Niklaus et al., *All for Jesus*, 43.
141. Simpson, *Gospel of Healing*, 136.
142. Niklaus et al., *All for Jesus*, 43.

its due relationship to the whole it will prove to be, like the Gospel itself, 'The power of God . . . to everyone that believeth.'"[143]

In the first three elements of the Fourfold Gospel, Simpson experienced three crises that brought about his experience of Christ as Savior, Sanctifier, and Healer. The last aspect of this fourfold presentation was Christ as our Coming King. Simpson taught that the second coming of Christ had a sanctifying influence on the believer. It also encouraged the believer to work for God's kingdom.[144] Simpson states that "it is one of the strongest influences to separate us from an evil world."[145] Fessenden makes the observation:

> At first glance, 'Christ Our Coming King' would seem to depart from the other three 'folds' in the Fourfold Gospel because its direct relationship to the daily walk of the individual believer is not as obvious and yet Simpson presented the personal return of Christ as the zenith of the believers pilgrimage and the complete fulfillment of the Gospel. All the blessings of salvation, sanctification and divine healing are merely the shadow of what is to come when Christ returns for his bride.[146]

Simpson wrote that the second coming was the glorious culmination of all the parts of the gospel—that of Christ as Savior, Sanctifier, Healer, and Coming King.[147] Simpson concludes, "So that the truth and hope of the Lord's coming is linked with all truth and life and is the Church's great and blessed hope."[148]

Simpson had grown up in the Presbyterian church and attended Knox College, which was a Presbyterian college. His eschatology growing up and throughout his years in seminary as well as during his first two pastorates was a "spiritualized amillennial" or "post-millennial" view of Christ's second coming.[149] Simpson attributed his conversion to premillennialism to the Lord, who revealed to him through the Word by the Holy Spirit the truth of Christ's second coming.[150] It is important to remember that the

143. Simpson, *Gospel of Healing*, 6.
144. Hartzfeld and Nienkirchen, *Birth of a Vision*, 16.
145. Ibid.
146. Fessenden, "Present Truths," 18.
147. Simpson, *Four-Fold Gospel*, 68.
148. Ibid., 67.
149. Nienkirchen, *A. B. Simpson and the Pentecostal Movement*, 70.
150. Ibid., 20.

popular view among many evangelicals, especially among Presbyterian pastors such as Arthur T. Pierson and W. J. Erdman, was premillennialism. Pierson was a close associate of Simpson's. He ministered at Simpson's missionary conventions and taught at the Missionary Training Institute. Although Simpson was a premillennialist, he was not a dispensationalist, which was a popular view at the time.

Another good friend of Simpson's was A. J. Gordon, who he considered to be his mentor in eschatology.[151] During the eulogy Simpson gave at Gordon's funeral, he stated that Gordon's book on premillennialism, *Ecce Venit: Behold He Cometh*, was "one of the best ever published on that theme."[152] Finally it was Major Daniel Whittle, the main speaker at the Louisville crusade, who was the outspoken premillennialist who may have most influenced Simpson's view of Christ's second coming.

Simpson was unique at this time in his eschatological views because he saw a direct correlation with Christ's second coming and the fulfilling of the Great Commission verses found in Matt 28:19–20 and Acts 1:8. He also was convinced that, along with these Great Commission verses, Christians had to fulfill Matt 24:14.[153] Matthew 24:14 states, "And the Gospel of the kingdom will be preached in the whole world as a testimony to all nations and then the end will come" (NIV). Simpson linked the return of Christ with the church's missionary responsibility.[154] Sawin comments that "Students at his [Simpson's] Missionary College and those who attended the conventions felt the urgency of this verse. Failure to take the Gospel where Christ was not known simply delayed His return. Therefore, to the work!"[155] Sawin goes on to say that Walter Turnbull, an associate of Simpson's, declared Simpson to be the only missionary leader that associated Christ's second coming with the completion of the missionary task.[156]

Missions and evangelism became the lifeblood of Simpson and the early Christian and Missionary Alliance. They were proclaiming the gospel to unreached people to help bring back the Coming King. Simpson writes in his book *Missionary Messages*, "We know that our missionary work is not in vain, but, in addition to the blessing it is to bring souls to Christ, it is to

---

151. Ibid.
152. Ibid., 22.
153. Hartzfeld and Nienkirchen, *Birth of a Vision*, 15.
154. Ibid
155. Ibid.
156. Ibid.

bring Christ himself back again."[157] He knew that not all would accept the gospel message. The goal was to gather a remnant for Christ's return. When this remnant was complete, then Christ would come. Simpson remarks, "We know that as many as are disposed to eternal life will believe and that when the last of this glorious company shall have been gathered home, the age will close and the Lord will come."[158] This motivation of bringing back the Coming King drove the early Christian and Missionary Alliance to become one of the great missionary forces in the late nineteenth century and early twentieth century, as it still is today.

Another aspect of Christ as the Coming King was that it had a sanctifying effect on Christians. It would cause believers to live holy lives and work for Christ.[159] In Simpson's *The Four-Fold Gospel*, he tells of the effect Christ's second coming has on believers: "It causes the Christian to be ready. Secondly, it causes us to be watching. Thirdly, it causes us to be faithful. Finally, it causes us to be diligent."[160]

Christ's second coming sanctifies believers and encourages them to live holy lives. Both of these aspects of Christ as the Coming King drove Simpson to serve God. He wanted to be involved in helping to bring back the King. He also wanted to be a faithful servant so that God would be pleased in his work for the Savior. The vision of Christ as the Coming King is what drove Simpson and the Christian and Missionary Alliance. It became a model and an example to other denominations and missionary organizations, which has impacted both North America and the world at large.

The Third Great Awakening made a tremendous impact on Christianity at the end of the nineteenth and early twentieth century. It was due to the Awakening that the church reached out to the masses in North America and the unreached peoples of the world. Moody, Phoebe Palmer, Gordon, Pierson, Torrey, Chapman, and Simpson were instrumental in the Great Awakening. Simpson was one of the leaders of the Awakening and well known in his day, but today he has been neglected by scholars despite the fact that he began the missionary church, helped found the Christian and Missionary Alliance, and helped popularize the Fourfold Gospel. The Fourfold Gospel and the missionary outreach of Simpson and the Alliance

---

157. Simpson, *Missionary Messages*, 167.
158. Ibid., 176–81.
159. Hartzfeld and Nienkirchen, *Birth of a Vision*, 16.
160. Simpson, *Four-fold Gospel*, 90–93.

impacted the Awakening as a movement. Evangelism was the key component in the spread of the Third Great Awakening, and the next chapter will examine the evangelism phase of the Awakening as well as Simpson's place in evangelism.

III

SIMPSON'S PLACE IN EVANGELISM

Simpson's passion for evangelism began with his own struggle during his conversion experience. He never forgot the distress he went through struggling to accept Christ as his Savior. Though he had grown up in a Christian family, the church he attended never explained the gospel to him. After his conversion, Simpson saw a dramatic change in his life that impacted him in all ways. His burden for reaching the lost on behalf of Christ blossomed in his ministry at the Chestnut Street Presbyterian Church in Louisville, Kentucky, and it culminated in his ministry at the Gospel Tabernacle in New York City. It was in Louisville that Simpson saw the importance of the centrality of evangelism in the church. He, along with other pastors as well as with Major Whittle and P. P. Bliss, organized the evangelistical crusade at which revival broke out. When the other pastors did not want to continue with the evangelistical outreach after Whittle and Bliss' crusade, Simpson and his church continued. This focus on evangelism continued for the next five years. It would be here that Simpson came to see what a united church could do through evangelism to reach not only an urban community, but also the world with the gospel.

While in New York City at the Thirteenth Street Presbyterian Church, Simpson's vision of evangelism clashed with that of the leaders of the church. He saw the church's primary function as reaching out in evangelism, but that was not the view held by most in leadership. Simpson resigned from the church and gathered a like-minded group of people with a vision to reach New York City and the world beyond. From this group, the Gospel Tabernacle was founded. It was from this body of believers that the missionary society that became the Christian and Missionary Alliance was formed. Evangelism became Simpson's and the church's primary passion. Although Simpson saw himself primarily as a pastor, he viewed evangelism as the most important ministry of his office.

The first fold of Simpson's Fourfold Gospel message was the truth that Christ had died for humankind and so had provided salvation for all of humanity.[1] Simpson believed that it this fold was the foundation of his evangelistic outreach. It would also become the main focus of the Christian and Missionary Alliance, the denomination he founded. As George Pardington, one of the early leaders of the Christian and Missionary Alliance, remarked,

> The primary message of the Alliance is Christ our Savior. Our first business for the king is the salvation of sinners. To win souls is our fundamental ministry. Indeed, to lie in wait for men like the Master Himself and with the wisdom and skill that are born from above to catch them in the net of the Gospel is the highest calling of the surrendered and consecrated Christian.[2]

Simpson fully embraced this primary message. As J. Edwin Orr explains, the Third Great Awakening can be divided into three phrases as follows. The initial phase was the outpouring of the Holy Spirit, which lasted from 1857 until 1859. The second phase was the evangelism phase, which took place shortly after the Civil War and lasted until 1899. The third phase began with the Welsh Revival between 1904 and 1905, and its evangelism phase lasted until World War I. As will be seen, Simpson was a part of each of these phases.

Simpson was converted at the beginning of the Third Great Awakening and ministered throughout the second and third phase of the Awakening until his death at the end of the Third Great Awakening. Joel Carpenter comments on Simpson and other leaders' involvement when he writes:

> Moody's partners in this new wave of popular outreach were a group of gifted and respectable urban pastors, such as Presbyterian A. J. Pierson of Philadelphia and A. B. Simpson of New York, and Baptists, A. J. Gordon of Boston and A. C. Dixon of Baltimore. These ministers modified their own genteel tastes and values and

---

1. Fessenden, "Present Truths," 5.
2. Pardington, *Twenty-Five Wonderful Years*, 52.

revamped their congregations to reflect the popular revivalistic style of urban evangelists.[3]

There were many men and women who were involved in the evangelism phase that helped spread the Awakening. A number of pastors and evangelists saw large numbers come to Christ including Simpson. Orr comments that it was during the Third Great Awakening that the church rediscovered evangelism.[4] He wrote:

> All things considered, the nineteenth century Awakening [the Third Great Awakening] represented no great discovery or rediscovery of doctrine. Its language was largely that of the New Testament stated in the language of the Reformers and the Revivalists of an earlier century. The great contribution of the Awakening was its application of these doctrines in the evangelization of the great mass of unchurched at home and the heathen abroad.[5]

This period would become the era of the evangelist. Nathan Hatch, commenting on the twentieth century, speaks about some of the leaders in evangelism at that time. He writes, "Evangelicals in this century, on the other hand have virtually organized their faith around the issue of communicating the gospel. Evangelism and missions were the principle burden of leaders such as A. B. Simpson, A. J. Gordon, R. A. Torrey, Charles E. Fuller, V. Raymond Edmans, Harold Ockenga and Billy Graham."[6]

Moody's Impact on the Awakening

Simpson, along with many others, poured his heart into evangelism. D. L. Moody became the primary leader of the revival and helped spread the Awakening. Through his campaigns, God transformed this former shoe salesman into one of the greatest evangelists in the later half of the nineteenth century. One scholar estimated that Moody presented the gospel to over one hundred million people in his lifetime.[7] This was more people than any evangelist had ever spoken to until Billy Graham came on the scene in the twentieth century—and Moody did all his preaching without

---

3. Carpenter, *Revive Us Again*, 35.
4. Orr, *Second Evangelical Awakening*, 121.
5. Ibid., 120.
6. Marty, *Fundamentalism and Evangelicalism*, 13.
7. Terry, *Evangelism: A Concise History*, 148.

the benefit of microphones and public address systems. This was true of all the evangelists and leaders of his era, including Simpson.

Moody preached a simple salvation message emphasizing the need for a personal relationship with Jesus Christ.[8] Moody had been brought to salvation by Edward Kimball, his Sunday school teacher in Boston. Kimball saw this young eighteen-year-old shoe salesman had an interest in spiritual things and went to him privately to share the message of Christ, and Moody was gloriously converted.[9] Moody recollects his conversion with the following words:

> When I was in Boston I used to attend a Sunday School class, and one day I recalled my teacher came around behind the counter of the shop I was at work in, and put his hand upon my shoulder, and talked to me about Christ and my soul. I had not felt I had a soul till then. I said to myself, "this is a very strange thing. Here is a man who never saw me till lately, and he is weeping over my sins, and I never shed a tear about them." But I understood it now, and know what it is to have a passion for men's souls and weep over their sins. I don't remember what he said, but I can feel the power of that man's hand on my shoulder tonight. It was not long after that I was brought into the Kingdom of God.[10]

Moody changed and put his whole heart and effort in reaching the lost for Christ, beginning with Sunday school children in Chicago.

Moody once said, "Christianity is not a creed; it is not doctrine, it is not feeling; it is not an impression; but it is a person." Moody saw that his purpose was to introduce others to the Savior.[11]

The theology of Moody can be summed up by the three Rs.[12] First, he believed humanity was *ruined by Adam's fall.* Moody believed in the total depravity of man. People were sinful. Moody said, "I look upon this world as a wrecked vessel; God has given me a lifeboat and said to me, 'Moody save all you can.'" The second R that Moody believed was that humanity was *redeemed by the blood of Christ.* He preached over and over again the necessity for the unsaved to come to God through Christ's blood. He also taught that it was because of God's love for sinners that he sent Christ to

---

8. Ibid., 151.
9. Dorsett, *Passion for Souls,* 46.
10. Ibid., 47.
11. Terry, *Evangelism: A Concise History,* 151.
12. Ibid., 152.

die on the cross for humanity. Moody's last R was *regenerated by the Spirit*. It is the Holy Spirit who brings people to the Savior. It is only through the power of the Holy Spirit that this can be accomplished, so one must look to the Holy Spirit to do the convicting work in a sinner's life.[13]

Moody saw his ministry as pointing sinners to the Savior, whether it was individually or in a crusade. What made Moody so effective? Moody's preaching was simple, and anyone could understand it. Although Moody's grammar was at times atrocious, he used short, simple sentences everyone could comprehend. He was a good communicator. Moody used numerous illustrations that people could identify with. He was also a great storyteller. He was very humorous in his preaching. He could also make people cry when he preached. His sincerity showed through, and people trusted him.[14] All these factors were appealing to people. This is why Moody appealed to simple factory workers and to seminary students such as R. A. Torrey at Yale. Gifted as he was in these areas, there was something Moody was missing that would ultimately make an even greater impact on his preaching.

Until his third trip to Great Britain, Moody had been involved in Sunday school work, the YMCA, and the founding of a church. He would speak at meetings, but it was not until his filling by the Holy Spirit that God began to work through him in a mighty way. Moody described his experience by writing, "Ah, what a day!—I cannot describe it. I seldom refer to it, it is almost too sacred an experience to share—Paul had an experience of which he never spoke for fourteen years.—I can only say God revealed Himself to me, and I had such an experience of His love that I had to ask him to stay his hand."[15]

It was after this experience of sanctification that Moody saw God work through his ministry in a great way. Moody and his soloist, Ira Sankey, were invited to go to England to preach at a number of meetings. They arrived in England in 1873 to find that two of the people who had invited them had died.[16] Moody and Sankey stayed, and with the help of others, they found places to preach. God began to pour out his Spirit on the meetings, and revival broke out.[17] It's been estimated that between June 1873 and August 1875, Moody and Sankey spoke and sang to over two-and-a-half million

13. Ibid.
14. Ibid., 155
15. Dorsett, *Passion for Souls*, 156.
16. Cohen, *Spirit of the Lord*, 117.
17. Hoffman, *Revival Times in America*, 131.

people.[18] It was advertised in the papers that Moody would preach the gospel and Sankey would sing it. The revival spread throughout all of Great Britain. Fred Hoffman comments:

> The revival spread rapidly through England and Scotland, and across to Ireland, resulting in many thousands of converts. This fruitful ministry in the British Isles continued for more than two years. Invitations came from the largest cities in Britain and the revival spread and increased in power, culminating in a great four months' campaign in the city of London. The whole city was profoundly stirred for God, and the church throughout the nation was graciously revived.[19]

As the news spread to America about the revival in the British Isles, Moody and Sankey received more speaking engagements than they knew what to do with.

When Moody returned to the United States after the evangelistic campaigns in England, he found that his reputation as an evangelist had been established. Moody's first campaign back in America was in Brooklyn in 1875. The meetings were held in a large facility called "The Rink," which had a seating capacity of five thousand. The crowds were so great that over twenty thousand people had to be turned away.[20] This would be a foreshadowing of the popularity Moody would enjoy for the next quarter of a century.[21] Moody returned to Great Britain in 1881 and stayed until 1884, during which time he saw even greater results than he did on his first tour.[22] Moody made his final evangelistic trip to Great Britain in 1891 and stayed until 1892.[23] Scharpff wrote, "His methods of evangelism greatly influenced Great Britain, and his writings left a deep impact on the Continent."[24]

Moody and Sankey continued their campaigns throughout the United States during this period and held campaigns in large cities such as Chicago, Baltimore, St. Louis, and Cincinnati, but they also went to smaller cities.[25] Moody continued his involvement with evangelistic crusades until

---

18. Scharpff, *History of Evangelism*, 175.
19. Hoffman, *Revival Times in America*, 131.
20. Muncy, *History of Evangelism in the United States*, 144.
21. Ibid.
22. Scharpff, *History of Evangelism*, 175.
23. Ibid., 174.
24. Ibid., 175–76.
25. Hoffman, *Revival Times in America*, 133.

his death in 1899.[26] Hoffman comments that "the last twenty-five years of his [Moody] ministry was largely in the great cities, resulting in a continuous spirit of revival throughout America."[27]

A fitting climax to Moody's evangelistic outreach was the campaign to evangelize those at the Columbian Exposition, the World's Fair that was held in Chicago in 1893. Moody organized and directed the six-month evangelistic outreach, and it was widely successful.[28] Moody brought a number of evangelists in for the World's Fair, which included Torrey, Wilbur Chapman, and a relatively unknown young evangelist by the name of Billy Sunday.[29] Many were converted at the Columbian Exposition directly through the efforts of Moody and the others.

Moody's influence during the Third Great Awakening was incalculable. God chose him to promote evangelism during this period. Certainly Moody did not act alone in this promotion: there were others such as A. J. Gordon, R. A. Torrey, Wilbur Chapman, A. B. Simpson, and A. C. Dixon, but Moody had the greatest impact. Scharpff remarks, "It would not be an overstatement to call Moody the greatest evangelist of his generation and one of the most fruitful soul-winners in kingdom history."[30] Moody's influence was seen not only in his ministry in the Third Great Awakening, but also in the impact he would have on those who came to be included in his evangelism after the Welsh Revival. Moody influenced most of those who would become leaders in the worldwide evangelistic outreach following the Welsh Revival—most notably, Torrey, Chapman, and Sunday. These three men would become key figures in the second evangelism phase,[31] with Torrey and Chapman becoming Moody's "first lieutenants."

Moody's Lieutenants

Torrey had come in contact with Moody while a student at Yale Divinity School. Torrey and some friends attended a service led by Moody to see

---

26. Ibid.
27. Ibid., 134.
28. Ibid., 135.
29. Dorsett, *Passion for Souls*, 390.
30. Scharpff, *History of Evangelism*, 177.
31. Orr, *Second Evangelical Awakening*, 263.

what this uneducated layman could teach them!³² Muncy gives us the story of Torrey's encounter with Moody:

> They [Torrey and his friends] went rather condescendingly to see what this uneducated layman might have to say. They were so impressed with Moody's message that they requested him to teach them how to win souls to Christ. Mr. Moody gave them some verses of Scripture to use and said, "You go at it, the best way to learn is to go at it. How to do it is to do it." This experience kindled the fires of evangelism in the soul of young Torrey and further prepared him for a career in evangelism.³³

In 1889, Torrey became Superintendent at Moody Bible Institute. He would also become the pastor of the Moody Church. Torrey continued in these two capacities until 1902.³⁴ After much prayer by himself and his church, he took a leave of absence at that time to take an evangelistic tour around the world.³⁵ Torrey took Charles Alexander as his soloist, and the two visited Australia, India, and Great Britain. Wherever Torrey and Alexander went, revival broke out.³⁶ Torrey and Alexander returned to America in 1906, continuing their evangelistic campaigns throughout the United States and Canada.³⁷ Between 1911 and 1921, Torrey made several evangelistic trips abroad to Great Britain and Asia.³⁸ From 1912 to 1914, Torrey served as Dean of the Bible Institute of Los Angeles and also served as the pastor of the Church of the Open Door in that same city. He spent his summers in Bible conference ministry and evangelism.³⁹ In 1924, Torrey resigned from his post as Superintendent at the Bible college and pastor of the church in order to give himself over fully to evangelism until his death in 1926.⁴⁰

This author had the privilege of meeting the evangelist Vance Havner late in Havner's life. I asked him if he had ever heard Torrey preach. Havner said he knew Torrey and had heard him preach often. He said that Torrey's

---

32. Muncy, *History of Evangelism in the United States*, 148.
33. Ibid.
34. Ibid., 149.
35. Hoffman, *Revival Times in America*, 147.
36. Ibid.
37. Ibid.
38. Ibid.
39. Ibid.
40. Ibid., 148.

messages were basic, but it seemed that whenever he spoke, the Holy Spirit worked in a great way, and many would come forward to receive Christ. There was a special sense of the Holy Spirit in his ministry, not unlike that of his mentor, Moody.

Moody also impacted Chapman in a great way. In fact, it was Moody who led Chapman to Christ. Moody's powerful influence was seen throughout Chapman's ministry.[41] In all the churches where Chapman pastored, revival would soon break out. Chapman finally resigned from pastoral work and went into full-time evangelistic work. Muncy comments:

> His [Chapman] success in pastoral evangelism brought urgent appeals for Mr. Chapman to vie all of his time to evangelistic meetings. In a five-year period he conducted simultaneous meetings in more than fifty American cities with gratifying results. There were seven thousand professions of conversion in one of these meetings and three thousand in another.[42]

God used Chapman and Torrey to help spread the Awakening. After the Welsh Revival, it was Chapman who gave Billy Sunday his start. Sunday would go on to influence millions as one of the best known evangelists in the United States. It is thought that over one million people shook Sunday's hand,[43] and it is estimated that over one quarter of a million people came to the Savior during Sunday's ministry.[44] Sunday's successful ministry continued to grow until it hit its peak just before World War I. It was this war that marked the end of the Third Great Awakening. After the war, there seemed to be less interest in Sunday's type of evangelism.[45] Muncy comments that it was the hatred and destruction of human life fostered by World War I that dealt a deathblow to the tabernacle-type of evangelism that Sunday promoted and espoused. Tabernacle evangelism was a type of outreach in which a popular evangelist such as Billy Sunday, Sam Jones, or Paul Rader would come into a town or city and conduct evangelistic crusades. They would begin by taking an old theater and refurbishing it or constructing an inexpensive auditorium called a tabernacle. The evangelist would conduct meetings in the tabernacle for four to six weeks, then move on to another town or city. The tabernacle would remain, and a resident pastor or evan-

41. Muncy, *History of Evangelism in the United States*, 147.
42. Ibid.
43. Ibid., 154.
44. Ibid.
45. Ibid., 156.

gelist would then continue with the outreach.[46] Joel Carpenter comments that one of the dangers of this outreach was that "the church was being reduced to a soul-saving station and an armory for mobilization cadres of lay evangelists."[47] This type of evangelism continued for a few years after the war, but its effectiveness diminished.[48] As a result of Sunday's evangelistic efforts and the fruit they bore, it is undeniable that he Sunday played a truly important role in the evangelism of the Third Great Awakening.

Simpson's Evangelism Efforts

Moody too would come to have an indirect impact on Simpson. Daniel Whittle, an associate of Moody's, had a tremendous influence on Simpson in his pastorate in Louisville. It was through Whittle that Simpson became burdened for evangelism and came to see it as the most important aspect of his ministry. Whittle also impacted Simpson's view of sanctification and eschatology.

When Simpson moved to New York City, he made it his goal to reach the city for Christ through evangelism. He made the Gospel Tabernacle an evangelistic center for the city. He never traveled as an itinerant evangelist, but his focus was on the city and the world. Moody helped to lay the foundation for Simpson's urban work by conducting evangelistic meetings in New York City at the Hippodrome in 1876. He saw great success, and approximately one million people came to the meetings in a span of ten weeks.[49] During the crusade, he had a falling out with some of the leaders because of their lack of commitment to the campaign. In his anger, Moody ended the crusade early.[50] Afterwards, he regretted his behavior and felt terrible about the outburst. A number of people who traveled long distances ultimately missed the meetings because of the cancellation, and Moody always felt badly about this.[51] Dorsett commented:

> Moody, in retrospect, sensed he had been terribly wrong. "I closed the meeting in the Hippodrome. In doing so I grieved the Holy

---

46. Carpenter, *Revive Us Again*, 78–79.
47. Ibid., 79.
48. Ibid.
49. Dorsett, *Passion for Souls*, 245.
50. Ibid.
51. Ibid.

Spirit." And even though New York City had been the "best [campaign] he had ever had" (approximately a million people attended in more than ten weeks), he was convinced God would never bless his work in that city again.[52]

Moody never returned to New York City to do a major crusade. Simpson went to New York after Moody's crusade and invested over half of his life trying to reach the city for Christ. Though Moody did not return, God rose up Simpson, an urban evangelist, to reach the city for the Savior. As T. V. Thomas and Ken Draper wrote:

> Simpson's Tabernacle at New York City, soon after its inception, was organized as an independent church. It served as a base for evangelistic meetings, including summer tent ministry. It ran several rescue missions, an orphanage, and home for unwed mothers, and housed the Missionary Training School, which provided trained workers for Simpson's evangelistic efforts.[53]

George Pardington stated that the primary purpose of Simpson and the Gospel Tabernacle was to save souls and train soul winners to reach New York City for Christ.[54] It was not enough for Simpson and the Alliance just to reach New York City for the Savior; they formed Alliance branches and independent churches to reach the United States and Canada for Christ. Pardington wrote, "Every Alliance branch, like every evangelical church, should be first and foremost a life-saving station for souls."[55] This burden for people was not only for North America, it was also what drove Simpson and the Alliance to focus on worldwide evangelization and mission work.

Simpson's role in the evangelism phase of the Third Great Awakening was to evangelize both at home and abroad. Through the founding of the Christian and Missionary Alliance, his churches and branches impacted whole towns and cities for the Savior. They took Simpson's Fourfold Gospel seriously—especially the first fold, Christ our Savior. This was not only true in North America, but also throughout the world.

Though Moody and his associates played major roles in the Awakening, there were many others who were integral in the Awakening. All were

---

52. Ibid.
53. Hartzfeld and Nienkirchen, *Birth of a Vision*, 199.
54. Pardington, *Twenty-five Wonderful Years*, 32.
55. Ibid., 53.

involved in the evangelism movement and saw tremendous results. The church is still benefiting from the ministries of Moody, Torrey, Chapman, Sunday, Gordon, Simpson, and many others who played important roles in the evangelistic outreach of the Third Great Awakening.

Prayer and evangelism would help spread the Third Great Awakening. Evangelism was the burden of all of the leaders of the Awakening. It was their desire to see the masses reached with the message of Christ, both in North America and abroad. Moody would end up being the undisputed leader in evangelism during this period. He would influence many others to follow his footsteps in evangelical outreach. One who would follow Moody's lead was Simpson. He would focus his efforts on New York City, then expand to the surrounding areas and the world. He would pour out his heart to the unreached, both nearby and to the ends of the earth.

Evangelism was integral to the Third Great Awakening. The holiness movement also played an important role. Those who preached the necessity of knowing Christ as one's Savior also stressed the importance of knowing Christ as one's Sanctifier. The next chapter will look at the holiness movement and its impact on the Third Great Awakening.

IV

SIMPSON'S IMPACT ON THE HOLINESS MOVEMENT

The holiness movement culminated during the Third Great Awakening. During this span of the fifty-year revival, the holiness movement was at its peak. Timothy Smith wrote, "At the high tide of revivalism, perfectionism [holiness] was at the crest of a wave."[1] The Third Great Awakening, which broke out in the fall of 1857 in New York City, was preceded by the ministry of Walter and Phoebe Palmer. Smith goes on to say,

> The Awakening of 1858 . . . was both the climax of these long trends and the result of united efforts by urban churchmen of many denominations. In the two years immediately preceding it, hundreds of these labored to precipitate a national Pentecost which they hoped would baptize America in the Holy Spirit and in some mystic manner destroy the evils of slavery, poverty and greed.[2]

The holiness movement in the United States was disseminated through the Methodist Church and the leaders of Oberlin College, notably Asa Mahan and Charles Finney. The Methodist Church's understanding of sanctification was defined and governed by the writings of its founder, John Wesley. He wrote that there was a definite second work of grace subsequent to conversion.[3] This is a free gift from God, much like the Christian's sal-

---

1. Smith, *Revivalism and Social Reform*, 142.
2. Ibid., 62.
3. Wesley, *Letters of John Wesley*, 222.

vation.⁴ After this experience, a believer can, by God's grace, live a holy life in obedience to God. Wesley described sanctification in the following manner:

> Entire sanctification, or Christian perfection, is neither more nor less than pure love; love expelling sin, and governing both the heart and life of a child of God. The Refiner's fire purges out all that is contrary to love, and that many times by a pleasing smart [to cause a sharp or stinging rebuke]. Leave all this to Him that does all things well, and that loves you better than you do yourself.⁵

Wesley taught that there comes a definite time when every believer should experience this second work of grace.⁶

Richard Riss describes Wesley's view of "complete" sanctification as "an instantaneous experience subsequent to conversion [that] enables a person to live a sanctified life, without conscious or deliberate sin."⁷ Melvin Dieter states that Wesley presented before his followers,

> The promise of a heart perfected in love, a personal restoration to the moral image of God, and the responsibility and power to express that love in relationship with God and neighbor. Through Christ and the indwelling Holy Spirit, the "bent to sinning" [could be cleansed from the repentant, believing heart, and a "bent to loving obedience"] could become a mainspring of one's life.⁸

According to Wesley, holiness is purity of intention in dedicating oneself completely to God.⁹ Wesley encouraged all new believers, immediately after conversion, to seek the experience of entire sanctification.¹⁰ Francis Asbury, the first bishop of the Methodist Episcopal Church in the United States, also urged all of his Methodist pastors to preach that every new believer should seek the experience of sanctification immediately after

---

4. Ibid., 268.
5. Wesley, *Works of John Wesley*, 432.
6. Ibid.
7. Riss, *Survey of Twentieth-century Revival Movements*, 17.
8. Gundry, *Five Views on Sanctification*, 21.
9. Ibid., 27–28.
10. Ibid., 37.

conversion.[11] The purpose of holiness is moral and ethical and not simply an opportunity for the believer to claim some special privilege before God.[12]

This characterization of sanctification was integral to the Methodist Church's evangelization of the lost. Robert Anderson remarks:

> Methodism entered the American religion environment during the Great Awakening of the eighteenth century, and from then until the close of the following century, revivalism and holiness were to march side by side. Revivalism had the dual purpose of converting sinners and rousing the faithful to a life of piety and service, in short, of holiness.[13]

Keith Hardman goes even further by stating, "The origins of the Third Great Awakening can be traced directly to the Methodists."[14] Charles Finney and Asa Mahan gave the doctrine of sanctification a new definition in the 1830s. They began teaching a new understanding of sanctification that was different than the Wesleyan view of sinless perfection. It had to do with the believer's perfect trust and consecration, and it resulted in social activism. Finney encouraged new believers to get involved in politics, Christian education, temperance, ending slavery, and helping the poor. He asserted that the spirit of the Christian is also that of the reformer.[15]

The Wesleyan and Oberlin movements had become the basis of the holiness movement of the Third Great Awakening. The holiness revival would permeate throughout the fifty years of the Third Great Awakening, affecting leaders from a large number of churches. As Vinson Synan states, "With Methodist and Oberlin perfectionists leading the way, the holiness crusade approaches a climax shortly before the Civil War. Ministers of most denominations joined the campaign for perfection."[16]

This would become a national movement that spread throughout North America. The holiness movement impacted the revival that broke out in 1857, and it was through this revival that holiness teaching continued to spread. Riss comments, "As the result of the revival of 1857–1860, Phoebe Palmer's teaching spread far and wide."[17]

11. Ibid.
12. Ibid., 32.
13. Anderson, *Vision of the Disinherited*, 28.
14. Hardman, *Seasons of Refreshing*, 172.
15. Anderson, *Vision of the Disinherited*, 28.
16. Synan, *Holiness-Pentecostal Movement in the United States*, 30.
17. Riss, *Survey of Twentieth-century Revival Movements*, 18.

The Higher Christian Life, written by W. E. Boardman in 1858, had a great impact on the Third Great Awakening. J. Edwin Orr wrote of Boardman:

> William Edwin Boardman had published at the height of the Awakening of 1858 a treatise upon the "Higher Christian Life." He was a zealous young Presbyterian businessman when he started his search in the 1840s for a holier life. His book was a huge success on both sides of the Atlantic (circulation, 200,000), being published in Britain in 1860. It produced its greatest effect in the old country.[18]

The Higher Christian Life provided new terminology and a new understanding of sanctification in Christian circles. Boardman interpreted sanctification for those outside the Wesleyan-Holiness tradition.[19] He presented sanctification in a simple way, without the Wesleyan or holiness terminology. Boardman did not present a systemic treatment of holiness, relying instead on his own experience and spiritual longings. This touched a similar vein in the religious public at the time, and they accepted his interpretation of sanctification.[20] Dieter remarks on his popularity in writing,

> This combination of both Methodist and Oberlin teaching and expression flowed through his work to produce a statement of the nature and reality of the life of holiness which was more widely received than the expositions on the more classic traditions.[21]

Boardman presented this biblical truth to Presbyterians, Baptists and Congregationalists. It was made acceptable in more reformed circles. As Dieter comments on *The Higher Christian Life*, "The book opened the doors of non-Methodist churches to the revival teachings [holiness revival] more widely than any volume which had preceded it."[22] Boardman's view of sanctification was welcomed by Baptist, Presbyterian, and Congregational churches that would not have accepted the Wesleyan-Holiness view of sanctification. Smith states:

> Meanwhile, a growing army of Revivalistic Calvinists who could not accept the second blessing adopted the view that true

---

18. Orr, *Fervent Prayer*, 142.
19. Riss, *Survey of Twentieth-century Revival Movements*, 18–19
20. Dieter, *Holiness Revival of the Nineteenth Century*, 49.
21. Ibid., 50.
22. Ibid., 49.

> conversion made one entirely free from sin. In the Awakenings which followed 1858 multitudes of them became convinced their justification in God's sight must be confirmed by their sanctification in their own and the eyes of the world. The goals were similar, only the method proposed for reaching them varied.[23]

Sanctification became paramount in the lives of Christians at this time and would be one of the two major building blocks for the Third Great Awakening. The salvation message was primary, but living a sanctified life would be the follow-up to that message.

During this time period, the first view of sanctification that was introduced was the Wesleyan-Holiness view. Some time later, the higher life, or deeper life, understanding of sanctification would become popular. These two views dominated the movement. Grant Wacker explains these two perceptions of sanctification by remarking,

> Both higher life and Wesleyan-Holiness leaders were committed to the idea that conversion ought to be followed by another landmark religious experience, and they both called that experience the baptism of the Holy Spirit. But there were significant differences between them regarding the purpose of the baptism experience. The higher life writers insisted that its main function was to empower believers to serve the church and to witness for Christ, whereas, Wesleyan-Holiness writers argued that its main function was to eradicate "inbred sin" and thereby to break the stronghold of selfish desires. The former, in other words, emphasized service, whereas, the latter stressed purity.[24]

The higher life, or deeper life, movement would spread from one denomination to another and would quickly move to the forefront of the holiness movement. Boardman and A. B. Earle both espoused the deeper life experience of sanctification. They were respected and accepted throughout America. They were welcomed, along with their view of sanctification, in Congregationalist, Baptist, and Presbyterian churches. They were the most popular evangelists in America until their fame was eclipsed by Moody in 1874.[25] The higher life, which was defined and explained by Boardman in *The Higher Christian Life*, was later popularized by D. L. Moody, A. J. Gordon, F. B. Meyer, R. A. Torrey, and A. B. Simpson.

---

23. Smith, *Revivalism and Social Reform*, 113.
24. Wacker, "Holy Spirit and the Spirit of the Age," 48.
25. Smith, *Revivalism and Social Reform*, 113.

In the 1870s, Boardman joined forces with two other popular deeper life advocates, Robert Pearsall Smith and his wife, Hannah Whitehall Smith. The Smiths spoke alongside Boardman all over the United States, Great Britain, and Western Europe preaching on "the deeper Christian life."[26] There were those in Great Britain and Europe who were seeking a similar experience and readily accepted their teaching.[27] The efforts of Boardman and the Smiths contributed to the founding of the first Keswick Convention in Great Britain in 1875.[28] This became an annual event that helped spread to other conferences the higher life or deeper life, which became known as "the Keswick Message." The Keswick message is not a doctrinal statement, and there has never been an exhaustive treatise on it.[29] The Keswick message is that all Christians have a fallen nature prone to sin, yet God requires holiness in Christians. God has provided the believer a provision of holiness, or a victorious Christian life, through union with Christ. It is not only Christ, but also the inner working of the Holy Spirit, that works to combat the downward pull of sin. The Holy Spirit provides a counterforce that enables the believer who has surrendered to trusting Christ to resist the downward pull of our fallen nature. Keswick does not teach the possibility of perfection in a Christian's life, but the message does teach the possibility that one can live in victory over sin and obey God's will.[30] The believer has to understand the inadequacy of trying to live the Spirit-filled life on their own before they can make that total commitment to God. The believer has to be filled and controlled by the Holy Spirit. It is the Holy Spirit that becomes God's provision for the Christian to live a life of holiness and to serve in God's work.[31] This is a moment-by-moment walk with God.[32] Dieter speaks of the impact of the Keswick message:

26. Blumhofer, *Restoring the Faith*, 32–33.
27. Ibid., 33.
28. Ibid.
29. Gundry, *Five Views on Sanctification*, 153.
30. Ibid., 154–55.
31. Ibid., 155.
32. Barabas, *So Great Salvation*, 84. Barabas, in his seminal work on the Keswick movement, gives the following definition of the Keswick message. It comes from the original "call" of the convention, a "Convention for the Promotion of the Practiced Holiness." He writes:

> In the very first issue of *The Christian Pathway to Power*, the editor stated what he conceived to be the practical possibilities of faith. 'We believe the Word of God teaches that the *normal* Christian life is one of uniform evident victory over sin;

> The higher life message of Keswick strongly influenced evangelical religious organizations around the world through such men as A. J. Pierson, Hudson Taylor, F. B. Meyer, Andrew Murray, Theodore Monod and Dr. Eugene Stock. The English evangelical community came under the continuing influence through the ministers and laymen who gathered annually at Keswick under the leadership of Webb-Peploe, Harford-Batterersby, and Handley Moule, later Bishop of Durham. Similar higher life conferences standing in an informal relationship to Keswick through their teaching and speaking personnel, were begun in Europe and the United States; through F. B. Meyer and others . . .[33]

The Keswick movement would reintroduce the deeper life movement to the United States.

The higher and deeper life message had come full circle. It had been brought to England by Boardman and the Smiths and was brought back to the United States by Moody and Ira Sankey. F. B. Meyer would later come to the United States and help popularize it. During the 1890s, Moody welcomed Keswick spokespersons to his Northfield Conferences. The Keswick message also found expression in hymns, devotional literature, periodicals, biographies, and spiritual tracts.[34]

While the Keswick message was becoming popular in Great Britain and Europe, the Wesleyan-Holiness movement continued to make an impact on the Awakening. Anderson observes:

> The resurgence of the Holiness movement was both international and interdenominational, but in America it was predominantly Methodist undertaking. The centennial year of Methodism, 1866, was commemorated across the nation by weekday prayer

---

and that no temptation is permitted to happen to us without a way of escape being provided by God, so that we may be able to bear it.' Keswick has never departed from this faith. From the beginning until the present it has been taught that a life of faith and victory, or peace and rest, are the rightful heritage of every child of God, and that he may step into it . . . 'not by long prayers and laborious effort, but by a deliberate and decisive act of faith.' It teaches that the normal experience of the child of God should be one of victory instead of constant defeat, one of liberty instead of grinding bondage, one of 'perfect peace' instead of restless worry. It shows that in Christ there is provided for every believer victory, liberty, and rest, and that this may be obtained not by a life-long struggle after an impossible ideal but by the surrender of the individual to God, and the indwelling of the Holy Spirit (ibid.).

33. Dieter, *Holiness Revival of the Nineteenth Century*, 158.
34. Blumhofer, *Restoring the Faith*, 40.

gatherings, conventions and camp meetings centering on the Holiness Movement. The following year, at Vineland, New Jersey, the National Camp Meeting Association for the Promotion of Holiness was organized, and over the next decade some three dozen national camp meetings and scores of regional and local ones were held under its auspices. Numerous other interdominational Holiness institutions were established, and Holiness periodicals proliferated.[35]

The Wesleyan-Holiness view of sanctification stayed in Methodist circles, where it failed to expand beyond the confines of Methodism. As a result of the holiness movement, over one hundred holiness denominations would come into existence worldwide within the next forty years.[36]

Moody, more than any other single individual, helped spread the holiness message through his preaching and through his Northfield Conferences. There were many others, including Simpson, who were also involved in spreading the message of sanctification. All of the leaders of the Third Great Awakening saw the Holy Spirit as key in the movement and in revival. As C. I. Scofield wrote at the end of the nineteenth century in his famous *Scofield Reference Bible*:

> We are in the midst of a marked revival of interest in the person and work of the Holy Spirit. More books, booklets and tracts upon the subject have issued from the press during the last eighty years than all the previous time since the invention of printing. Indeed, within the last twenty years more has been written and said upon the doctrine of the Holy Spirit than the preceding eighteen hundred years.[37]

The leaders of the revival recognized the centrality of the Holy Spirit in the Awakening and realized if the Awakening was to continue, they needed to be filled or baptized in the Holy Spirit. Anderson, writing about the leading evangelists in the Third Great Awakening, stated that these leaders were not only evangelists, they were also promoters of holiness. He states:

> The leading revivalists were first and foremost evangelists, but all were recognized advocates of holiness as well, and many of their converts swelled the ranks of the holiness hosts. Most prominent among these were Dwight L. Moody, sometimes salesman and

---

35. Anderson, *Vision of the Disinherited*, 29.
36. Riss, *Survey of Twentieth-century Revival Movements*, 20.
37. Dayton, *Theological Roots of Pentecostalism*, 78–79.

YMCA worker who dominated revivalism for the last quarter of the Nineteenth Century; Reuban A. Torrey, sometime president of both the Moody Bible Institute of Chicago and the Los Angeles Bible Institute; Adoniram J. Gordon, founder of the Gordon Bible Institute; Albert B. Simpson, father of the Christian and Missionary Alliance; and J. Wilbur Chapman, evangelist of international renown. All of these men professed to have been baptized in the Holy Spirit, and all preached and wrote extensively on the subject ....[38]

The leaders of the holiness movement saw that it would be Spirit-filled men and women who would have a key role in the Third Great Awakening and that was essential in order for the revival to continue. Simpson wrote the following words about R. A. Torrey: "Dr. Torrey in a recent address in the city of Chicago remarked that the greatest need of the church today was an army of spirit-filled men to go forth and ring in the ears of the professing Christians of America this old question, 'Have ye received the Holy Ghost since ye believed?'"[39] Simpson recognized the centrality of the Holy Spirit in his life and his ministry. Like Torrey, he saw the great need of the church of his day was to be Spirit-filled. Simpson's experience of sanctification while serving as the pastor of the Chestnut Street Presbyterian Church in Louisville, Kentucky, was life-changing.

Simpson believed that the indication of Christ as sanctifier was integral in fully understanding the gospel. Simpson felt that next to Christ as Savior, Christ as Sanctifier was next in importance. In fact, the second fold of the Fourfold Gospel espoused by Simpson was "Christ our Sanctifier." One had to experience Christ as Sanctifier before one could live a holy life and serve Christ effectively. According to Simpson, although salvation was the beginning of the Christian life, sanctification was necessary to grow in the Christian faith. He saw that many Christians stopped at regeneration and therefore never grew in holiness or in their walk with Christ. Simpson described the necessity of sanctification in the treatise *The Four-Fold Gospel*, where he uses the analogy of a plant and a house. He writes:

> Regeneration is the beginning. It is the germ of the seed. But it is not the summer fullness of the plant. The heart has not yet gained entire victory over the old elements of sin. It is sometimes overcome by them. Regeneration is like building a house and having

---

38. Anderson, *Vision of the Disinherited*, 37.
39. Gilbertson, *Baptism of the Holy Spirit*, 312.

the work done well. Sanctification is to have the owner come and dwell in it and fill it with gladness, and life and beauty. Many Christians are converted and stop there. They do not go on to fullness of their life in Christ, and so are in danger of losing what they already possess.[40]

Simpson described sanctification in his book *Wholly Sanctified* in the following manner: "Sanctification is thus God's own life in the spirit that is yielded up to Him to be His dwelling place and instrument of His power and will."[41] John Sawin explained Simpson's view of sanctification as follows:

> Simpson used the term "sanctification" as if pertaining to the Fourfold Gospel in its objective sense of "holiness," not in its more frequent objective sense of "setting apart." The two meanings are interrelated but as far as the second "fold," sanctification refers to holiness of heart and life that results from the abiding presence of Christ or from the indwelling of the Holy Spirit . . . the indwelling Spirit and the Christ who abides within are simply different expressions of the same truth. It is the truth that prompted Simpson to preach the sermon, "Himself" and to write the poem/hymns of the same title. To Simpson, this was the essence of the second "fold," sanctification. He believed that to enter this experience necessitated a critical decision, but he also knew that growth and deeper fillings of the spirit ought to characterize the sanctified life. Subjective sanctification, then, to Mr. Simpson, was a distinct experience.[42]

Simpson was both definite and precise in his understanding of Christ as Sanctifier. In 1885, Simpson had been invited to be one of the speakers at the International Convention of Holiness and Divine Healing in Bethshan, England. This convention had been organized and lead by Boardman. Simpson addressed the conference and also listened to many of the other speakers on their view of holiness. After hearing their views on sanctification, Simpson asked for a special privilege to address the conference. The sermon he preached became known as "Himself."[43]

"Himself" is a short sermon that concisely describes Simpson's understanding of Christ in sanctification. The focus is on Christ himself and

40. Simpson, *Four-Fold Gospel*, 28.
41. Ibid., *Wholly Sanctified*, 39.
42. Hartzfeld and Nienkirchen, *Birth of a Vision*, 8–9.
43. Ibid., 116.

on what he did on the cross for all believers. What a Christian needs is not doctrine or theology, although these things are important. What one needs is Jesus Christ himself. One does not need to seek after healing or sanctification but to look instead for the Sanctifier, Christ. One does not look for healing but instead looks for the Healer, Jesus Christ. Instead of looking for what Christ can do for a Christian, the Christian needs to look to Christ himself.

Simpson continued emphasizing that it is Christ who fills the believer with his Holy Spirit. It is Christ's work in the Christian. The Christian's part is to surrender their will completely to God and permit Christ to live his life through their own. The believer needs to be filled by Christ moment by moment. It is not something one can do on one's own—it has to be Christ. Simpson says he learned to take his spiritual life from Jesus moment by moment when Simpson asks the Christian,

> Is not that a terrible bondage, to be always so dependent? What? A bondage to be dependent on the One you love—your dearest Friend? Oh no! It comes naturally, spontaneously, like a fountain, without consciousness, without effort. True life is always easy and overflowing.[44]

For Simpson, the key to sanctification and the Christian life was simply surrendering one's all to Christ and letting him live through the Christian.

Simpson goes on to say that Christ, and not our own faith, is where our focus has to be. One does not have faith in faith but rather faith in Jesus Christ. Simpson shares his experience of surrendering to Christ. He took Christ as his Healer, and Christ healed him by becoming his strength and health. Simpson also mentions how Christ quickened his mind and gave him strength for ministry. Simpson ends the message by saying he is still learning of the secret of Christ in the believer. He closes with this statement: "I feel I have only begun to learn how well it works. Take it and go on working it out, through time and eternity—Christ for all, grace for grace, from strength to strength, from glory to glory, from this time forth and even for evermore."[45]

Samuel Stoesz summarizes the message of Simpson's "Himself" in the following manner: "He [Simpson] emphasized that the Christian's need was not blessing or healing or sanctification but Christ Himself. The question

---

44. Bailey, *Best of A. B. Simpson*, 8.
45. Ibid., 14.

was not what people thought of Bethshan or about divine healing but what they thought of Christ."[46] The message of "Himself" was printed in a tract, and it is still in print today. Simpson also made his sermon into a poem that became a hymn called "Himself," which is still sung in Alliance churches today. Simpson understood Christ as Sanctifier very well, and he poured his life into writing and speaking about Christ as Sanctifier. Sawin comments, "Simpson, in his printed sermons (books), articles and editorials, sought to define precisely his view of sanctification and he sought to lead people into the experience of it."[47] Simpson kept Christ as Sanctifier at the forefront of his preaching and his writing.

As one of the spokesmen for the holiness movement, Simpson was a bridge between the Wesleyan-Holiness perspective of holiness and the deeper life and Keswick view of sanctification.[48] Simpson's view of holiness was a combination of both camps. He held that it was necessary for the believer to have a crisis experience in which the believer totally surrendered to Christ and was filled with the Holy Spirit. This experience happened subsequent to conversion. This was similar to the Wesleyan-Holiness view that it was necessary to have a second work of grace. But unlike proponents of the Wesleyan-Holiness view, Simpson did not believe in the possibility of the eradication of either sin or sinful nature in a believer's life. Simpson not only believed that sanctification was a crisis, but he also saw sanctification as progressive. When the believer makes the decision to surrender all to Christ and is filled by the Holy Spirit, sanctification has just begun. It is also progressive because a Christian has to grow in sanctification. This is similar to the Keswick view, which speaks to the importance of a believer's union with Christ helping Christians grow in holiness. At the conferences Simpson led, he invited both Wesleyan-Holiness speakers such as Phoebe Palmer and Keswick speakers such as F. B. Meyer. He also invited writers of both camps to submit articles to his periodical. Because of Simpson's gracious attitude and treatment toward both groups, there was very little tension between members of either camp. Instead, they worked together to promote sanctification in both their camp meetings and literature.

Simpson's great burden and desire was to see people sanctified. He was willing to overlook small differences in the views of sanctification in order to see men and women become Spirit-filled. Although Simpson was

46. Ibid.
47. Ibid.
48. Blumhofer, *Restoring the Faith*, 34.

concerned about doctrine, he was more concerned about people's lives. He saw that their greatest need, next to salvation, was sanctification, and Simpson would do anything he could to make sure that they came to know Christ as their Sanctifier.

Edith Blumhofer comments that Simpson "was far less interested in doctrines such as healing, sanctification, and enduement with power than he was cultivating a mystical relationship with Christ."[49] Simpson had a pastor's heart, and that is where his focus was. He was not a theologian but a pastor. The Christian public saw Simpson as a spokesman for the Wesleyan-Holiness movement and the Keswick movement. He was affiliated with both sides, and that fact made Simpson well received in both groups.

J. B. Culpepper, a Wesleyan-Holiness writer who was a contemporary of Simpson's, wrote, "I first read of this [Keswick] movement two or three years ago, my animadversions [a critical and usually censorious remark] led me to ask . . . why cross the Atlantic Ocean and publish as a great discovery, that which every Methodist held . . . it is similar to what Mr. A. B. Simpson teaches."[50]

In the beginning of the Keswick movement, there were numerous Wesleyan-Holiness theologians who argued against the Keswick movement. The problem they saw in the Keswick message was their denial of the eradication of believers' sinful nature at the moment of sanctification.[51] As time went on, the Wesleyan-Holiness camp began accepting the Keswick view of spirituality.[52] They saw those in the Keswick movement as an ally against the modernist movement.[53] David Bundy writes, "Wesleyan/Holiness readers happily read the work of A. B. Simpson, F. B. Meyer, W. H. Griffith Thomas, Geddes H. C. MacGregor, and others. Today most Wesleyan/Holiness Christians hold a Keswick theory of sanctification along with a premillennial eschatology."[54] George M. Marsden echoes the unity of the holiness movement in the late nineteenth century. He comments, "Until the 1890s almost all of those who were rediscovering the work of the Holy Spirit had viewed each other as allies. Keswick teachers, A. B. Simpson, the Salvation Army, and the holiness camp meeting movement all gave each

---

49. Ibid.
50. Blumhofer and Balmer, *Modern Christian Revivals*, 132.
51. Ibid.
52. Ibid., 133.
53. Ibid.
54. Ibid.

other approving nods and borrowed methods and emphasis."[55] Although leaders in both groups would argue over fine points of doctrine, the average Christian saw little difference, and Simpson helped unite the Christian public in a shared understanding of sanctification.

Simpson's Promotion of Holiness

How did Simpson promote the message of holiness? He did it in three ways: first, in his preaching; secondly, through conventions and conferences; and finally, in his writings. First of all, Simpson preached the message of sanctification at the Gospel Tabernacle and throughout the branches and churches affiliated with the Christian and Missionary Alliance. He also spoke at conventions and conferences. Many of his books, especially *Wholly Sanctified* and *A Larger Christian Life*, were messages preached at the Gospel Tabernacle that were written down stenographically and published in book form.[56]

Simpson's most important work on sanctification was a two-volume work on the Holy Spirit. They were originally a series of messages first preached at the Gospel Tabernacle. The first volume, *The Holy Spirit: The Old Testament*, was a series of messages that began in September 1894 and was completed in April of 1895. The second volume, *The Holy Spirit: The New Testament*, also originated as a series of messages, beginning in May of 1895 and finishing in April of 1896.[57] Walter Turnbull observes that these messages had a tremendous impact on the members of the church. They were preached to lead each member into a deeper walk with God, and they were successful.[58] Turnbull goes on to say that Simpson's "own life flamed with the reality of the messages his lips proclaimed."[59] Simpson made Christ as Sanctifier one of the most important themes in his preaching. His passion was to see people filled with the Holy Spirit so that they might live holy lives and serve the Master in power.

Another way Simpson helped to spread the holiness message was through his conventions and summer conferences. This may have been one of the most effective ways for Simpson to reach a wider audience with his

---

55. Marsden, *Fundamentalism and American Culture*, 94.
56. Hartzfeld and Nienkirchen, *Birth of a Vision*, 279.
57. Ibid., 287.
58. Simpson, *Holy Spirit*, 1:3.
59. Ibid.

message of sanctification. Conference ministries were widely used in the holiness movement to bring the message of sanctification to the Christian public. Simpson hosted a number of conventions not only at the Gospel Tabernacle in New York City, but also throughout the country. Simpson would speak at these conventions, but he also brought in a number of holiness and deeper life speakers. The list of speakers at his conferences looked like a "Who's Who in the Holiness and Deeper Life Movement." The list of speakers who attended his conventions and summer conferences included Andrew Murray, F. B. Meyer, Hudson Taylor, Otto Stockmayer, Charles Townsend, A. J. Gordon, A. J. Pierson, R. A. Torrey, D. L. Moody, D. W. Whittle, C. I. Scofield, James M. Gray, and Phoebe Palmer.[60] There were many more speakers who were not as famous but were just as powerful nevertheless.

The conventions held at the Gospel Tabernacle in New York City impacted the city and the surrounding areas. As A. E. Thompson observed, "Frequently the attendance of the New York City conventions overflowed the Gospel Tabernacle and the services had to be held in some large neighboring theater or Carnegie Hall."[61] Thompson writes, "One of the proofs of the power of these great conventions was the attention given to them in the daily press."[62] The publicity was not always positive, but the message went out to the public. For the most part, the publicity given by church periodicals was positive, which helped spread the message of Christ as our Sanctifier.[63]

The main summer conferences for Simpson and the Christian and Missionary Alliance were held at Old Orchard, Maine. There, Simpson would frequently share speakers with D. L. Moody's Northfield Conferences. Speakers such as F. B. Meyer, Andrew Murray, and Charles Inwood would speak at both conferences.[64] Both Northfield and Old Orchard had a tremendous impact in popularizing the holiness message among Christians. Christian leaders of the period recognized the power of these conventions and summer conferences to spread the message of holiness among Christians who attended. These conventions and conferences transformed Christians' lives. Thompson comments:

60. Thompson, *A. B. Simpson*, 110.
61. Ibid., 111.
62. Ibid.
63. Ibid., 107.
64. Gilbertson, *Baptism of the Holy Spirit*, 180.

Simpson's Impact on the Holiness Movement

> The conventions in other cities have been one of the great outlets for the testimony of the Alliance. Unnumbered multitudes have heard the message who otherwise would never have been touched by it. Most of these have remained in their churches, themselves, quickened into new life and their lives empowered for hitherto unthought of service. The ministry of many a pastor has been transformed. Hundreds have been called into Christian service who had never dreamt of such a life.[65]

Simpson had an impact on other Christian leaders not only in the Christian and Missionary Alliance, but also in other churches and denominations.

Simpson also linked missions with the holiness movement. Therefore, his messages on holiness and missions at the conventions encouraged people not only to be filled with the Holy Spirit, but to also support worldwide missions outreach.[66] Thompson recognized that these conferences and conventions did more than anything else to spread Simpson's message. He comments, "These conventions have done more than any other single agency, except Dr. Simpson's pen to disseminate the truth which he so loved and call men to service in which his own life burned it."[67] Simpson taught that no person was fit for Christian service unless he or she had met Christ as Sanctifier. Simpson also spread the message of holiness with his pen.

Simpson wrote extensively about the ministry of the Holy Spirit. Gilbertson comments:

> A. B. Simpson was a prolific writer. He used the written word as an inexpensive way to spread the teachings and activities of the Christian and Missionary Alliance movement. Simpson published over one hundred books, the majority of them compilations of sermons that had been stenographically recorded. In addition, he edited and wrote for a series of periodicals from 1880 until his death in 1919.[68]

Simpson preached and wrote extensively on sanctification, which he called "the baptism of the Holy Spirit" or "being filled with the Holy Spirit." Gilbertson states, "The baptism of the Holy Spirit accordingly was a significant experience in Simpson's life and a dominant motif in his writing and

---

65. Thompson, *A. B. Simpson*, 112.
66. Taylor, *Global Missiology for the 21st Century*, 119.
67. Thompson, *A. B. Simpson*, 105.
68. Gilbertson, *Baptism of the Holy Spirit*, 49–50.

teaching."[69] Simpson would also invite others who held similar views on sanctification to contribute to his periodicals. Gordon and Torrey were frequent contributors to Simpson's periodicals.[70] During this time, paperback books became popular, and Simpson published many of his books using this cheap new method. This way, every Christian could afford the book and the message could be disseminated as widely as possible. This was a successful strategy to spread the Fourfold Gospel, especially the message of sanctification.

Stephen Merritt, a leader in the holiness movement, had spoken to Simpson about a book on the Holy Spirit. It was Merritt who wrote the introduction to the first volume of Simpson's book on the Holy Spirit. Merritt writes:

> It was a cause of great joy to my soul to read the announcement that the first volume of *The Holy Spirit, or Power From On High*, would soon be issued. You will remember that at the Old Orchard Convention last year I was led to exclaim, "The book of the Holy Ghost is yet unwritten" and to request the vast audience to rise and pray that the Holy Spirit might inspire Rev. A. B. Simpson to write the work of the age for Him. That this petition is now being answered is the delight of my life.[71]

This was only one of Simpson's books on the Holy Spirit, but it made an impact on the holiness movement as a whole. The written works of Simpson, Boardman, Gordon, Pierson, and Torrey all impacted the holiness movement and helped spread the message of sanctification.

Simpson also impacted another group during the Third Great Awakening that evolved out of the holiness movement: the emerging pentecostal movement. Many of those in the pentecostal movement saw Simpson as one of the forefathers in the pentecostal revival.

Simpson's Influence on the Pentecostal Movement

Simpson not only impacted the holiness movement, he is also considered by many to be one of the forerunners of the pentecostal movement. Blumhofer wrote:

69. Ibid., 4.
70. Ibid., 42.
71. Simpson, *Holy Spirit*, 1:7.

> Through the institutions and associations he founded as well as by his writings and the gospel songs he composed, A. B. Simpson powerfully influenced the early Pentecostal Movement. His focus on "Jesus Christ the same yesterday and today and for ever." (Hebrews 13:8) that supported his teaching on healing found enduring expression in the song, *Yesterday, Today, Forever, (Jesus Is the Same.)* (More than any other text, those words became basic to American Pentecostalism. They were often displayed on the walls of Pentecostal storefront missions.) . . . A premillennialist who stressed holiness, Spirit baptism, divine healing and missions, Simpson articulated a message with which emerging Pentecostals easily identified.[72]

Simpson influenced one of the founders of pentecostalism, Charles Fox Parham. Most pentecostal historians see Simpson as one of the most important contributors to the pentecostal movement.[73]

Parham opened Bethel Bible College in Topeka, Kansas, on October 15, 1900, at a mansion called "Stone's Folly." Parham's theology came from many sources. Just before Parham opened his college, he traveled to Chicago to hear Alexander Dowie. From there, he went to Nyack, New York, to speak to Simpson and then to Shiloh, Maine, to visit Frank Sanford's Holy Ghost and Us Church. After talking to these men, Parham felt there was something beyond the experience of sanctification they were missing.[74] By December of 1900, Parham was leading his students through a study of the holiness movement and divine healing. They were studying the second chapter of Acts when Parham asked his students to find scriptural evidence of the baptism of the Holy Spirit. They became convinced that speaking in tongues was the evidence of that experience.[75] At a watch night service on December 31, 1900, a student by the name of Agnes N. Ozman asked Parham to lay hands on her and pray that she receive the baptism of the Holy Spirit, as evidenced by speaking in unknown tongues. He did so, and Ozman began to speak in other tongues. It was reported that she spoke another language, possibly Chinese, and could not speak English for three days. This was the beginning of the pentecostal movement.[76] Ozman had

---

72. Blumhofer, *Assemblies of God*, 31.
73. Synan, *Holiness-Pentecostal Movement in the United States*, 101.
74. Ibid.
75. Ibid.
76. Ibid.

been a student at Simpson's Missionary Institute at Nyack. She recalled her days at Nyack with fondness.[77] She wrote:

> Our teachers were A. B. Simpson, Farr, Funk, Wilson and Stephen Merritt. The latter had learned much about the workings of the Holy Ghost, and our hearts were blessed as we were admonished to trust Him to use us ... At the Christian Mission Alliance Bible School, we were privileged to bid farewell to many dear hearts who laid their lives down going to Africa, China, India and Jerusalem.[78]

Another one of Parham's students was William J. Seymour, an African American Methodist holiness preacher. He was baptized in the Holy Spirit and spoke in tongues, and he took the message back to Houston and then to Los Angeles.[79] It was in Los Angeles, under the ministry of Seymour, that the Azusa Street Revival broke out. It began in April of 1906.[80] The pentecostal movement exploded soon afterwards, spreading like wildfire. The revival began in Seymour's house but could not be contained there and moved to a dilapidated former African Methodist Episcopal church. The church building was located at 312 Azusa Street in downtown Los Angeles. This is how the revival became known as the Azusa Street Revival. Meetings were held at the church three times a day, seven days a week for three-and-a-half years. Seymour sent out a revival newspaper called the *Apostolic Faith,* free of charge, that helped spread the news of the revival to over fifty thousand people.[81] Shortly after the Azusa Street Revival broke out, Seymour and Parham's relationship fell apart. Up until this time, Parham had been cordial to African Americans and had preached to mixed congregations. It is not clear what caused the rupture, but it has been suggested that the emotionalism Parham witnessed at Azusa and elsewhere among African Americans and white pentecostals repulsed him. He linked this emotionalism to that of Southern blacks in general.[82] Wacker comments,

> Using crude racial slurs, Parham denounced white women who consorted with black men in worship at the Azusa mission, and deplored that white and black men and women knelt together and

---

77. Hartzfeld and Nienkirchen, *Birth of a Vision,* 127.
78. Ibid.
79. Riss, *Survey of Twentieth-century Revival Movements,* 27.
80. Wacker, *Heaven Below,* 6.
81. Synan, *Century of the Holy Spirit,* 4.
82. Wacker, *Heaven Below,* 232.

fell across one another. Such "foolishness" he charged, had followed the Azusa work everywhere.[83]

Later, in 1927, Parham publicly praised the Ku Klux Klan. The falling out between Seymour and Parham also may have had to do with Seymour eclipsing him in leading the revival at Azusa. Seymour became more important than Parham. Eventually, the Azusa Revival would begin to separate along racial lines. This was not only true at Asuza, but also in the pentecostal churches. White and black pentecostal denominations emerged at a time when there were strong social pressures toward racial separation, and most of the pentecostal churches followed suit. They bowed to social pressures.[84]

During the three years of the Azusa Revival, thousands of people received salvation and were baptized in the Holy Spirit. Ministers from all over the country and the world visited Azusa and brought the pentecostal revival back to their churches. The revival rapidly spread to cities such as Indianapolis, Akron, Winnipeg, Dallas, Cleveland, San Francisco, and even Nyack, New York.[85] Riss wrote, "By the time the Azusa Street Mission closed in 1909, Pentecostalism had begun to make significant inroads into the mainstream of American religious life. Those effects continued with increasing force throughout all of the twentieth century."[86] Today the charismatic and pentecostal movement has grown to become the second largest group of Christians in the world. The only group larger is the Roman Catholic Church. Over five hundred and twenty-five million people claim to be pentecostal or charismatic.[87]

The Christian and Missionary Alliance was one of the first religious bodies to feel the impact of the pentecostal movement.[88] A pentecostal revival broke out in 1907 in Alliance churches in Akron, Ohio; Indianapolis, Indiana; Nyack, New York; Cleveland, Ohio; Rocky Springs Park, Pennsylvania; and San Francisco, California.[89] In 1908, a pentecostal revival broke out in Alliance, Ohio, at the Christian and Missionary Alliance's summer conference. The conference was dominated by those who believed

83. Ibid.
84. Ibid., 235.
85. Hardman, *Seasons of Refreshing*, 243.
86. Riss, *Survey of Twentieth-century Revival Movements*, 72.
87. Wacker, *Heaven Below*, 8.
88. Riss, *Survey of Twentieth-century Revival Movements*, 72.
89. Ibid., 72–77.

in the pentecostal experience. It received a great deal of unfavorable coverage in the press.[90] Simpson was beginning to come to be at odds with the pentecostal leaders in the Alliance. Simpson opposed the "evidence doctrine," which said the evidence of being filled or baptized with the Holy Spirit was speaking in tongues. Simpson wrote in his annual report of 1907–1908:

> One of the greatest errors [of pentecostals] is a disposition to make special manifestations evidence of the baptism of the Holy Spirit, giving to them the name of Pentecost as though none had received the spirit of Pentecost but those who had the power to speak in tongues, thus leading many sincere Christians to cast away their confidence, and plunging them in perplexity and darkness, or causing them to seek after special manifestations other than God Himself.
>
> To say that the gift of tongues is the only proper evidence of having been baptized with the Holy Ghost is rash and wholly unscriptural; and places a mere manifestation of the Holy Ghost above His higher ministry of grace.[91]

Simpson sent his assistant Henry Wilson to investigate the pentecostal outbreak in Alliance, Ohio, in 1908. A. W. Tozer describes the incident:

> There were many good people in the Pentecostal movement, and many admirable qualities about its adherents. Mr. Simpson did not want to pass judgment upon them till he had sufficient evidence, so he appointed Dr. Henry Wilson to visit Alliance, Ohio, a hotbed of the new phenomenon, to study the meetings and report back. After a careful study, Dr. Wilson made the following report and it stands today as the crystallized utterance of the Society: "I am not able to approve the movement, though I am willing to concede that there is probably something of God in it somewhere."[92]

Simpson would later make his view public and denounce the "evidence doctrine" that required believers to speak in tongues in order to be filled with the Holy Spirit.[93] Charles Nienkirchen writes, "His opposition to this distinctive tenet of pentecostalism set the stage for numerous individuals

---

90. Ibid., 77.
91. Gilbertson, *Baptism of the Holy Spirit*, 229.
92. Tozer, *Wingspread*, 133.
93. Hartzfeld and Nienkirchen, *Birth of a Vision*, 125.

and congregations with pentecostal sympathies to withdraw from the Alliance and align themselves with the pentecostal movement."[94]

It is important to note that some pentecostals did not accept the evidence doctrine. The most famous was Seymour himself, the leader of the Azusa Street Revival. Wacker writes, "William J. Seymour's steady tumble into obscurity after 1912 probably stemmed from several sources, including white racism and his own lack of leadership inclinations. But Seymour's decision to renounce his earlier insistence on tongues as the initial evidence of the Holy Spirit baptism surely contributed to his eclipse."[95] F. F. Bosworth, one of the leaders of the early pentecostal movement, also left the Assemblies of God in 1918 because of his rejection of the evidence doctrine.[96] The Assemblies of God was one of the first pentecostal denominations; it combined a number of independent pentecostal churches together in one denomination. Synan remarks on Bosworth:

> By September 1918, the debate [surrounding evidence doctrine] boiled over in the General Council Assemblies of God with two former members of the Christian and Missionary Alliance (CMA), Fred F. Bosworth and D. W. Kerr, leading the discussions. Bosworth who had spoken in tongues under Charles Parham at Zion City, Illinois in 1906, attacked the teaching as "a doctrinal error," charging that Charles Parham was "the first man in the history of the world to publicly teach it." Leading the opposing forces was Kerr who argued that "it is the Word of God, not the experience of famous men, that is the touchstone for the Pentecostal belief concerning the immediate evidence of the baptism."[97]

Bosworth would return to the Christian and Missionary Alliance and go on to minister with them until his death in 1958.[98]

Because of Simpson's openness to the gift of tongues as a legitimate spiritual gift and because of the Alliance's general openness to this gift, it was not until 1914 that the Alliance adopted an official policy. Alliance leaders at the time tried to treat speaking in tongues like they did other matters of doctrine such as baptism, church government, and other differences in

---

94. Ibid., 125–26.
95. Wacker, *Heaven Below*, 43–44.
96. Ibid., 43.
97. Synan, *Holiness-Pentecostal Tradition*, 164.
98. Ibid.

belief with personal liberty.[99] This freedom was one of the early strengths of the Alliance. Unfortunately, it also caused problems. The general openness to the pentecostal movement created a need to make an official policy.[100] On April 13, 1914, the Christian and Missionary Alliance adopted an official motion on tongues:[101]

> We believe that the gift of tongues or speaking in tongues did in many cases in the apostolic church accompany or follow the baptism of the Holy Spirit. We believe also that other supernatural and even miraculous operations on the part of the Holy Spirit through His people are competent and possible according to the sovereign will of the Holy Spirit Himself throughout the Christian age. But we hold that none of these manifestations are essentially connected with the baptism of the Holy Spirit, and that the concerned believer may receive the Spirit in His fullness without speaking in tongues or any miraculous manifestation whatever.[102]

The Alliance's official policy states that tongues are a legitimate spiritual gift but not necessarily the evidence of being filled with the Holy Spirit. The dictum of "seek not, forbid not" became the Alliance's official policy on tongues.

Simpson's and the early Christian and Missionary Alliance's openness to the pentecostal movement and the gift of tongues made them unusual among early leaders in the evangelical movement. G. Cambell Morgan, an important Bible teacher and preacher at this time, called the movement "The vomit of Satan."[103] Torrey proclaimed that it was "emphatically not of God, and founded by a Sodomite."[104]

In 1912, Harry Ironside denounced the pentecostal movement in his book *Holiness, the False and the True*, where he described the pentecostal movement as "superstition and fanaticism of the grossest character find a hotbed among 'holiness' advocates. Witness the present disgusting 'Tongues Movement,' with all its attendant delusions and insanities."[105]

---

99. Blumhofer, *Restoring the Faith*, 104.
100. Ibid.
101. Ibid.
102. Ibid., 105.
103. Synan, *Holiness-Pentecostal Tradition*, 144.
104. Ibid.
105. Ironside, *Holiness, the False and the True*, 38.

Ironside goes on to say that the result was lunacy and infidelity.[106] Oswald Chambers, speaking of the pentecostal movement, said, "In the modern tongues movement the responsibility is with the teachers. May God have mercy on them!"[107] Pierson, another leader in the holiness movement who was integral in the Third Great Awakening, also had a less-than-positive outlook on the pentecostal revival. Blumhofer wrote of Pierson:

> Arthur Pierson shared Torrey's concern over an emphasis on glossolalia; in two articles in the *Missionary Review of the World*, he cautioned readers against unduly coveting this gift. Tongues speakers seemed to him to be too often unsuccessful in separating the genuine from the spurious. He noted a tendency among Christians to become too absorbed in "Holy Spirit manifestations" and warned that overemphasis on the Spirit might "hinder His revelation of Christ."[108]

Pierson was less critical than many of the others. Simpson, as one of the leaders in the holiness movement, seemed to be the most open to the pentecostal movement, except in his rejection of the "evidence doctrine."

Simpson's influence is seen in the very beginning of the pentecostal movement with his impact on Parham and Ozman. Many of the leaders of the pentecostal movement came out of the Alliance. The early pentecostal leaders adopted Simpson's Fourfold Gospel. Nienkirchen observes that

> Donald Gee, the astute British Pentecostal leader and theologian credits Simpson with originating the slogan, "Fourfold Gospel" observing the Pentecostals adopted it for their own purposes by substituting the baptism of the Holy Spirit for sanctification. Gee bemoans the lack of attention given to holy living in the Pentecostal Assemblies and prefers to have "a fivefold gospel [including] sanctification [to] a fourfold gospel without it."[109]

Many of the pentecostal leaders were trained at Simpson's Missionary Training Institute at Nyack, New York. Of those who served as missionaries with the Assemblies of God, the largest number had come as alumni of Nyack.[110] Many of the most educated men and women of the pentecostal

---

106. Ibid., 39.
107. Chambers, *Biblical Psychology*, 225.
108. Hart, ed., *Reckoning with the Past*, 298.
109. Hartzfeld and Nienkirchen, *Birth of a Vision*, 128–29.
110. Ibid., 129.

movement came out of the Christian and Missionary Alliance.[111] It is interesting to note that a number of Simpson's hymns were adopted by the early pentecostals, even though these songs were very difficult to sing.[112] Gary McGee, a pentecostal theologian and a professor at the Assemblies of God graduate school, wrote:

> The Assemblies of God has a marvelous heritage, and part of it is traced back to the ministry of A. B. Simpson, the Alliance and the school at Nyack. Through these means the Spirit of the Lord prepared a surprising number of leaders to guide the Assemblies of God in the early years. In addition, these leaders, both men and women, brought with them sound Bible teaching on salvation, the deeper life of the Spirit, divine healing, the second coming of Christ and the importance of world evangelization.[113]

Carl Brumback, an Assemblies of God Church historian, states that the pentecostal movement owes the Christian and Missionary Alliance a sevenfold debt:[114]

> Doctrines borrowed from the Alliance; 2) the hymns of Simpson; 3) the books of Simpson, Pardington, Tozer and others; 4) the terminology "Gospel Tabernacle" which when supplemented with "full" became a popular name for churches among Pentecostals; 5) the polity of the early Alliance Society, after which the Assemblies of God was styled; 6) a worldwide mission vision; and 7) numerous leaders converted and trained in Alliance circles.[115]

Simpson and the early Alliance had a tremendous impact on the pentecostal movement. It can be said that Simpson was one of the forerunners of the movement.

Although Simpson did not accept the "evidence doctrine," he is still looked on with respect and admiration by the pentecostal movement for the early influence he had on the movement. Simpson's writings are still popular today in pentecostal circles. Nienkirchen makes an astute comment on Simpson's impact on the pentecostal movement: "A. B. Simpson's life and teaching embodied several of the strains of spiritual awakening that flowed through the second half of the nineteenth century and ultimately

---

111. Wacker, *Heaven Below*, 152.
112. Blumhofer, *Assemblies of God*, 61.
113. Hartzfeld and Nienkirchen, *Birth of a Vision*, 128.
114. Ibid., 129–30.
115. Ibid., 130.

emptied into the river of pentecostalism."[116] Simpson's impact on the pentecostal revival was integral, and his important influence is still being felt today in both the pentecostal and charismatic movements.

The holiness movement was an integral part of the Third Great Awakening. Most of the leaders in the Awakening were also leaders in the holiness movement. They saw the necessity of being filled with the Holy Spirit to not only live a holy life, but also to evangelize and see the revival spread. Evangelism and holiness went hand in hand in the spread of the revival. Simpson was one of the leaders of the holiness movement and helped spread the message with his emphasis on Christ the Sanctifier. From the holiness movement, the pentecostal movement was born. The pentecostal and charismatic movements ultimately eclipsed the holiness movement in the twentieth century. Those in the pentecostal movement would look to Simpson as one of their forerunners. From the holiness movement emerged the divine healing movement. At holiness conventions and camp meetings, there would be a divine healing service, and the divine healing movement grew and spread to became an important part of American Christianity.

The next chapter will look at the divine healing movement and its influence on the Third Great Awakening.

---

116. Ibid.

V

SIMPSON'S INFLUENCE ON THE HEALING MOVEMENT

The healing movement played an important role in the Third Great Awakening. Of the five movements in the Awakening—evangelism, holiness, premillennialism, and urban as well as missionary outreach—the healing movement was probably the least emphasized. Almost all the leaders of the Third Great Awakening were either directly or indirectly involved in the movement as proponents of divine healing. Many leaders of the holiness movement were also involved in the healing movement. D. L. Moody, W. E. Boardman, R. A. Torrey, A. J. Gordon, A. T. Pierson, Andrew Murray, and A. B. Simpson were all advocates of divine healing, with Simpson becoming one of the movement's chief spokesmen.

The holiness and healing movements were deeply intertwined, which became evident at the holiness conferences and conventions. Often there would be a message on holiness followed by another service for those who were sick. Ray Cunningham comments, "The intimate connection between perfectionism and 'faith cure' [divine healing] is clearly revealed in the interwoven ministries of the leading practitioners of faith healing, Charles Cullis, William E. Boardman and Albert B. Simpson."[1] Paul Chappell writes, "Essentially, during the early years of the healing movement acceptance of the holiness doctrine preceded and prepared the way for faith healing."[2] Chappell goes on to say, "By the time of Cullis' death in 1892, the

---

1. Cunningham, "From Holiness to Healing," 500.
2. Chappell, "Divine Healing Movement in America," 72.

doctrine of divine healing was firmly rooted in the expansive landscape of American Christianity. Through the aggressive outreach of Cullis' ministry, this neglected doctrine had been brought to the forefront of the American Christian community and made a permanent feature."[3] By the early 1880s, the religious news media was reporting on this new movement, which was spreading rapidly throughout the United States.[4] Although the movement was new, the phenomenon was not.

Divine healing had been practiced by the church through the centuries. It was practiced by the New Testament church and continued down through the period of the church fathers. The practice of divine healing began to decline within the church at the onset of the Middle Ages. It never totally ceased, but it became less common.[5] There were some in the Reformation period, such as Martin Luther, who taught it and preached it, but it never became widespread.[6] It soon became a forgotten doctrine. By the mid-nineteenth century, divine healing was again preached in Europe by Pastor Johann Blumhardt at Bad Boll, Germany, where he had a "healing home." A healing home was a place where the sick—whether physically, mentally or spiritually—could come and stay and receive instruction on what Scripture said about healing. The sick would meditate on Scripture and search their hearts to seek God's leading for healing, even as others within the healing home ministry would pray that God would heal them.[7] People would go there for spiritual and physical help. Dorothea Trudel operated a similar healing home in the Swiss village of Minnedorf on Lake Zurich.[8] Reports of what was being accomplished through the ministry efforts of these two people began to circulate throughout the English-speaking world.[9] Evangelist Otto Stockmayer helped spread the message of divine healing beyond the borders of Germany.[10] Keith Bailey comments on Stockmayer:

> This popular evangelist and Bible teacher made a deep impression on the evangelical community of Great Britain on his visits

3. Ibid., 192.
4. Ibid.
5. Bailey, *Children's Bread*, 211.
6. Ibid., 213.
7. Ibid., 217.
8. Dayton, *Theological Roots of Pentecostalism*, 120–21.
9. Ibid., 121.
10. Bailey, *Children's Bread*, 219.

there. Stockmayer visited the United States and preached in many churches and conferences. It seems that England forms the link by which the renewal of physical healing eventually came to America.[11]

These three figures were the main instruments used to spread the message of divine healing in North America.

In North America, Charles Cullis rediscovered divine healing and became its most important spokesman and advocate in the United States. Cullis was a homeopathic physician in Boston in the mid-1800s. He was brought to a deeper walk with God through the death of his young wife. Her death helped him focus on God, and he turned to God for comfort and encouragement. In 1862, Cullis was filled with the Holy Spirit and began a ministry preaching holiness and divine healing.[12] Cunningham describes this special work:

> Two years later he began his "faith work," as it was called, by establishing a consumptive's home, supported by volunteer work and unsolicited donations, on Beacon Hill. The undertaking flourished and by the mid 1880s it had become a great enterprise consisting of numerous medical, nursing and children's facilities, as well as rescue missions, in and about Boston. The outreach of the faith work extended to activities among Negroes in Virginia, Chinese in California and several missions in India.[13]

In addition to this ministry, Cullis also established a publishing company known as the Williard Tract Repository to publish holiness literature and material on divine healing.[14] Cullis became interested in divine healing when patients considered incurable were sent to him by other physicians.

Cullis went to Switzerland to visit Dorothea Trudel's healing home in Minnedorf, Switzerland, where he became persuaded that divine healing was meant to be experienced through all generations. Cullis became convinced that Jas 5:14-15 was just as applicable for the believers of his day as it was for those in New Testament times. The passage tells of how someone who is ill can seek divine healing. It states that if anyone is sick in the church, they are to call for the elders of the church. The elders would pray over the sick person, then anoint the sufferer with oil in the name of

11. Ibid., 219-220.
12. Cunningham, "From Holiness to Healing," 500.
13. Ibid.
14. Ibid.

the Lord. The prayer offered in faith would raise the sick person up. In other words, God would heal them. Cullis began to practice this form of divine healing with patients who were considered incurable. He saw some of them miraculously healed. This began Cullis' healing ministry, which led him to become the period's most important proponent of divine healing.

Cullis brought W. E. Boardman, as one of the leaders of the holiness movement, to the divine healing movement in the early 1870s. According to Cunningham, "Cullis' influence was a major factor in bringing Boardman's long standing interest in spiritual healing to the point of conviction."[15] Boardman moved to England, and in 1881 he wrote a book on divine healing called *The Great Physician*.[16] In 1885, Boardman organized the International Convention on Holiness and Divine Healing held at Bethshan, London, England that was attended by delegates from all over the world.[17] This conference helped to further popularize the holiness and healing movements.

Cullis influenced Boardman and many others through his conventions and summer conferences. Cunningham observed, "The most dramatic manifestation of Cullis' commitment to faith cure, however, was the annual Summer Faith Convention, which had become, by the mid-1800s, 'a recognized feature of the religious life of New England.'"[18]

It was at one of these conventions at Old Orchard, Maine, in 1881 that Simpson heard the message on divine healing and claimed its promise for himself. After hearing Cullis' message, Simpson went out alone in the woods and prayed for God's healing; God healed him of both his heart problem and his difficulty with his nerves. How would modern medicine diagnose Simpson's illness? There has not been any research on what he may have suffered from. This is because once God healed him of his disease, it was no longer was a factor in his life and ministry. Dan Evearitt explains that some have suggested that Simpson suffered from chronic

---

15. Ibid., 501.
16. Ibid.
17. Nienkirchen, *A. B. Simpson and the Pentecostal Movement*, 15.
18. Cunningham, "From Holiness to Healing," 502.

fatigue syndrome,[19] since some of the symptoms of his illness were similar to this disease.[20]

Simpson and his ministry would never be the same. His personal experience and biblical understanding of divine healing contributed to him becoming the second most influential leader in the divine healing movement, next to Charles Cullis.[21] While Cullis would be considered the "Apostle of Divine Healing," Simpson would be considered its chief spokesman.

Divine healing would become the third fold of Simpson's Fourfold Gospel: Christ as our Healer. Simpson was careful to keep divine healing in its proper place in the gospel message. He wrote, "Divine healing is not the most important truth of the Gospel, but it is a truth that God has shown to us. Holding it in its subordinate place, let us hold it fearlessly and confess it manfully."[22] Simpson realized the importance of divine healing and wanted to keep it in its proper perspective. In his classic work on healing, *The Gospel of Healing*, Simpson writes in his preface: "It is most important that it should be ever held in its true place in relation to other parts of the Gospel. It is not the whole Gospel, or perhaps the chief part of it, but it is a part, and in its due relationship to the whole it will prove to be, like the Gospel itself, 'the power of God . . . to every one that believeth.'"[23]

Simpson taught that divine healing was part of the redemption of Christ. He saw this demonstrated in Isa 53:4–5 and Matt 8:17. Here, healing was shown to be a part of Christ's atoning work on the cross. Simpson did not see this work, however, the same way he saw the free offer of salvation. Whereas one was free for anyone who would believe, divine healing was only available to God's children—to those who knew Jesus as Lord and Savior.[24] Simpson wrote in his book *The Four-Fold Gospel*:

19. Beers et al., *Merck Manual of Medical Information*, 1717. *Merck Manual of Medical Information* states that "Chronic fatigue syndrome refers to longstanding severe and disabling fatigue without a proven physical or psychological disease" (ibid.). It is not clear what causes chronic fatigue syndrome. There is some recent evidence that suggests it might be due to abnormalities of the immune system that might be the cause. It also seems that in most cases the symptoms of chronic fatigue syndrome may also lessen over time. The methods of treatment may include aerobic exercise, psychotherapy, and drug therapy. It is thought that excessive periods of rest, in fact, may worsen the illness (ibid., 1718).

20. Daniel J. Evearitt, interview with the author, November 4, 2003.

21. Dayton, *Theological Roots of Pentecostalism*, 128.

22. Hartzfeld and Nienkirchen, *Birth of a Vision*, 11.

23. Simpson, *Gospel of Healing*, 6.

24. Hartzfeld and Nienkirchen, *Birth of a Vision*, 12.

Simpson's Influence on the Healing Movement

> Divine Healing is part of the redemptive work of Jesus Christ. It is one of the things he came to bring. Its foundation is the Cross of Calvary. "He redeemeth thy life from destruction." "Deliver him from going down to death, I have found a ransom." Surely that healing comes from Himself alone. "By His stripes we are healed." This is the redemptive work of Christ. You have a right to it, beloved, for his body bore all the liability of your body on the cross.[25]

Christ as Healer became an important message of Simpson's, but it never superseded his messages of Christ as Savior and Sanctifier. There were proponents of divine healing, however, who made divine healing their main thrust.

One such proponent was John Alexander Dowie. Dowie, the founder of both the city of Zion, Illinois, and of the Christian Catholic Church headquartered in Zion, made divine healing the main focus of his messages. Dowie became as well known as Simpson on the teaching on divine healing, and many pentecostals look on him as one of their forerunners. Chappell classified Dowie as one of the more extreme and vocal leaders in the divine healing movement. To Dowie, divine healing was the main message. Dowie would put healing above all other aspects of Christ's ministry. Dowie held two basic presuppositions in his view of healing. First, Jesus Christ "is the same yesterday, today and forever, and being so, he is unchanged in power and will," and second, "Disease, like sin, is God's enemy, and the devil's work, and can never be God's will."[26] When someone became ill, it was because the devil usurped Christ in the sick person's life.[27] Dowie also insisted that divine healing always occurred instantaneously, and he was opposed to consulting physicians or any use of medicine. He preached a famous message titled "Doctors, Drugs and Devils; or the Foes of Christ the Healer."[28] His message equating the medical world with the devil often sparked riots in the United States and overseas.[29] During one of his attacks against the medical establishment in Chicago, over two thousand physicians and medical students rioted and had to be restrained by police.[30]

25. Simpson, *Four-Fold Gospel*, 60.
26. Chappell, "Divine Healing Movement in America," 300.
27. Ibid.
28. Ibid., 286.
29. Ibid., 287.
30. Ibid.

Later on in his ministry, Dowie became convinced that he was a modern-day Elijah. As a result, Dowie was removed from leadership in the Christian Catholic Church and the city of Zion, Illinois. Because of Simpson's understanding of divine healing, Dowie asked Simpson if he would go around the country with him to preach on the subject. Simpson replied, "No brother Dowie, I have four wheels on my chariot. I cannot agree to neglect the other three while I devote all my time to the one."[31]

Afterwards, Dowie turned on Simpson and began attacking him.[32] Tozer describes Dowie's attacks:

> Impulsive and violent as he always was, Dowie promptly turned against Simpson and set out with the express intention of discrediting him in the eyes of the public. He arranged throughout some of the principal cities of the United States a series of lectures in which he would tear Simpson to shreds and then tramp on the shreds. Simpson refused to fight back. Pittsburg was the place chosen for the opening of the shredding campaign. Crowds filled the huge auditorium to hear the famous John Alexander Dowie. That evening, an hour or so before time for the opening lecture, Dowie was eating a fish dinner when a tiny bone became lodged cross-wise in his throat. The crowds waited, time went on and the speaker did not appear. He never showed up. It must have been an eloquent piece of bone, for it completely changed the plans of Mr. Dowie. He cancelled his series of lectures and crept back to lick his wounds. When Simpson was informed of the turn things had taken, he said simply, "Oh, Dowie. Yes, I committed that man to God long ago."[33]

Simpson tried to keep the sensational out of his message on divine healing. He tried to keep the discussion biblical and away from the bizarre. Norris Magnuson comments, "Because claims were sometimes bizarre . . . a woman testified at Old Orchard, for example, that 'God had filled a tooth for her'—Simpson and others cautioned against abuses and misunderstanding."[34] Simpson was more concerned that people were living right and walking with God so that healing could then be seen in its proper perspective. Simpson wrote, "God is much more concerned to have

---

31. Tozer, *Wingspread*, 134–35.
32. Ibid., 135.
33. Ibid.
34. Magnuson, *Salvation in the Slums*, 71–72.

you right than to have you well."[35] Simpson believed that sometimes people were not healed because they were praying for healing for the wrong reasons. Healing could not be received for selfish reasons. It could only be received by those who where completely committed to the Lord, who were living for God's glory, and who desired to serve the Lord.[36]

Although Simpson tried to be balanced in his preaching on divine healing, he was still criticized for his views. This probably hurt him more than anything else. Friends he held dear abandoned him when he embraced divine healing. Some Christian periodicals would print articles criticizing his view on healing. One periodical reprinted a chapter from his *Gospel of Healing* and accused him of not recognizing the importance of the redemption of the body in heaven.[37] Mrs. H. Grantham Guiness, whose husband founded the East London Institute for Home and Foreign Missionaries, blamed Simpson for the deaths of three young missionaries associated with the Kansas Mission to the Soudan (Sudan). She said he had corrupted them with his views of divine healing, which resulted in their deaths.[38] Simpson also received criticism from some of the Keswick tradition, notably Griffith Thomas and Herbert Lockyear, for his belief in healing in the atonement.[39]

Simpson was an able defender of divine healing when the need arose. One such incident occurred when James Buckley, editor of the *New York Christian Advocate*, wrote an article critical of divine healing in *Century Magazine*.[40] Buckley's article was titled "Faith-Healing and Kindred Phenomena." Buckley contended that the doctrine of divine healing practiced among Christians was no different than that practiced by spiritualists, pagans, and other healers. Those who practiced divine healing used the same methods and practices as those of non-Christian religions and the occult. Buckley proclaimed that all healing came from natural causes and that God did not directly intervene and heal anyone.[41] He concluded that divine healing was "a probable superstition, dangerous in its final effects."[42] Buckley believed that divine healing detracted from the moral and spiri-

---

35. Ibid., 72.
36. Ibid.
37. Hartzfeld and Nienkirchen, *Birth of a Vision* 17.
38. Ibid., 18.
39. Ibid.
40. Chappell, "Divine Healing Movement in America," 269.
41. Ibid., 269–70.
42. Ibid., 270.

tual transformation that is the heart of Christianity.[43] Buckley also said it destroys the "ascending of reason."[44] He felt the doctrine of divine healing could lead to "mental derangement."[45] Simpson wrote a rebuttal in his periodical, *The Word, the Work and the World*, and defended the doctrine of divine healing. His two-part article was entitled "Divine Healing and Demonism Not Identical: A Protest and Reply to Dr. Buckley . . ."[46] Simpson first dismissed the importance of Buckley's views, arguing they were not a threat to the divine healing movement. Secondly, he quoted from another periodical that attacked Buckley's credentials. The periodical called Buckley that "eminent Methodist secularist."[47] Thirdly, Simpson dismissed the idea that divine healing and healing of non-Christians was the same thing. They are different. Simpson asserts that healing in pagan religions is done through the power of Satan. They are demonic miracles. He explains this by referring to Matt 24:14, where false prophets will perform signs and wonders that deceive even the elect. Simpson concludes with an attack on the very basis of the article.[48] He writes, "The article makes no attempt to answer the Scriptural argument for divine healing. This is its most fatal defect. From a Christian minister this omission is ominous and with Christian readers it is a fatal objection."[49] Simpson also wrote more articles in his periodical on the biblical evidence for divine healing.[50] Simpson was so successful that Buckley set apart a large portion of his next article answering Simpson's rebuttal and other articles.[51]

Simpson promoted divine healing in a number of ways. Often, divine healing seemed to get more publicity than the other folds of the gospel because newspapers tended to sensationalize the healing services. Each week at Simpson's Gospel Tabernacle, there was a Friday afternoon healing service. The service was quite popular, and Simpson would preach a message on healing and then follow with the instructions given in Jas 5:14–16 to anoint the sick and pray for them. Simpson specifically chose to hold his

43. Ibid.
44. Ibid.
45. Ibid.
46. Ibid.
47. Ibid., 271.
48. Ibid.
49. Ibid.
50. Ibid., 270–71.
51. Ibid., 272.

healing services on Fridays because he did not want the message of healing to dominate the Sunday morning service. He also felt that many listeners on Sunday morning, especially those who were not as mature in their faith as others, were not ready for divine healing.

John Sawin wrote, "Simpson believed that teaching on divine healing in particular, should not be crowded upon the popular audiences who were not prepared for strong meat."[52] Therefore, he chose Friday to keep the service available, yet slightly obscure.[53] But the meetings became anything but obscure. The Friday healing service became the largest weekly religious meeting in New York City.[54] The attendance at these services was between five hundred and one thousand people at each service.[55] Cunningham wrote of the Friday afternoon healing service's positive impact on New York City that "one clerical associate declared that his weekly healing service 'became' a shrine for thousands of people connected with the churches of the city and its suburbs."[56] The Friday afternoon healing meetings went uninterrupted for thirty-eight years.

Besides praying for those attending the meeting, prayer requests were taken from all over the country.[57] Simpson and his teaching on divine healing were well known all over the country. In fact, Joshua Cravett, a former student of Moody's whose wife had been diagnosed with a case of terminal tuberculosis medical authorities had declared hopeless, was urged by Moody to contact Simpson.[58] Moody wrote, "why not go see A. B. Simpson, if she has faith, and let him anoint her as God is able to raise her up. We here will be praying . . . You will find Rev. Simpson near . . . 6th Avenue [New York] most any Christian can tell you. Keep me posted."[59] The Cravetts followed Moody's advice, and Lyle Dorsett reported what happened: "The Cravetts took Moody's advice and attended 'a simple anointing service' held on a Wednesday evening at Simpson's church. A. B. Simpson spoke on Romans

---

52. Niklaus et al., *All for Jesus*, 55.
53. Travis, *Christ Our Healer Today*, 115.
54. Ibid., 116.
55. Niklaus et al., *All for Jesus*, 55.
56. Cunningham, "From Holiness to Healing," 503.
57. Chappell, "Divine Healing Movement in America," 267.
58. Dorsett, *Passion for Souls*, 334.
59. Ibid.

8:11, laid hands on Charlotte Cravett, and prayed. She lived for fifty-three more years and never again showed a trace of tuberculosis."[60]

Some of the people who came for healing needed more instruction and special preparation than a public service could provide. As a result, Simpson began a home for those who were seeking healing. In this retreat center, people had time to read, pray, and receive instruction on healing.[61] The healing home was called the Berachah House, which meant the "House of Blessing."

The Berachah House was patterned after Johann Blumhardt's healing home in Bad Boll, Germany; Dorothea Trudel's home in Minnendorf, Switzerland; and Charles Cullis' Healing Home in Boston. The Berachah House began in 1884 and was in existence for fifteen years, with over ten thousand people "transformed" through the ministry of the home.[62] The Berachah House was so successful that a number of other homes sprung up all over the United States that were patterned after it. There were over a dozen of these homes that were directly or indirectly connected with Simpson and the Alliance.[63] These healing homes had a tremendous impact on the American evangelical churches in North America.

Simpson's pen played an important role in helping popularize the doctrine of divine healing. Chappell comments, "Simpson's gifted writing ability provided him yet another means to share the message of divine healing with the masses."[64] Simpson wrote numerous articles on divine healing for his own periodical, *The Word, the Work and the World*.[65] In fact, there was a special section for testimonies from those who had been healed in his periodical. Many of Simpson's articles were reproduced and reprinted in other magazines as well.[66]

Simpson also wrote a number of books that helped popularize divine healing. Simpson's most important work on healing was *The Gospel of Healing*. The book was a collection of eight articles written between 1887 and 1888. It was slightly revised in 1915.[67] The book, along with A. J. Gordon's

---

60. Ibid.
61. Niklaus et al., *All for Jesus*, 56.
62. Magnuson, *Salvation in the Slums*, 70–71.
63. Chappell, "Divine Healing Movement in America," 261.
64. Ibid., 269.
65. Ibid.
66. Ibid.
67. Travis, *Christ Our Healer Today*, 117.

Simpson's Influence on the Healing Movement

The Ministry of Healing, had a strong impact on the Christian public's view of divine healing. As Magnuson writes of the impact of Simpson's *The Gospel of Healing*,

> The conventions and local gatherings of the Alliance as well as its periodicals, featured a constant stream of testimonies. One person wrote of being freed from morphine and other troubles; another of deliverance from "nervous prostration"; still another professed release from twenty-five years of dependence upon drugs, besides insomnia and inability to take solids. The latter person credited her healing to Simpson's book, *The Gospel of Healing*. "I have stopped reading it again and again," she declared, with the kind of reaction Simpson's writing and preaching often evokes, "to weep and praise God for the blessing it has been to me."[68]

The Gospel of Healing was often offered to those who came to the Berachah House so they could be instructed on the basics of divine healing.[69]

Simpson also published a number of other books that dealt with divine healing. They were *The Discovery of Divine Healing, Inquiries and Answers Concerning Divine Healing, A Cloud of Witnesses*, and his three-volume *Friday Meeting Talks*.[70] Simpson's book *A Cloud of Witnesses* was so popular that its first printing sold out in just a few weeks.[71]

Simpson also helped spread the divine healing message through his summer conferences and conventions. Chappell wrote:

> These summer revivals led Simpson in 1884 to begin annual interdenominational conventions at the downtown church. So successful were these conventions that invitations came from across the nation for him to conduct similar meetings. Within a year, city-wide conventions in the major cities of America had become a normative part of Simpson's ministry. In addition, during the summer of 1886, Simpson began conducting ten-day crusades at Old Orchard Beach on "Christian Life and Work and Divine Healing." His conventions were to continue for thirty-two years, thus maintaining faith healing meetings at Old Orchard for over twenty years following the suspension of Cullis' conventions.[72]

---

68. Magnuson, *Salvation in the Slums*, 71.
69. Travis, *Christ Our Healer Today*, 118.
70. Chappell, "Divine Healing Movement in America," 264.
71. Ibid., 267.
72. Ibid., 265.

At these conventions and conferences, thousands reported being healed.[73] These conventions were not only for healing, but also for evangelism, holiness, and missions. The healing service was just one part of the conventions and the conferences.

Tozer stated that one of the main reasons these conventions and conferences were successful was the teaching on divine healing and the practice of prayer for the sick.[74] He goes on to say that by 1887, these conventions had become famous.[75] At these conventions and conferences, Simpson would also invite some of the most prominent advocates of divine healing to be featured speakers.[76] Men and women such as A. J. Gordon, Andrew Murray, Otto Stockmayer, A. T. Pierson, R. A. Torrey, and Carrie Judd spoke at Simpson's conventions and summer conferences.[77] This was probably one of the most effective ways of getting Simpson's message out, and it helped popularize the third fold of the Fourfold Gospel, Christ as our Healer, to the Christian public. Drake Travis concludes, "Simpson is credited with enlightening countless people to the truth of divine healing. The notable change in the awareness and exercise of this truth during his era testifies to the effect of the one man, Simpson."[78] Chappell states:

> For thirty-seven years, A. B. Simpson stood as one of the most effective and popular propagators of the divine healing message in America. His conventions, Friday meetings, healing home, and prolific publications on the topic made him one of the most significant figures of the movement . . . No single individual in a movement who was influenced by Charles Cullis, touched as many lives with the message of healing as Simpson or persuaded as many individuals to enter full-time ministry with faith healing as a vital aspect of that ministry.[79]

Simpson and the early Christian and Missionary Alliance made an important contribution to the divine healing movement as the twentieth century began.[80] It was through the preaching of divine healing that many

---

73. Ibid., 266.
74. Tozer, *Wingspread*, 96.
75. Ibid.
76. Chappell, "Divine Healing Movement in America," 266.
77. Thompson, *A. B. Simpson*, 100.
78. Travis, *Christ Our Healer Today*, 125.
79. Chappell, "Divine Healing Movement in America," 277.
80. Ibid., 283.

people came into the Christian and Missionary Alliance. Sawin comments on this fact when he writes:

> Many of the leaders in the Alliance during the formative years were men and women who had been delivered from life threatening and incapacitating sickness. Though Simpson was cautious and though he kept the doctrine of healing subordinate to evangelism for lost souls and the spirit-filled life, nevertheless, God's healing grace and power exercised toward hundreds of people during early Alliance history accounts in some measure for the remarkable ministry and influence of Simpson and the Alliance. Many healed persons gave themselves unstintingly to the ministry of the Gospel. They served in churches, in Alliance branches, in rescue missions, and in overseas missionary work.[81]

Chappell wrote, "By the time of Cullis' death in 1892, the doctrine of divine healing was firmly rooted in the expansive landscape of American Christianity."[82]

Divine healing was here to stay, and the message was not only adopted by Simpson's Christian and Missionary Alliance, it would also become a cornerstone in the emerging pentecostal movement. Some of these newer groups would not keep the balance of divine healing, as Simpson had directed, but instead followed Dowie's and Charles Parham's perspective on healing.

Simpson's view on divine healing always remained balanced. He considered his experience of divine healing to be the third greatest crises in his life. It was his belief that Christ provided healing in his redemption for humankind. Healing was part of Christ's atonement. He saw this in two Scripture passages: Isa 53:4–5 and Matt 8:17. Divine healing was only for believers, and it was for all believers. It was for all Christians. Simpson incorporated divine healing in the church by following the dictum in Jas 5:14–15. It stated that all those who were sick in the church should call for the elders of the church, who would anoint with oil and pray for the sick one. This teaching would become an integral part of Simpson's ministry.

It is ironic that Simpson is now most remembered for his teaching on divine healing, even though divine healing was the fold he least emphasized in his preaching of the Fourfold Gospel. Simpson, as a spokesman for divine healing, is still having an impact today through his books and

---

81. Hartzfeld and Nienkirchen, *Birth of a Vision*, 14.
82. Chappell, "Divine Healing Movement in America," 192.

his denomination, the Christian and Missionary Alliance. Chappell wrote: "With [Simpson's] publications still being widely circulated and the fourfold Gospel still the foundation of his 1.3 million member denomination, A. B. Simpson continues to spread the message that divine healing is the heritage of every Christian believer."[83]

Although divine healing was the least emphasized of the movements in the Third Great Awakening, it still played an important role. Divine healing had been practiced in the church down through the centuries, but it became popular again in the second half of the nineteenth century. Charles Cullis helped bring it to the forefront in American Christianity. Simpson became one of the movement's chief spokesmen. He helped popularize it to the Christian public through his healing services at the Gospel Tabernacle, through his conventions and summer conferences, and through his writings. Divine healing became an integral part of the American church. The leaders of the Third Great Awakening not only helped popularize divine healing, they were also involved in the premillennial movement that rose to prominence in the second half of the nineteenth century. The following chapter will deal with Simpson and his involvement in the premillennial movement.

---

83. Ibid., 277.

VI

SIMPSON'S INVOLVEMENT IN THE PREMILLENNIAL MOVEMENT

As we consider Simpson and the premillennial movement, an explanation should be given concerning Christian millennialism as a whole. As Timothy Weber writes, "Christian millennialism is the belief that there will be a long period of unprecedented peace and righteousness closely associated with the second coming of Christ."[1] Most Christians can be divided into three groups, depending on how their view interprets Christ's millennial reign in terms of whether Christ will reign literally and when they anticipate Christ's return in relation to his reign. Amillennialists, who do not believe in a literal millennium, understand Christ's references to his return figuratively. They believe that Christ's return will be in the hearts of believers. Postmillennialist's believe that after the church establishes the millennium, Christ will return. The church establishes the millennial kingdom through preaching the gospel. Premillennialists believe Christ will return before the millennium, at which time Christ will establish it.[2]

A majority of the leaders in the Third Great Awakening were, as it pertained to the second coming of Christ, premillennialists. The premillennial movement was an important part of the Awakening, and it encouraged its leaders to evangelize the unsaved around them. These leaders felt that prophetic events were lining up to usher in Christ's imminent return, and they wanted to bring as many people as possible into the kingdom of God

---

1. Weber, *Living in the Shadow of the Second Coming*, 9.
2. Ibid.

before this happened. The premillennialists saw wickedness in the world increasing and believed they needed to bring in as many lost sinners as possible before the evil times reached their pinnacle and Christ returned. D. L. Moody, a prominent premillennialist, was fond of saying, "I look upon this world as a wrecked vessel, God has given me a lifeboat and said to me, 'Moody, save all you can.'"[3] Moody, along with R. A. Torrey, Wilbur Chapman, A. J. Gordon, A. T. Pierson, and A. B. Simpson, were all premillennialists. They recognized that premillennialism was important for the continuance of the revival. Simpson wrote in 1891: "England is permeated with the [premillennial] truth. Nearly, if not all, the evangelists in this land, who are most used by the Master, hold the blessed hope as the motive of their lives and work."[4]

Premillennialism began to take hold after the Civil War, and by the end of the First World War, premillennialism was fast becoming the predominant eschatological perspective. It became the most popular evangelical view of the end times and continues to hold that position in the Evangelical Church in the United States today.[5]

During the first three centuries of the church, most of the early church fathers were premillennial, including Papias, Irenaeus, Justin Martyr, Tertullian, Hippolytus, Methodius, Commodianus, and Lactertius. The church's eschatological outlook did not change until the fourth century, when Constantine made Christianity legal and gave it favored status. The amillennial position then became supreme.[6] Robert Clouse comments that "the millennium was reinterpreted to refer to the church, and the thousand-year reign of Christ and his saints was equated with the whole history of the church on earth making for the denial of a future millennium."[7] Augustine popularized the position, and it became the dominant eschatological belief in the medieval period. This teaching became so popular that the Council of Ephesus in 431 condemned all other views.[8] Thus, amillennialism became the predominant view of eschatology in the Roman Catholic Church and in the churches that came out of the Reformation.[9]

3. Marsden, *Fundamentalism and American Culture*, 38.
4. Simpson, "How I Was Led," 6.
5. Weber, *Living in the Shadow of the Second Coming*, 9.
6. Clouse, *Meaning of the Millennium*, 9.
7. Ibid.
8. Ibid.
9. Van Hoogen, "Premillennialism and the Alliance Distinctives," 49–50.

Daniel Whitley introduced postmillennialism in the seventeenth century. This view would be promoted in America by Jonathan Edwards during the Great Awakening.[10] The postmillennial view held that Christ would return after a period of millennial blessing and not before, as was taught by the premillennial view.[11] John Davis writes,

> While in the postmillennial view Christ is not physically present on earth during the millennial period, he is the active agent and primary cause of the church's victorious advance and expansion, sending forth the Spirit to bless in a dramatic way the proclamation of the Word of God.[12]

Postmillennialism also became the dominant view among Christians from the American Revolution until the Civil War.[13] There were a number of prominent nineteenth-century American theologians who were postmillennialists. The list includes Charles Hodge, A. A. Hodge, Robert L. Dabney, W. G. T. Shedd, A. H. Strong, and Benjamin B. Warfield.[14] Postmillennialists were optimistic about America and saw the United States as God's postmillennial kingdom in the world. This perspective was similar to the Puritan view of the New England Colony as God's light on the hill.

Postmillennialism began to lose popularity during the Civil War and the years that followed because it did not seem to fit with what was happening in the world. Many Christians felt things were getting worse. After World War I, postmillennialism lost most of its followers. Davis comments, "the pessimism and disillusionment engendered by wartime conditions contributed heavily to the demise of the once dominant view in American Christianity. The optimistic and hopeful outlook of the postmillennial vision no longer seemed suited to the times."[15] In the 1870s, premillennialism became widely accepted by the evangelical Christians in North America.[16] It steadily grew in popularity, even on into the present.[17]

---

10. Marsden, *Fundamentalism and American Culture*, 49.
11. Davis, *Victory of Christ's Kingdom*, 11.
12. Ibid.
13. Ibid.
14. Ibid., 12.
15. Ibid., 21.
16. Ibid., 51.
17. It must be mentioned that William Miller, the founder of the Adventist movement, was the first significant American premillennialist. His failed historical understanding of Christ's return in 1843 and 1844 helped set the stage for a more "futuristic"

Weber states that premillennialism can be further divided into two subgroups on the basis of their approach to prophetic texts.[18] He explains:

> Historicist premillennialists believe that the prophetic Scriptures, especially those in Daniel and Revelation, give the entire history of the church in symbolic form. Thus, they look into the churches, past and present, to find prophetic fulfillments and to see where they are in God's prophetic timetable.
>
> Futurist premillennialists argue that none of the prophecies of the "last days" have been fulfilled in the history of the church, and they expect them to come to pass within a short period just before the return of Christ. For them, all the events prophesied in the Bible still await fulfillment.[19]

In futurist premillennialism, there is general agreement on the events of the future, but there is also disagreement on the exact timing of when the church will be taken away to meet Christ in the air. The futurist premillennialist call this doctrine of taking the church out of the world the "rapture." They find this "rapture" expression in the Latin translation of 1 Thess 4:15–17.[20] There is disagreement on when the rapture will occur, but most agree that it is associated with the tribulation period. Among dispensationalist premillennialists, there are three common understandings of the tribulation period: pretribulationist, midtribulationist, and posttribulationist. These are all views of the church and its relationship to the tribulation.

This tribulation is seen to be the period of "Jacob's Trouble" (Jer 30:7), of the great pressure or tribulation (Matt 24), and of the wrath of God. Weber writes:

---

understanding of premillennialism. In his book *Millennial Fever and the End of the World*, George Knight gives an excellent history of Miller and the Adventist movement. Knight comments that Miller, up until the faithful date of 1843, had a large following and helped popularize the premillennial view of Christ's return. Although Miller founded the Adventist movement, Miller always considered himself a Baptist and kept his Baptist doctrine (Knight, *Millennial Fever*, 82). William Miller and his views would have been perfectly acceptable, except for his date-setting, by most of the evangelical churches in the late nineteenth century. One of the groups that came out of Adventist movement was the Evangelical Adventists, and they were largely assimilated with conservative Protestantism in the late nineteenth century because they were so similar to the evangelical churches of the time (ibid., 327–28).

18. Weber, *Living in the Shadow of the Second Coming*, 9.
19. Ibid., 9–10.
20. Ibid., 11.

Simpson's Involvement in the Premillennial Movement

Pretribulationists believe that the church will be raptured before the rise of the Antichrist and the beginning of the tribulation. Midtribulationists, on the other hand, contend that the church will be raptured during the tribulation after the Antichrist's rise to power, but before God begins to pour out a series of preliminary judgments on the earth in anticipation of Christ's return. Posttribulationists say that the church will live through the entire period and rescued at the end of the tribulation by the rapture at the time of second coming.[21]

A doctrine within premillennialism that gained a large following among American evangelicals in the 1870s was dispensationalism, which was both futuristic and pretribulational. It quickly overcame and supplemented the posttribulational brand of premillennialism.[22]

Dispensationalism was developed and promoted by John Nelson Darby and his Plymouth Brethren movement in Great Britain. The Plymouth Brethren were founded by Christians who were unhappy with the spiritual condition of the Anglican Church in Great Britain. The Plymouth Brethren were a loosely organized group of Christians who met together for communion, prayer, and the study of the Scriptures.[23] Darby was a gifted teacher and formulated dispensationalism into a theological system. C. I. Scofield, one of Darby's American disciples, promoted and helped popularize dispensationalism in America.[24] Scofield defined a dispensation as "a period of time during which man is tested in respect of obedience to some specific revelation of the will of God." He continues: "These periods are marked off in Scripture by some change in God's method of dealing with mankind, in respect to two questions: of sin, and of man's responsibility. Each of the dispensations may be regarded as a new test of the natural man, and each ends in judgment-making his utter failure in every dispensation."[25] Weber explains what separated dispensationalists from other premillennialists when he writes,

> What separated dispensationalists from their fellow futurists was their strict literalism when interpreting biblical prophecy, their absolute separation of Israel and the church as two distinct

21. Ibid.
22. Ibid.
23. Ibid., 17.
24. Ibid.
25. Ibid.

peoples of God, and some conclusions which grew out of these presuppositions.

Everything in the dispensationalist system seemed to rest on the conviction that God has two completely different plans operating in history, one for an earthly people (Israel) and one for a heavenly people (the church). Thus "rightly dividing the word of truth" meant more than keeping one's dispensations straight. At all costs, the dispensationalists insisted, one must maintain the distinction between the two peoples of God.[26]

D. L. Moody helped bring dispensationalism to America by promoting Darby and his brand of premillennialism. Although Darby and the Plymouth Brethren movement never became popular in the United States, their brand of premillennialism did. Moody spent a great deal of time with the Plymouth Brethren on his evangelistic trips to Britain. He invited John Nelson Darby and other Plymouth Brethren to preach at his Illinois Street Church.[27] Moody wrote a pamphlet, *Second Coming of Christ,* that helped promote the doctrine. By the 1800s, his publishing house, run by his brother-in-law Fleming Revell, had printed an entire line of books under the heading of "Premillennial Works."[28] Lyle Dorsett explains that Moody

> ... helped recruit his St. Louis pastor friend, J. H. Brooks, as well A. J. Gordon and George Mueller to help fill out a list of nearly a dozen titles. Premillennialism, like the Holy Spirit, Bible applications, personal work and evangelism, became the hallmarks of Moody's teaching, and these were reflected in Revell's lists as long as Moody lived.[29]

At this time, many American Christians were quite willing to accept premillennialism and its new form, dispensationalism. Dispensationalism was seen as an ally against theological liberalism.[30] It was a buffer for the orthodox faith. The historian Paul Boyer comments:

> Dispensationalism arrived at a time of mounting evangelical concerns over challenges to the Bible's divinely inspired status by liberal theologians in the United States and by historical-critical scholars in Germany. The formation of the Evangelical Alliance

26. Ibid., 17–18.
27. Dorsett, *Passion for Souls,* 136.
28. Ibid., 335.
29. Ibid.
30. Marsden, *Fundamentalism and American Culture,* 51.

in England in 1846 and of an American branch in 1867 signaled the rising uneasiness at the founding convention in London, the eight hundred delegates adopted a creedal statement affirming the Bible's inspiration and authority. Many emboldened evangelicals thus welcomed Darby's strong emphasis on Biblical authority and his literal reading of the prophetic texts.[31]

The dispensational premillennial movement encouraged average Christians' confidence that they could understand Scripture and that Scripture was literal and historically accurate.[32] The prophecies in the past had been fulfilled, and the prophecies in the future would also be fulfilled. Dispensationalism was a hedge against the liberal encroachment that was affecting the church.[33] Marsden states,

> It is clear that the views of John Nelson Darby as accepted by the American adherents of the Niagara and International Prophecy conferences of the late nineteenth century, popularized by W. E. Blackstone's, *Jesus Is Coming* and systematized by James H. Brooks and then by his protégé C. I. Schofield, opposed liberal trends at almost every point.[34]

Although the premillennial message spread through the printed word and was taught at Bible colleges, it was spread most effectively through summer conferences and conventions. The most important was the Niagara Bible Conference. According to Sandeen, it was the "mother of all Bible conferences, and the Monte Cassino and Port Royal of the movement."[35] Sandeen states, "Known during its first several years as 'The Believers' Meeting for Bible Study', this conference can properly be called the earliest, most expressively, most influential and most difficult to describe."[36] The Niagara Bible Conference was integral in promoting premillennialism throughout North America.[37]

After the initial meeting in 1875, the conference changed its name from the Believer's Meeting for Bible Study to the Niagara Bible Conference. In 1878, the conference adopted a statement of faith that included

---

31. Van Hoogen, "Premillennialism and the Alliance Distinctives," 55.
32. Ibid., 56.
33. Marsden, *Fundamentalism and American Culture*, 51.
34. Ibid.
35. Sandeen, *Roots of Fundamentalism*, 132.
36. Ibid.
37. Reiter et al., *Rapture: Pre-, Mid- or Post-Tribulational*, 18.

the doctrine of premillennialism.[38] The conference later came to be dominated by prophetic concerns. The conference would meet annually over the course of one or two weeks, usually at a resort. It met from 1883 to 1899 at the resort at Niagara-on-the-Lake, Ontario, and that is how it got its name.[39] Sandeen states, "Virtually everyone of any significance in the history of the American millenarian movement during this period attended the Niagara Conference."[40] The Niagara creed was tolerant of different premillennial beliefs, but it became dominated by the dispensationalists' view.[41]

A. J. Gordon and James Brooks were voices of moderation at the Niagara Conference. After their deaths, dispensationalism took over and crowded out the other forms of premillennialism.[42] This controversy over premillennialism was disrupting the Niagara fellowship. Even Moody could not heal the division. After Moody's death in 1899, there was a break between the different groups over premillennialism. Richard Reiter writes that Moody's "death left an irreplaceable gap in evangelicalism, and affected the Niagara Bible Conference. Forces of moderation and tolerance suffered losses at the front rank while those of polarization gained strength."[43] The dispensational form of premillennialism became the dominant form of premillennialism, and it remains popular even to this day.

Christ the Coming King

The fourth fold of Simpson's Fourfold Gospel was Christ as the Coming King. Simpson saw this as the pinnacle of the gospel. Christ's second coming fulfilled the rest of the gospel. Simpson wrote in his book *The Fourfold Gospel* that "the second coming of the Lord Jesus Christ is a distinct and important part of the Apostolic Gospel."[44] He explained further that the second coming "is the glorious culmination of all other parts of the Gospel."[45] Simpson felt the other three folds of the gospel prepared the church and the believer for the return of Christ. He saw Christ as the Com-

---

38. Weber, *Living in the Shadow of the Second Coming*, 26–27.
39. Sandeen, *Roots of Fundamentalism*, 134.
40. Ibid.
41. Ibid., 141.
42. Reiter et al., *Rapture: Pre-, Mid- or Post-Tribulational*, 18–19.
43. Ibid., 19.
44. Simpson, *Four-Fold Gospel*, 68.
45. Ibid.

ing King. The return of Christ was something the believer and the church looked forward to. If the church was doing what God had called it to do, and if the believer was walking with God, the return of Christ would be looked at with joyful anticipation. His return had a purifying effect on both the believer and the church.

Simpson came to know Christ as Coming King while pastoring in Louisville, Kentucky, and it was there that he became a premillennialist. Simpson writes of his discovery:

> I was trained in the Scottish school of theology, and was taught to consider Christ's coming to mean his manifestation to the soul of the believer by the spirit, his coming at death to the saint and his coming spiritually by the spread of the Gospel. I so believed for fifteen years, and during my early ministry so taught.
>
> Twelve "years" ago I received the Holy Spirit, and new light was thrown upon the Word. I saw how weak and insufficient for service I had been in the old way, and, as I waited before the Lord, I found Him pressing the truth upon me, and I was forced to be willing to believe that the old axioms I had accepted were false, and the personal reign of Christ was clearly taught in Scripture.[46]

Simpson became a strong advocate of Christ's premillennial return. Samuel Stoesz wrote that Simpson could be critical of the other eschatological views. He remarks, "Simpson objected to amillennial and postmillennial positions saying that the rejection of a restored earthly kingdom 'takes out of God's Book all reality and makes everything merely a dream as vague as the fooleries of Christian Science.'"[47] Simpson, though critical of these other eschatological views, worked with Christians who differed on these issues in the promotion of the gospel. He did not impose his premillennialism as a criterion for fellowship.[48] Simpson's pragmaticism could be seen in his belief that getting the gospel out was more important than theological differences. This did not mean that Simpson or the early Alliance did not think Christ's return was unimportant. To the contrary, Christ's return was seen as paramount because it constituted the fulfillment of the gospel message. George Pardington wrote, "The crowning message of the Alliance is the crowning message of the Gospel, and that is the return to earth of the

---

46. Simpson, "How I Was Led," 6.
47. Foster and Fessenden, *Essays on Premillennialism*, 44.
48. Nienkirchen, *A. B. Simpson and the Pentecostal Movement*, 24.

Lord Jesus Christ. The Alliance believes that Jesus is coming again, and that his coming is personal, pre-millennial, and imminent."[49]

Simpson was a true premillennialist. Although he had been influenced by dispensationalism, he himself was not a dispensationalist. Simpson was a close friend of dispensationalists such as James Gray, the president of Moody Bible Institute, A. T. Pierson, R. A. Torrey, and C. I. Scofield, and Simpson spoke at one of the conventions at Scofield's Congregational Church in 1892. Yet he never accepted the whole dispensational scheme.[50] Simpson did believe in the pretribulation rapture, but he differed with dispensationalists in that he did not know how long the tribulation period would be. He also did not believe the Lord could come at any moment.[51] Simpson believed certain historical events had to occur before Christ returned.

The first of these events was the return of the Jews to their homeland in Palestine. This pilgrimage began occurring in the late 1800s with the Zionist movement. It was crystallized with the Balfour Declaration that promised the Jews a Palestinian homeland in 1917. Then five weeks after the Balfour Declaration was signed, the Turks surrendered Jerusalem to the British forces under General Alleby.[52] Simpson, along with the other premillennialists, rejoiced when this happened because they saw the restoration of the Jews in Palestine pointing to Christ's second coming.[53] When Simpson heard the news of the capture of Jerusalem in 1918, he rejoiced even to the point of tears. He believed that there was only one thing that needed to be done before Christ would return, and that was the fulfillment of Matt 24:14—that the gospel was to be preached to all nations.

Simpson also saw the return of Christ as having a sanctifying or purifying effect on the believer and the Church. Simpson wrote: "[Premillennialism] is an interesting practical truth—a great lever that will uplift the world into fitness to receive Him. It is intimately associated with holiness. 'He that hath this hope purifies himself even as he is pure' (1 John 3:3). It is a motive to Christian work. Everything in our church life links itself with that blessed hope."[54]

---

49. Pardington, *Twenty-five Wonderful Years*, 61.
50. Hartzfeld and Nienkirchen, *Birth of a Vision*, 30.
51. Ibid.
52. Weber, *Living in the Shadow of the Second Coming*, 129.
53. Ibid., 132.
54. Simpson, "How I Was Led," 6.

Simpson always stressed the second coming of Christ with a motivation for holiness.[55] He stressed that the believer was always to be watching for the Lord's return. He was to be busy at God's work. Franklin Pyles tells of an illustration that Simpson used: "He loved to tell A. J. Gordon's story of how his daughters knew he would return on a train sometime during a given week, but they did not know on which particular day. So every day that week, they dressed in their finest and waited at the station, hoping each time that this train would bring their father."[56] This was meant to demonstrate that believers were ever to be watching and waiting for the Lord so that Christ would find them ready.

The last event that needed to occur before Christ's return was the preaching of the gospel to the ends of the earth. Simpson's deep burden for the lost sinners of the world and his desire to preach the gospel to the unreached both at home and abroad drove the Alliance missionary outreach. Simpson loved the unsaved, but he also desired the fulfillment of Jesus' prophesy that once the gospel had been preached to all the earth, then Christ would return (Matt 24:14).

Simpson was not alone among the premillennialists, who saw evangelization of the world as the last event before the ushering in of Christ's return. Dana Robert wrote:

> Prominent mission leaders such as A. T. Pierson, A. J. Gordon, A. B. Simpson, and others felt they were living during a "crisis of missions." The Holy Spirit in the late nineteenth century was opening the world to Christianity in preparation for the second coming of Jesus Christ. It seemed probable that their generation would be the one to preach the Gospel from one end of the world to another in fulfillment of Matthew 24:14, "And the Gospel of the Kingdom shall be preached in all the world for a witness unto all nations and then shall the end come."[57]

Simpson's passion became promoting missionary outreach—the denomination he founded would continue this outreach. Simpson's burden for missions and his desire to see the Great Commission fulfilled would be his most compelling contribution to the premillennial movement. Pyles wrote that "eschatology was the lifeblood of Simpson's missionary theology. That the imminent return, not in the sense of 'any moment,' but in the

---

55. Hartzfeld and Nienkirchen, *Birth of a Vision*, 31.
56. Ibid.
57. Carpenter and Shenk, *Earthen Vessels*, 31–32.

sense of an event that could be soon, could be within this generation, if the church obeys, was the wellspring of his missionary movement."[58] Simpson felt the church could be involved in determining the return of Christ. If they worked to take the gospel to the local areas and to the ends of the earth, they could help "bring back the King." This was a great motivating force among many Christians and local churches. Simpson and the Alliance saw that through their mission effort, they "could bring back the King." They understood that all the other events for Christ's return had been fulfilled, and this was the last event that needed to be brought about. In fact, this is still the rallying cry for missions in the Christian and Missionary Alliance. Simpson felt Christ's return could be hurried or delayed, depending on the obedience of the church in this matter.[59] Simpson recognized the great responsibility that was placed on the church. He wrote:

> The Lord has left to us in some degree the determination of the time of His coming. There is a sense in which our chronology may be condensed into briefer limits by intense acting . . . There is such a thing as accelerated as well as retarded time and we may accelerate the time of the Lord's return by meeting the spiritual conditions and preparing the way.[60]

Simpson's passionate desire for Christ's return was illustrated in a message given at a convention: "I am sure the Master would be disappointed in this convention if it did not send up a deep cry for his coming. Only think what it means for us and what it will bring us. Perfect life. We shall know perfect holiness then, for 'we shall be like him when we shall see him as He is' (1 John 3:12)."[61]

Simpson kept Christ as the Coming King as a priority in his life, as did the Christian and Missionary Alliance, the society he founded. Simpson's objective was to preach the gospel in New York City as well as to the ends of the earth. He did this because of his burden for souls and their lost condition. He also did this because of his belief that by preaching the gospel to all the world, Christ's return would be accomplished. As a means to fulfill this objective, Simpson began urban ministries at the Gospel Tabernacle in New York City. He also established the Missionary Training Institute there to train pastors, urban workers, and missionaries to reach New York City,

---

58. Hartzfeld and Nienkirchen, *Birth of a Vision*, 41.
59. Ibid., 51.
60. Ibid.
61. Simpson, "How I Was Led," 6.

North America, and the unreached peoples of the world. He established missionary conferences and conventions as well to inspire Christians to pray, to give, and to go to the unreached peoples both at home and abroad. As Weber remarks in his discussion of the Christian and Missionary Alliance's focus, "The Christian and Missionary Alliance combined a firm conviction in the premillennial coming of Christ and an aggressive social and missionary program. For them, belief in the imminent return of Christ and missionary effort went hand in hand."[62]

There have been a number of eschatological interpretations of Christ's return in the last two thousand years. In the early church, the premillennial view reigned supreme; later, the amillennialist view became the dominant view of the church. In the eighteenth century, the postmillennial view gained popularity and became the most important understanding of Christ's return in the United States until the Civil War. After the Civil War, the premillennialist view became the most popular. Most of the leaders of the Third Great Awakening adopted this perspective, including Simpson. Simpson and a few others tied their premillennialist view of Christ to missions. He understood that Matt 24:14 stated that when the gospel has been preached to all nations, then Christ will return. Therefore, he and the early Alliance put all their effort into evangelism, both at home and abroad to, "bring back the King."

In the next chapter, we will look at the outcome of this missionary burden and zeal to see Simpson's impact on urban and worldwide evangelism.

---

62. Weber, *Living in the Shadow of the Second Coming*, 79.

VII

SIMPSON'S CONTRIBUTIONS TO URBAN AND WORLDWIDE EVANGELIZATION

Simpson's Burden for Souls

A. B. Simpson made an impact on the nineteenth century by his concern for the urban masses, especially in New York City. Along with his concern for the evangelization of the world, Simpson's whole life was poured into ministering to the neglected and lost people of the world. His entire focus and energy was concentrated into this great quest. The society that he founded, the Christian and Missionary Alliance, would carry on his vision and burden up to the present time.

Simpson, speaking about the necessity of world evangelism, wrote, "This is not merely a duty. It is the supreme task of every Christian. This is not merely a question of Christian obligation. It is not merely an opportunity. It is an emergency the true servant of God is 'redeeming in time'—buying up the opportunity."[1] He saw the primary purpose of the Christian and the church was to reach the lost next door and across the world. Simpson's burden and his passion was for the unreached people of the world.

Where did Simpson get this great concern for the lost souls around him? As a young man, he himself struggled with his own lost condition. It nearly drove him to despair. Upon his conversion, Simpson was assured of

---

1. Simpson, *Missionary Messages*, 4.

his own salvation, but he did not yet seem to have the same burning desire to see others come to Jesus Christ that he would develop years later. During his time at Knox College and subsequently at his first church in Hamilton, Ontario, it is hard to see the great passion for souls he would later have in Louisville, Kentucky, and New York City. While at Knox Church, Simpson saw the church grow. During his tenure, 750 new members were brought in.[2] For the most part, his focus was on those within the church and not on those outside its walls. He poured most of his attention on his church and had a very localized view of the ministry.[3] A. E. Thompson describes this period in Simpson's life in a way that shows his very narrow conception of evangelistic outreach. Thompson writes:

> In those days few Presbyterian ministers engaged in special evangelistic campaigns however earnest they might be as preachers of the Gospel. Dr. Wardrobe, of Guelph, Ontario, was one of the exceptions. An incident, which he recalled in his later years, is illuminating: "I had just returned to Ontario from a pastorate in the Maritime Provinces, and, being in Hamilton for a day, I decided to call upon a young preacher there and ask him, as the most likely man I could think of, to come and assist me in a series of revival meetings. With much dignity he replied, 'I believe in the regular work of the ministry.' What was my surprise, therefore, to learn not many years later that my young friend, Simpson, had left the 'regular work of the ministry' to give himself to the evangelization of the neglected masses of the American metropolis."[4]

Why did Simpson have this great burden for lost souls after he left Knox Church in Hamilton, Ontario? What would cause such a change in his philosophy of ministry? After leaving Knox Church, Simpson answered a call to pastor the Chestnut Street Church in Louisville, Kentucky. It was in Louisville that Simpson experienced two crises, or turning points, that precipitated his burden for the lost.[5] The first crisis came about when he was filled by the Holy Spirit. Simpson saw this crisis as not only integral to his own personal sanctification, but also essential to his evangelistic ministry. When Simpson described his experience, he spoke of how he "had received a profound spiritual blessing in the midst of an ambitious and

2. Thompson, *A. B. Simpson*, 50.
3. Hartzfeld and Nienkirchen, *Birth of a Vision*, 196.
4. Thompson, *A. B. Simpson*, 44.
5. Hartzfeld and Nienkirchen, *Birth of a Vision*, 197.

half-consecrated ministry, how the baptism of the Holy Spirit awakened in his heart an intense longing for the salvation of souls and simpler methods of reaching the masses with the Gospel."[6] Simpson saw this as the Holy Spirit working through him, and it was the Holy Spirit that gave him this burden for lost souls. He writes, "the Lord Jesus Christ tells us that we are sanctified in order to serve him here."[7] It was at this same time that Simpson experienced his second crisis, through which he developed his vision for the lost of the world.

Shortly after Simpson's arrival in Louisville in 1874, he called together the pastors of the city to meet at his Chestnut Street Presbyterian Church. He wanted to invite these pastors to participate in a citywide evangelistic crusade.[8]

Simpson began by gathering the pastors together to pray for revival. They invited Major D. W. Whittle to preach and P. P. Bliss to sing. As a result, hundreds were converted. The campaign had a tremendous impact on the city.[9] Whittle and Bliss illustrated to Simpson the importance of the Spirit-filled life and ministry in reaching the masses for Christ. Simpson and his ministry would never be the same. He was no longer content to do the "regular ministry of the church." He now had to reach the masses; whether poor or rich, black or white, he wanted to see all people come to the Savior. George Pardington comments on this evangelistic campaign: "As a result, Louisville was visited with a great religious awakening. Mr. Simpson himself was deeply stirred by these meetings and the Lord gave him an intense desire to preach the Gospel to the non-churchgoing masses."[10]

After the Whittle and Bliss campaign, Simpson wanted to continue with the evangelistic outreach on Sunday evenings, but he could not get the support from the other pastors, so he and his congregation decided to continue by themselves.[11] They continued to carry out the evangelistic outreach for two winters. They met every Sunday evening, first in the Public Library Hall and later on in Maculey's Theatre.[12] Evangelism had become Simpson's central focus. T. V. Thomas and Ken Draper wrote about this change:

6. Niklaus et al., *All for Jesus*, 13.
7. Simpson, *Serving the King*, 26.
8. Tozer, *Wingspread*, 46.
9. Ibid., 47.
10. Pardington, *Twenty-Five Wonderful Years*, 20.
11. Thompson, *A. B. Simpson*, 55.
12. Pardington, *Twenty-Five Wonderful Years*, 20.

Simpson's Contributions to Urban and Worldwide Evangelization

"No longer content to be secure in a comfortable church of social equals, he [Simpson] sought to mobilize the whole church for evangelization."[13] Pardington comments that at this time Simpson was convinced the Lord wanted him to be a full-time evangelist.[14] Later, Simpson said that God closed the door for him to be a full time evangelist, even though that was his primary ministry in both Louisville and New York City.

Simpson was not satisfied with the location and the size of his Louisville church or with renting facilities for the evangelistic campaigns. He wanted a facility that was centrally located within the city and would hold the masses that would come to the campaigns.[15] The church agreed with Simpson's plan to build a "tabernacle-type" building that would hold up to 2,500 people.[16] In the end, the church leaders built a facility much more elaborate than Simpson had wanted. They spent more than the budgeted amount and went into significant debt.[17] Simpson believed it was wrong to borrow money to build the structure and felt that the money could have been better spent in the advancement of the gospel. With a $50,000 debt on the building, Simpson refused to dedicate the tabernacle until the debt was paid off.[18]

In addition to this point of contention, Simpson and the leaders of the church differed in their vision of what they wanted to accomplish. Simpson felt the leadership of the church was hindering him from accomplishing all that he wanted to do for God in terms of evangelism in Louisville. He felt the church leadership was limiting what God could do.[19] Simpson described how the Holy Spirit had put in his heart an intense burden for souls as well as a desire for a simpler method to reach the masses with the gospel.[20] He wrote of the obstacles that leadership put before him. He stated, "After attempting for several years to accomplish the purpose [reach the masses] in a fashionable Presbyterian church during which something was accomplished but much was hindered by the social exclusiveness and

---

13. Hartzfeld and Nienkirchen, *Birth of a Vision*, 197.
14. Pardington, *Twenty-Five Wonderful Years*, 20.
15. Ibid.
16. Niklaus et al., *All for Jesus*, 12.
17. Ibid., 13.
18. Hartzfeld and Nienkirchen, *Birth of a Vision*, 197.
19. Niklaus et al., *All for Jesus*, 13.
20. Ibid.

the conventional religious methods about him [Simpson]."[21] As a result, Simpson felt it was necessary to find another church. Ironically, he would face the same problem in the next church. They too did not share Simpson's vision of reaching the masses for Christ.

It was during his time in Louisville that Simpson experienced another crisis in his life. This new crisis was the development of his great burden for world evangelism. When Simpson was a baby, the famous Canadian Presbyterian missionary to the South Sea Islands, John Geddie, had baptized him. In Geddie's prayer, he had committed young Simpson for missionary service. On a furlough roughly twenty-one years later, Geddie visited Simpson at Knox Church to remind him of that prayer and that Simpson had been set apart for the proclamation of the gospel.[22] Shortly after Simpson graduated from Knox College, he had thought about offering himself for missionary service. After talking to his future wife, however, he decided to accept a call from Knox Church.[23] Thompson comments on how Simpson's heart for missions nonetheless impacted his pastorate at Knox: "A marked increase in missionary interest was noted in that congregation during his ministry."[24] Simpson definitely had a keen interest in missions before he ever faced his crisis with missions in Louisville.

In 1877, while serving in Louisville, Simpson went to a Believer's Conference at Watkins Glen, New York, to be rejuvenated both spiritually and physically. At the conference, the speaker spoke on the importance of a closer walk with God and issued a missionary challenge. This pierced both Simpson's conscience and his heart for the unreached masses of the world.[25] Later, while staying with some friends in Chicago, Simpson had a vision of the lost of the world. Later, he described it:

> Never shall I forget how, eighteen years ago, I was awakened one night from sleep, trembling with a strange and solemn sense of God's overshadowing power, and on my soul was burning the remembrance of a strange dream through which I had that moment come. It seemed to me that I was sitting in a vast auditorium and millions of people were sitting around me. All the Christians in the world seemed to be there, and on the platform was a great

21. Ibid.
22. Thompson, *A. B. Simpson*, 119.
23. Ibid.
24. Ibid.
25. Niklaus et al., *All for Jesus*, 13.

multitude of faces and forms. They seemed to be mostly Chinese. They were not speaking, but in mute anguish were wringing their hands, and their faces wore an expression that I can never forget. I had not been thinking or speaking of the Chinese or the heathen world, but as I awoke with that vision on my mind, I did tremble with the Holy Spirit, and I threw myself on my knees, and every fiber of my being answered, "Yes, Lord, I will go."[26]

Immediately after having this dream, Simpson wrote to his wife, Margaret, about the vision and told her he wanted to immediately go to the mission field. She answered him right away.[27] Recalling the letter, Mrs. Simpson later commented, "I wrote to him that it was all right—he might go to China himself—and I would remain at home and support and care for the children. I knew that would settle him for awhile."[28] Simpson saw that it was impractical for him to go to China, but he felt he had to do something. He had this great burden for the world, but he did not know what to do about it. He wrote, "I tried for months to find an open door, but the way was closed. Years afterward God showed me that he had laid the question on my heart, and until he allowed me to go forth, if I ever did, I was to labor for the world and the perishing heathen just the same as if I were permitted to go to them."[29]

How could Simpson be involved in the worldwide mission outreach? What could he do? He began to notice that there was little communication between the different missionary agencies. Often, one agency would not know what the other was doing.[30] Additionally, the Christian public was ignorant of what was going on around the world. They were limited to local denominational boards, and they did not know what other mission agencies were doing either. The Christian public had a myopic view of missions and worldwide evangelization. John Sawin wrote that Simpson saw a solution to this: "A plan crystallized in Simpson's thoughts—one that seemed impractical or impossible to those he consulted: He proposed publishing an illustrated missionary journal that gathered into its pages the work of missionaries in all lands. The project became a driving force in his life."[31]

26. Thompson, *A. B. Simpson*, 120.
27. Niklaus et al., *All for Jesus*, 14.
28. Ibid.
29. Thompson, *A. B. Simpson*, 10.
30. Niklaus et al., *All for Jesus*, 14.
31. Ibid.

As a result of his burden for the world and for the masses, Simpson saw that it was time to expand his horizons. When the Thirteenth Street Presbyterian Church in New York City called him as their pastor, Simpson saw this as a divine invitation. New York City was the largest city in the United States, teeming with immigrants who had never heard the gospel. There were literally millions of men, women, and children who had never heard of Christ's atoning work. New York City was also the center of mission activity for many missionary agencies. It would be a perfect place to launch an illustrated missionary periodical. God had used Louisville to change Simpson and enlarge his vision to prepare him for the work in New York.

Sawin comments on Simpson's ministry in Louisville: "Simpson's ministry in Louisville determined the course of the rest of his life. Almost every major aspect of his message, his ministry and the movement he founded can be traced to his experiences while pastor of Chestnut Street Presbyterian Church."[32] After Simpson's arrival in New York City, he was exposed to the great need of the urban masses in that city. His ministry would never be the same. He could not ignore the neglected people of the city, and his ministry there reflected it.

Simpson's Concern for the Urban Masses

Gerald McGraw, writing about the environment A. B. Simpson found himself in when he arrived in New York City, said it was the perfect place for Simpson. He remarks:

> Where should a pastor locate if his highest priority for the 1880s included missionary promotion and the evangelizing of unreached masses? From what American port did overseas missionaries sail? To what harbor were nearly a million immigrants arriving annually to start a new life? The answer, obviously, was New York City, which was both the haven for new settlers and the hub of missionary departures, arrivals, and information.[33]

God could not have placed Simpson in a more strategic place for missions and urban outreach. His dream of seeing the urban masses reached on behalf of Christ and of becoming actively involved in worldwide missions

---

32. Ibid., 15.
33. McGraw, "Legacy of A. B. Simpson," 69.

would be fulfilled in his long and fruitful ministry in New York City. Simpson began his ministry at the Thirteenth Street Presbyterian Church in Manhattan on December 9, 1879.

Over the decade of the 1880s, the American urban population increased by 50 percent.[34] This was due to a tremendous influx of immigrants from Europe. More than five million immigrants came to New York in that decade.[35] This produced a tremendous challenge for New York City's Christians and their churches. The masses needed to be reached for Christ, although most of the city's Christians and churches were not meeting this challenge. Even Simpson's own church would not support his efforts to reach out to these urban masses. Simpson had originally come based on assurances from the Thirteenth Street Presbyterian Church leadership that they were supportive of his evangelistic endeavors. But when their young and enthusiastic pastor wanted to bring one hundred poor Italian immigrants into their fashionable middle-class church, they had second thoughts. Consequently, Simpson began to have problems with the church leadership. McGraw writes:

> Although he had energetically served that traditional Thirteenth Street parish for two years, at the same time he kept pursuing cross-cultural ministries in public halls and on the streets. Reputed to constitute the metropolis' most wealthy, fashionable parish, his congregation refused to welcome hundreds of Italian immigrants he was winning to Christ. Consequently, despite the remonstrating of his denominational colleagues, the wonder of the press and the criticism of his loyal wife, Margaret, Simpson forsook a comfortable salary to become, as he explained, an evangelist who would remain on the scene and follow up his converts, who refused to trust anyone but God for his support.[36]

Simpson gave up all financial security, as well as the prestige of his church, to try to reach the needy that were surrounding him. Leaving the Presbyterian ministry seemed ludicrous to Simpson's wife, Margaret. It seemed shortsighted and impractical. How would they support their family? Without Simpson's pastorate, they did not even have a place to live because they were living in the church's parsonage. She had her feet on the ground, while Simpson's mind was often in the heavens. Over the years,

---

34. Ibid.
35. Reitz, "A. B. Simpson, Urban Evangelist," 19.
36. McGraw, "Legacy of A. B. Simpson," 69.

Margaret gradually came to trust her husband's vision and judgment. Sawin wrote, "In her younger years as Simpson's wife, Margaret had opposed him on some key decisions and at times made his life difficult. But once she caught up with his vision and became convinced he was a man sent from God, Dr. Simpson had no finer, more loyal and hardworking associate than his wife."[37] Shortly after the Alliance was organized, Margaret was elected to serve as financial secretary on the Board of Managers. She served at this capacity until her death at the age of eighty-two.[38] She also served in the beginning of the Alliance on the Foreign Missions Committee. She had a burden for missionaries and corresponded with almost all the Alliance missionaries. Shortly before she died, she told E. J. Richards, the home secretary of the Alliance, that she had eight trunks filled with correspondence written to her by foreign missionaries and friends from North America.[39] She also served as the superintendent of assignments for missionaries, and she was considered a good judge of whether a young person was fit for missionary service.[40] Margaret became an integral part of the Christian and Missionary Alliance.

Having left his Presbyterian charge, Simpson, along with thirty-five others, formed the Gospel Tabernacle on February 10, 1882, with the goal of reaching the unreached people in the city and throughout the world who had never heard the gospel.[41] The local churches were not reaching these people. The urban challenge was not being met. George Reitz writes of the challenge and burden Simpson felt for those around them:

> Yet to meet this challenge, the urban church of New York City was weak. A. B. Simpson faulted the apparently 480 evangelical Protestant churches with nearly 80,000 members and adherents not so much for their quantity as for their quality. He claimed that the church was more concerned about nice theories, beautiful sermons, church decorations, and personal pleasures than thousands of lost men and women.[42]

In January of 1882, Simpson noted that the urban population had grown by sixteen thousand in five years, and there was not a single new

37. Niklaus et al., *All for Jesus*, 157.
38. Ibid.
39. Ibid.
40. Ibid.
41. Reitz, "A. B. Simpson, Urban Evangelist," 20.
42. Ibid.

Simpson's Contributions to Urban and Worldwide Evangelization

church planted during that time.[43] Simpson also condemned the flight of the evangelical Protestant churches that were then moving from urban neighborhoods to nicer uptown areas.[44] Simpson noted that "almost half of New York's population, or a total of 542,000, live below Fourteenth Street, and yet, in all this densely populated region, the former home of nearly all the churches, there are but 112 Protestant churches, of which many are only missions"[45] He saw a great need, and the goal of his new church would be to reach these masses.

The Gospel Tabernacle moved a number of times using temporary facilities. In 1889 a permanent church building was erected in Hell's Kitchen, right in the middle of one of the neediest areas in New York City.[46] Walter Rauschenbusch, author of the book *A Theology for the Social Gospel* and one of the chief architects of the Social Gospel movement, pastored the Second German Baptist Church in the Hell's Kitchen area near the Gospel Tabernacle.[47] Rauschenbusch spent ten years pastoring in Hell's Kitchen and later taught about the Social Gospel at Rochester Theological Seminary. Although Simpson and Rauschenbusch served churches in proximity, there is no evidence they were personally acquainted.[48] Of the two, it was Simpson who stayed in New York City and continued to minister at the Gospel Tabernacle until his death.[49]

While working in New York City one of Simpson's favorite verses in the Bible became Acts 1:8: "But you will receive power when the Holy Spirit comes on you; and you will be my witness in Jerusalem and in all Judea and Samaria, and to the ends of the earth" (NIV). Simpson had a unique interpretation of the verse as well as a broad definition of the application of the text.[50] He did not see the Samaria of the text as a geographical location such as New York, Connecticut, or New Jersey; rather, it was found in the outcasts of the city.[51] Reitz writes, "Simpson went on to identify these outcast types as the drunkard, harlot, thief, convict, foreign population, and the

43. Ibid.
44. Ibid.
45. Ibid.
46. Evearitt, "Social Gospel vs. Personal Salvation," 10.
47. Ibid., 2–3.
48. Ibid., 1.
49. Ibid., 3.
50. Reitz, "A. B. Simpson, Urban Evangelist," 22.
51. Ibid.

multitude 'struggling in the dark underworld of poverty.'"[52] Simpson's goal was not to reach either the poor or the rich; it was to reach the unsaved. He did not want anyone to be neglected. He wanted to preach the gospel to all who would hear it. Pardington, a contemporary and close friend of Simpson, wrote of Simpson's vision and passion for the masses. He explains:

> The vast throngs of non-church goers in New York City were laid heavily on Mr. Simpson's heart. He desired to preach the Gospel to them on the street or in public halls, as he had done in Louisville. He made a personal canvas of the North Ward, visiting every home. In prayer and planning he conceived a church without pew rents and for all classes and conditions of man, something like Newman Hall's Church, or Spurgeon's Tabernacle in London, England.[53]

The purpose of the founding of the Gospel Tabernacle was to reach the unevangelized masses. There would be no discrimination. Pardington goes on to remark that the purpose of the Gospel Tabernacle was to save souls and train people in evangelistic work or missionary service.[54]

Simpson was primarily concerned with the condition of people's souls. His greatest focus and concern was with the spiritual, but he did not let his focus on the spiritual aspects blind him to the physical needs of those to whom he was ministering. This was essential to the perspective of all the evangelicals who worked among the poor and needy in the urban centers of America in the late nineteenth century. Their primary immediate focus was on the soul, but they did a tremendous amount of work to alleviate the physical suffering of the downtrodden in the slums. Donald Dayton comments on the social outreach of evangelical groups:

> Norris Magnuson has carefully surveyed the activities and convictions of such revivalist movements as the Salvation Army, the Volunteers of America, the Christian and Missionary Alliance, the "rescue mission" movement, the circles around the *Christian Herald* and the Florence Criterton homes for "fallen women" during the period from 1865 to 1920. He details how the commitment of the "slum workers" to "saving souls" did not preclude their involvement in a wide range of social concerns (food, shelter, recreation, health, unemployment, and so forth) among such dwellers of the

---

52. Ibid.
53. Pardington, *Twenty-Five Wonderful Years*, 22.
54. Ibid., 32–33.

inner-cities as the poverty-stricken, recent immigrants, racial minorities—as well as among the more socially deviant derelicts, prisoners and prostitutes.[55]

According to Dayton, "Out of Simpson's work grew the Christian and Missionary Alliance, a movement that originally understood itself to have a special call to serve the 'neglected classes' both at home and abroad."[56] The goal of every social outreach ministry led by Simpson and the Gospel Tabernacle—whether it was the rescue mission, work in hospitals, orphanages, industrial missions, missions to fallen women, or ministry to prisoners—was to lead lost souls to Christ.[57] Daniel Evearitt stated that the focus of Simpson and all the other evangelists involved in the Social Gospel outreach was to convert souls, not to reform society.[58] This was how D. L. Moody saw Christian ministry, and it was also how most evangelicals in this period understood their social outreach ministry. Yet, as a consequence of redeeming souls, they were also transforming society.

Evangelicals have had a significant impact on reforming society, but they did not receive as much credit as those from the more socially liberal churches. While more liberal churches set up rescue missions in poorer areas, most members were not personally involved in the work and hired social workers to staff them. In contrast, the evangelical churches *were* a mission and took this role seriously. The Gospel Tabernacle was the hub of ministry activity in the Hell's Kitchen area of New York City.

One of Simpson's most interesting qualities was his ability to attract gifted leaders to help him in his work. Norris Magnuson attributed the rapid growth of the early Alliance to this quality. He explains:

> Among the reasons for the continuous growth of the Alliance was the caliber of men whose cooperation Simpson attracted. A list of speakers at the New York and Old Orchard annual conventions constitute something of a "Who's Who" of the evangelicalism of the day. Andrew Murray and F. B. Meyer from abroad, and A. J. Gordon, A. T. Pierson, R. A. Torrey, D. L. Moody, J. Wilbur Chapman, S. H. Hadley, Francis Williard and Robert E. Speer from the

---

55. Magnuson, *Salvation in the Slums*, 5.
56. Dayton, *Discovering an Evangelical Heritage*, 113.
57. Evearitt, "Social Gospel vs. Personal Salvation," 12.
58. Ibid., 12–13.

United States. Others officially united with the Alliance in the missionary endeavors.[59]

Simpson also attracted quality leaders for the staff at the Gospel Tabernacle. One such man was Henry Wilson. Wilson was Simpson's associate pastor at the Tabernacle and was seen as perhaps Simpson's closest friend. Next to Simpson, Wilson is considered the most important leader in the early years of the Alliance.[60] Wilson was involved in a number of social outreach programs, serving as the president of the Seaman's Christian Association and chaplain of the Magdalene Home for Girls.[61] Simpson made this comment about Henry Wilson: "'Few men' in New York were 'in closer touch' and more helpful friends to the city missionaries."[62] Wilson was also the chief organizer for the annual "Rescue Day" featuring city missionaries and their work at the New York conventions.[63] Rescue Day came out of the Gospel Tabernacle monthly all-night prayer meetings for the city missionaries of New York City.[64] This became an important event for not only Alliance workers, but also for many other groups and welfare workers from the surrounding area.[65]

One of the quality female leaders Simpson worked with was Emma W. Wittemore, who founded the Door of Hope ministries for "fallen women."[66] This ministry evolved into a nationwide ministry in thirteen years, and by 1903 there were sixty-one Door of Hope missions throughout the United States.[67] Another woman Simpson had a great influence on was Carrie Judd-Montgomery. She was a renowned speaker on healing and holiness. She was also active in rescue and welfare work.[68] Carrie Judd-Montgomery founded Faith Rest Cottage in Buffalo to minister to the physical and spiritual needs of the downtrodden. Later she and her husband moved to San Francisco, where they founded the City of Refuge, which was a village of

---

59. Magnuson, *Salvation in the Slums*, 18.
60. Ibid., 19.
61. Ibid.
62. Ibid.
63. Ibid.
64. Ibid., 17.
65. Ibid.
66. Reitz, "A. B. Simpson, Urban Evangelist," 23.
67. Hartzfeld, and Nienkirchen, *Birth of a Vision*, 53.
68. Magnuson, *Salvation in the Slums*, 70.

welfare institutions.[69] She also published the periodical *Triumphs of Truth*, which continued to her time of death.[70] Simpson attracted men and women who took seriously the motto of the Gospel Tabernacle, "A work for everyone and everyone at work."

How much impact did Simpson and the early Alliance have on New York City and the surrounding area? John Dahms wrote: "Due to the influence of the Alliance and its leadership, the ministry in 'hospitals, almshouses, and charitable institutions' in New York City was so considerable by 1894, that it was said that even A. B. Simpson would have been at a loss to tell 'how much the Alliance was doing for all [such] agencies of Christian work in that city.'"[71] In 1907, the weekly Alliance periodical, *The Christian and Missionary Alliance Weekly*, said, "Many of the charitable institutions 'within the limits of New York City, and indeed for many miles around' had benefited from the influence of the Gospel Tabernacle, and that many of their leaders were adherents of the Christian and Missionary Alliance."[72] Simpson and the early Alliance members had an important impact on New York City in the late nineteenth and early twentieth century. Since very little has been written about it outside of a few academic books, these efforts have been largely forgotten.

Simpson and the early Alliance took the social needs of the neglected masses of the city to heart. They saw themselves as not only responsible for saving souls, but also for helping to alleviate physical needs when possible. Robert Glover, writing shortly after the death of Simpson, stated that more than seven hundred people had entered full time church work or rescue work from the Alliance.[73] This statement shows the emphasis training rescue workers placed on reaching the neglected masses.

What social ministries were Simpson and the early Alliance actually involved in? Within three years after the founding of the Gospel Tabernacle, two rescue missions were opened to reach those in need of health care, particularly sailors and prostitutes near the church.[74] The Gospel Tabernacle opened another mission in 1899 on Eleventh Avenue near Thirty-eighth

---

69. Ibid., 70.
70. Niklaus et al., *All for Jesus*, 269–70.
71. Hartzfeld, and Nienkirchen, *Birth of a Vision*, 52.
72. Ibid., 52–53.
73. Magnuson, *Salvation in the Slums*, 16.
74. Evearitt, *Body and Soul*, 64.

Street that became known as "Eleventh Street Mission."[75] There would be a total of seven rescue missions—three for the homeless and four for "fallen women"—that would be operated and supported by the Gospel Tabernacle.[76] The church also founded the Berachah Orphanage to care for homeless children.[77] The orphanage opened in 1886 at College Point, Long Island in New York, before relocating to Nyack, New York.[78] There were also other orphanages in the United States that received support both directly and indirectly from the Alliance.[79] This ministry to orphans extended overseas. During the 1890s, there was a famine in India, and Alliance missionaries in India provided for a number of orphans during that difficult time.[80]

In 1894, Simpson opened the Berachah Home. This was a home intended for rest and healing. The focus at the home was divine healing without the aid of physicians.[81] Simpson described the Berachah Home as a "delightful" place of rest and spiritual blessing.[82] During the first fifteen years of his ministry, it was reported that ten thousand souls had been transformed through "rest," quickening, and divine healing.[83] Other healing homes were established all over the United States that patterned themselves after the Berachah Home. These homes were connected to Alliance people or people who had ties with the Alliance.[84]

The Alliance was also involved in health ministries in New York City. The Second Berachah Mission was established in the Hell's Kitchen neighborhood. Evearitt commented, "At the time, it was 'the best equipped mission in the city,' with work among sailors and a free medical dispensary for the poor of the neighborhood."[85] Amelia Barnett, who was a member of the Gospel Tabernacle, was one of a number of physicians who made their services available for free to all who were in need.[86] Dr. George Dowkonut,

---

75. Ibid.
76. Reitz, "A. B. Simpson, Urban Evangelist," 23.
77. Ibid.
78. Hartzfeld, and Nienkirchen, *Birth of a Vision*, 54.
79. Ibid., 53.
80. Ibid., 54.
81. Ibid., 55.
82. Ibid.
83. Ibid.
84. Ibid.
85. Evearitt, *Body and Soul*, 64.
86. Magnuson, *Salvation in the Slums*, 72–73.

who was involved with the Berachah mission, trained a number of physicians in their dispensaries, and many of them went overseas as medical missionaries.[87] These medical dispensaries not only helped the needy of New York, they also impacted the world for Christ through missionary doctors.

Simpson and the early Alliance leadership were also involved in industrial missions. In the rescue missions, they tried to help the needy find employment and provide job skills.[88] In New York City, the Door of Hope establishments trained their residents in homemaking, dressmaking, and fancy serving.[89] There was a Woman's Industrial Center, which was an integral part of the Door of Hope Center, in Fort Worth, Texas.[90] In Buffalo, New York, there was an Industrial School for Girls that was affiliated with the Alliance.[91] These industrial missions were not limited to the United States. Overseas, the Alliance founded an industrial school and workshop in Akola, India. At this school, young people were taught useful skills that they could use to support themselves. The Alliance also began an industrial farm where children were taught farming methods and "help[ed] supply food for the Alliance orphanages."[92] Famines throughout India in the 1890s opened the door for Alliance missionaries to care for a large number of orphans who benefitted from this training and education. Later, as the famines ceased to be a problem, the Alliance missionaries gradually removed themselves from the care of orphans and industrial education in India.[93]

One of the first things Simpson did when he went to New York City was to get involved in evangelism with the European immigrants who surrounded his church. Members of the church were involved in helping newly arrived immigrants from Germany as early as 1887.[94] Albert Funk, who was an assistant pastor at the Gospel Tabernacle, provided German language services for German immigrants.[95] Evangelism among the Ital-

---

87. Ibid., 73.
88. Hartzfeld, and Nienkirchen, *Birth of a Vision*, 56.
89. Ibid., 57.
90. Ibid.
91. Ibid.
92. Magnuson, *Salvation in the Slums*, 98–99.
93. Ibid., 99.
94. Hartzfeld and Nienkirchen, *Birth of a Vision*, 58.
95. Niklaus et al., *All for Jesus*, 61.

ian immigrants was what ultimately led to Simpson's resignation from the Thirteenth Street Presbyterian Church. Simpson and the early Alliance concentrated much of their time and energy on working with Italian immigrants. Magnuson wrote:

> The Alliance opened a mission in 1890 in a funeral home in "little Italy." A "faith" work, the mission included by 1895 an Italian church on 112th Street as well as a home for girls at Tivoli-on-the-Hudson. Students and faculty at Nyack Missionary Institute held Italian services regularly at nearby towns and conducted night school sessions three times weekly.[96]

The Italian evangelist Michele Nardi attended the Gospel Tabernacle and graduated from the Alliance Training School in New York City. He was a close friend of Simpson's his whole life. Simpson regularly reported Nardi's ministries in the *Alliance Weekly*[97] and later wrote a biography about Nardi's death.[98] Nardi had a tremendous ministry among the Italian people in the United States and Italy.[99] Simpson and the early Alliance poured their hearts and efforts into reaching as many of the neglected immigrant population as they could.

It was not only immigrants who constituted the "neglected masses." Another group of people Simpson was involved in reaching out to in a number of ways was African Americans. According to Reitz,

> There didn't seem to be any color barrier to Simpson. Even though there was no work among blacks in New York City, Simpson wholeheartedly supported ministries in Ohio, Pennsylvania, and North Carolina where churches were planted. Diaconate outreaches were opened: Love-Joy Missions Institute in 1906 in North Carolina, a ministry assisting black families in Nashville, Tennessee, an innercity children's work in Chattanooga.[100]

As Simpson wrote in 1898, "One of the most unique and encouraging features of the Alliance work in Ohio and Pennsylvania is the successful organization of a number of strong branches of our beloved colored

---

96. Magnuson, *Salvation in the Slums*, 129.
97. Ibid.
98. Ibid.
99. Ibid., 130.
100. Reitz, "A. B. Simpson, Urban Evangelist," 4.

brothers."[101] Simpson goes on to say, "They are attracted to the heart-stirring truths and deep spirituality of the Alliance movement."[102] The early Alliance leadership held their African American brothers and sisters in high regard. Simpson stated in 1899, "Much excellent work is being done among our colored brethren in various parts of the country. Some of our best Alliance branches in Ohio and Pennsylvania are exclusively among them and are supporting several missionaries."[103] African Americans became an integral and important part of the early Christian and Missionary Alliance. They were involved in reaching other African Americans in northern cities through their effective ministry, which earned the respect of their white colleagues as well.[104] African American believers also volunteered for missionary service, especially in Africa, where white missionaries often suffered severe health problems.[105] Some believers were also involved in rescue ministry work and educational efforts in the South.[106] African American involvement in the Christian and Missionary Alliance has continued to the present. This is especially true in the district this author serves in. The Metropolitan District of the Christian and Missionary Alliance encompasses the New York City metropolitan area and the entire state of New Jersey. There are a number of ethnic churches still being planted, and some are being planted by African American pastors in predominately African American neighborhoods. There are also a number of African American pastors in leadership positions in the district. They serve on both the District Executive Committee and the License and Ordination Committee. One goal of the Alliance, both locally and nationally, is to get more African Americans involved as missionaries, pastors, and in leadership positions in both district and national levels.

Simpson was also involved in the early temperance movement. The Women's Christian Temperance Union Evangelistic Training School met at the Alliance's Berachah mission in New York City in the 1890s.[107] Simpson gave the daily Bible lectures at the Women's Christian Temperance Union

---

101. Evearitt, *Body and Soul*, 72.
102. Ibid.
103. Magnuson, *Salvation in the Slums*, 121.
104. Niklaus et al., *All for Jesus*, 166.
105. Magnuson, *Salvation in the Slums*, 122.
106. Ibid., 123.
107. Ibid., 135.

Training School during the 1890s.[108] There was also a regular article on temperance in the Christian and Missionary Alliance periodical, *The Alliance Weekly*.[109]

Simpson had an impact on Frances Williard, who was the well known leader of the temperance movement. She wrote a letter to *The Alliance Weekly* and told of her earlier experience of sanctification at Old Orchard, Maine, where the Alliance met annually.[110] Simpson wrote at her death "that her loss would be felt 'as widely as any break in the ranks of Christian workers during the century.'"[111] Simpson, in his tribute to Williard, went on to say that her friends and fellow laborers "were loyal friends and members of the Alliance."[112]

Magnuson commented about Simpson's involvement with the temperance movement by writing,

> Despite A. B. Simpson's conviction that there were plenty of people "to run social reform and temperance societies" his Alliance followers were prominent in the W.C.T.U. (Women's Christian Temperance Union) and generally active in the cause of temperance. *The Alliance Weekly*, which he edited, for years featured a "temperance column," as did most rescue journals. Students at his training school in New York City spent their afternoons and evenings in tenement houses, saloons and rescue missions, claiming many converts from "drink." Simpson's influential colleague, Henry Wilson, was president of a mission, which stresses the abstinence "pledge." Joseph Pullis, a convert from apparently hopeless drunkenness who became a spiritual leader in the Alliance in New York, served on the staff of the Christian Home for Intemperate Men, where he had himself found shelter.[113]

Though Simpson was highly involved in the outreach to the urban masses, there has been some criticism that as he got older and as the Alliance movement matured, there was generally less interest in the downtrodden and needy. According to David Moberg, "The intense interest in social service on the part of the early Christian and Missionary Alliance members was soon subtly opposed by its founder, possibly because this competed

---

108. Hartzfeld, and Nienkirchen, *Birth of a Vision*, 59.
109. Ibid.
110. Magnuson, *Salvation in the Slums*, 136.
111. Ibid.
112. Ibid.
113. Ibid., 136–37.

with institutional goals of the new fellowship."[114] Evearitt, responding to this criticism, states, "He [Moberg] gives no specific examples for the 'subtle' opposition of Simpson to social work."[115] Evearitt goes on to give an explanation of Simpson's waning interest in social work. He writes, "There is in the material written toward the end of Simpson's life less of an emphasis on social concerns, and, indeed, by the end of his life some of the social welfare work was being curtailed. Orphanages were phased out and as children grew to adulthood and left the facilities and some Alliance works were taken over by others."[116] It also has to be remembered that for Simpson and his followers, as well as for other evangelicals working in social welfare, the primary concern was the spiritual need.[117] They were there to save souls, and social outreach was the byproduct of that purpose. Therefore, social welfare was important, but it was not the primary focus. As Evearitt explains, "What social activity Simpson and his followers became involved in was on a personal level. It was a person-to-person, compassionate concern for needy individuals . . . He saw social needs and attempted to aid its victims on an individual basis. It was never his intention to try to make this world into a utopian society."[118] When Simpson went to New York City, he saw the need and, in turn, responded to it.[119] Moberg was right to note the change in Simpson's focus and in his interest in social outreach. This change was not because Simpson opposed social outreach or saw it as a threat to worldwide outreach. His focus changed because he saw even greater needs.

Was there another reason for the "subtle waning of interest" in social needs with Simpson? There seems to be a simple explanation to this question. In 1897, the Missionary Training Institute moved from New York City to Nyack, New York, twenty miles north of the metropolis. Nyack was a beautiful, sleepy little village overlooking the Hudson River. Simpson also moved to Nyack and had a home built on the campus. As a result, Simpson was no longer rubbing shoulders with immigrants and the poor, as he had been for so many years in New York City. He was no longer a resident of the city—he had become a commuter. Reitz agreed that this might have lessened Simpson's burden for the urban masses in New York

---

114. Moberg, *Great Reversal*, 30.
115. Evearitt, *Body and Soul*, 138.
116. Ibid., 139.
117. Ibid.
118. Ibid.
119. Ibid.

City.[120] Evearitt also felt this was one of the reasons for waning interest in the poor in the vicinity of the church. Another reason for lessening concern was that the area around the Gospel Tabernacle was changing, becoming less impoverished and a little better off.[121] Rather than lessening his burden for the urban masses, this move seemed to have shifted Simpson's focus away from the urban outreach aspect of the Alliance to one of worldwide evangelization. The change in emphasis was gradual but steady. When one does not see an immediate need, it becomes easy to change one's emphasis and focus, and that is what gradually happened to Simpson. The worldwide expansion of the ministry became more important and urban outreach less so. The question one might ask is: If Simpson had stayed in New York City, would the focus of the Alliance be different today? We will never know, but it is interesting to ponder.

Simpson's Impact on Worldwide Evangelization

The Third Great Awakening saw tremendous growth in missionary interest. The missionary movement reached its pinnacle in the United States in the period from 1890 to 1917 and ultimately became an integral part of the Awakening. In terms of the number of missionaries serving at that time, financial support and popular support missions together warranted the term "crusade."[122] The missionary endeavor was on everybody's lips. It was felt this generation could be reached for Christ. The missionary endeavor of the day could be encapsulated by the slogan of the Student Volunteer Missionary Movement, whose goal was to preach the gospel to the world in their generation. Their motto was "The evangelization of the world in this generation." This motto was the vision of thousands of college and seminary students who were involved in reaching the world with the message of Christ. It was also the goal of the women's missionary organizations. The Layman's Movement, which was an organization of over 100,000 men who helped promote foreign missions in their local churches, also adopted this motto.[123] Simpson was one of the leaders of this missionary movement. Mark Noll describes Simpson as one of the "missionary entrepreneurs" of the second half of the nineteenth century and the beginning

---

120. George W. Reitz, interview with the author, February 12, 2003.
121. Daniel J. Evearitt, interview with the author, February 12, 2003.
122. Marty, *Missions and Ecumenical Expressions*, 3.
123. Ibid.

Simpson's Contributions to Urban and Worldwide Evangelization

of the twentieth century. Simpson—along with D. L. Moody, A. T. Pierson, and A. J. Gordon—was a key figure in the missionary outreach.[124] Ruth Tucker explains the role Simpson played during the missionary endeavor in North America at this time when she writes, "Like the great missionary statesmen Samuel Mills and John R. Mott, Simpson never served as a foreign missionary himself, but like Mills and Mott, his influence for missions was enormous, particularly in the growth of the late nineteenth and early twentieth century mission societies in America."[125]

Tucker describes Simpson's contribution in this way: "Largely through [Simpson's] influence, foreign missions in the twentieth century became the most vital outreach of the North America Evangelical Churches."[126] At the time of his death, Simpson was recognized for his impact on worldwide missions.[127] *The Sunday School Times* states that "he probably had no superior in missionary appeal."[128] Even the *New York Times* recognized his important influence on foreign missions in writing that he was "one of the leading executives in foreign missionary work."[129] Simpson had a significant impact on the worldwide evangelization of his day, and his impact is still being felt through the denomination he founded.

What were some of the major contributions Simpson made to the evangelization of the world? His first and most obvious contribution was the founding of a missionary denomination, the Christian and Missionary Alliance. The only other Protestant denomination that has been as zealous for missions was the Moravian Church of the eighteenth century. The Moravian Church was founded at Herrnhut in Germany in 1722 and was led by Count Nicolaus Ludwig von Zinzendorf. Five years after its founding, the group experienced a great revival. They began a prayer vigil that would continue twenty-four hours a day, seven days a week. This phenomenon lasted for one hundred years. After the start of the revival, the Moravians began sending missionaries throughout the world.[130]

The late missiologist J. Herbert Kane wrote that in the eighteenth century, the Moravians became the nerve center of a worldwide network of

---

124. Noll, *History of Christianity in the United States*, 2.
125. Tucker, *From Jerusalem to Irian Jaya*, 290–91.
126. Ibid., 291.
127. McGraw, "Legacy of A. B. Simpson," 76.
128. Ibid.
129. Ibid.
130. Tucker, *From Jerusalem to Irian Jaya*, 71.

missionary outreach.[131] Kane went on to say that members of the church were prepared to go to the ends of the earth at a moment's notice when the need arose.[132] He wrote, "Whenever a call came, they drew lots and the one or ones on whom the lot fell left as soon as possible for some remote part of the earth."[133] Kane explained that the key to their success was that they were convinced "that world missions [was] the supreme task of the church, and that the responsibility for carrying out the task rests with every member of the Christian community, not just the leaders."[134] Kane felt that it needed to be done again and that the Christian and Missionary Alliance were doing it. He remarked, "In more recent times the Christian and Missionary Alliance has come as close as anyone to achieving this idea. After one hundred years the Christian and Missionary Alliance is still predominately a missionary organization."[135]

J. Edwin Orr made the same observation about Simpson and the Alliance. He wrote, "Albert Simpson, a convert of the 1858 Revival in Canada, founded the Christian and Missionary Alliance in 1886, at first as an interdenominational organization but later itself becoming a denomination as missionary minded as the Moravians."[136]

A second major contribution Simpson made to worldwide evangelization was the founding of the Missionary Training Institute in New York City. It was one of the first Bible colleges in the United States. He founded the Institute in 1882 with twelve students.[137] The first commencement at the Missionary Training Institute was held in 1884, and that November a missionary team of seven left for the Congo.[138] The Missionary Training Institute was developed with the goal of training laypeople to reach the unsaved both in North America and abroad. The Missionary Training Institute trained a number of Christian workers and missionaries, both for the Christian and Missionary Alliance and also a number of independent faith mission boards.

---

131. Kane, *Wanted: World Christians*, 207.
132. Ibid.
133. Ibid.
134. Ibid., 208.
135. Ibid.
136. Orr, *Light of the Nations*, 273.
137. Gangel, "Bible College," 34.
138. Pardington, *Twenty-Five Wonderful Years*, 30.

Simpson's Contributions to Urban and Worldwide Evangelization

Another key contribution Simpson made to the missionary movement was his emphasis on reaching unevangelized people of the world. This tremendous burden for the lost was a driving force in Simpson's life. In fact, Simpson was once found in his study on his knees with his arms around a globe, weeping for the unevangelized masses of the world. This zeal for those who had yet to come to know Jesus would extend farther than Simpson ever dreamed. It would influence the lives of many others who would, in turn, contribute to one mission society after another.

Simpson, like Hudson Taylor, the founder of the China Inland Mission, wanted to try to share the gospel with the unreached people of his time. During the late nineteenth and early twentieth century, most of the missionary activity was focused on the coastal regions of countries that had already been colonized. China was one such country. Feeling the burden to reach the Chinese in the interior of the country, Hudson Taylor founded the China Inland Mission. Simpson too was compelled to try to reach neglected inland people. He passed on this burden to Roland Bingham, who had been one of his students at the Missionary Training Institute and who would later found the Sudan Interior Mission.[139]

Another young missionary who would come to be impacted was Peter Cameron Scott, who went to the Missionary Training School and then served as a missionary with the Christian and Missionary Alliance to the West Coast of Africa. Scott would later come back to the United States and found the African Inland Mission.[140] Simpson also influenced the founder of The Evangelical Alliance Mission, more commonly know today as TEAM. William Franson was a Swedish-American who was captivated by Simpson and his missionary vision. Franson was involved with taking Swedish missionaries to work with Alliance missionaries in China and later founded TEAM.[141]

Simpson, along with a few others of his time, saw the great need to reach the people and groups that were not being reached by other missionary societies. He writes:

> Our chosen fields are the "regions beyond" in unoccupied portions of the heathen world, and so our missionaries have been led into the most difficult and remote regions and enabled to introduce the Gospel to many sections where Christ had not been

---

139. Tucker, *From Jerusalem to Irian Jaya*, 291.
140. Ibid., 291–92.
141. Hartzfeld, and Nienkirchen, *Birth of a Vision*, 269.

named, such as Kwang-si in South China, the province of Hunan in Central China, the borders of Tibet [and recently the country of Annom], the tribe of Mongolia; the unoccupied region of Congo and the Niger in Africa and some of the neglected republics in South America"[142]

It was not the goal of either Simpson or the early Alliance to duplicate what other missionary organizations were doing; therefore, they would look for the most neglected and destitute parts of the earth.[143] The fact that one hundred missionaries died overseas during the first twenty-five years of the Alliance's missionary work illustrates the sacrifice these early missionaries made. Louis L. King comments about the early Alliance work:

> The areas the new organization [CMA] originally sought to enter were blocked by unfriendly governments, hostile people and impossible living conditions. But undeterred, with unparalleled bravery and an enormous toll by death, Alliance missionaries soon penetrated Congo, India, and China. Within five years, work had been started in twelve countries, with forty stations manned by 180 missionaries. Twenty-three missionaries had died. Further, the cost of accomplishment can be seen in 45 deaths in India and the Congo between 1893 and 1900 and in the 36 martyrs' graves in China in 1900.[144]

Simpson and the early Alliance wanted to reach these neglected people no matter what the cost. Simpson saw the overwhelming need as well as the lack of workers available to accomplish the task. He states in his book *Missionary Messages* that the church in North America had the resources to do the job, but the focus of North American churches was in the wrong places. He comments, "While the wealth of our people increases and our Christian agencies are crowded with professional workers, the mission fields are neglected and even the workers that would go are hindered for lack of means. The Lord's heart aches as he cries, 'The harvest truly is great, but the labourers are few.'"[145]

Simpson was able to share this vision with the North American church through his missionary conventions. As a result of these conventions, by 1914 the Alliance had almost three hundred missionaries and rose close to

---

142. Pardington, *Twenty-Five Wonderful Years*, 105.
143. Goddard et al., *Encyclopedia of Modern Christian Missions*, 133.
144. Ibid., 33.
145. Simpson, *Missionary Messages*, 133.

Simpson's Contributions to Urban and Worldwide Evangelization

four million dollars to support these missionaries.[146] Simpson was able to write that year about the progress of the Alliance. He reported, "Although the work is still but a beginning, yet we thank God for a consecrated army of more than a thousand men and women in our home and foreign fields, where the supreme watchword is the fullness of Jesus for His people and the evangelization of the world in the present situation."[147] All this was accomplished in a brief, twenty-five-year span. The driving passion to reach the lost led to the great sacrifices made by the early Alliance missionaries and members.

With this fervor within them, Alliance missionaries became the first to pioneer missions work in a number of countries. Alliance missionaries planted the first churches in the provinces of Hunan and Kwang-si in the country of China.[148] Robert Glover, commenting on the Alliance and their pioneering work in China, wrote, "The Society, patterned largely after the China Inland Mission in its principles and practice, had a worthy share in the pioneer work of several of the last provinces of China to be entered with the gospel.[149] During the Boxer Rebellion in 1900 in China, 189 missionaries and children were put to death. The two missions that lost the most missionaries were the China Inland Mission with seventy-nine deaths and the Christian and Missionary Alliance with thirty-six deaths.[150] As Kenneth Scott Latourette wrote of Simpson and the early work of the Alliance in the Congo, "In 1885 A. B. Simpson, out of whose labour in the United States came what was eventually the Christian and Missionary Alliance, sent his first band to the Congo. Illness brought to the venture a tragic interruption, but in 1888 another party came and succeeded in establishing a station which was a continuous undertaking."[151] The Christian and Missionary Alliance built the first American church in Jerusalem, and by 1914 the Alliance had three mission centers in Palestine.[152]

The Alliance began work in South America in areas not being reached by Protestant churches in the 1890s. They worked in Chile, Argentina, and Ecuador. Alliance missionaries were also the first to go into Indochina. As

146. Pardington, *Twenty-Five Wonderful Years*, 7.
147. Ibid., 6.
148. Goddard et al., *Encyclopedia of Modern Christian Missions*, 133.
149. Glover, *Progress of Worldwide Missions*, 155.
150. Ibid.
151. Latourette, *History of the Expansion of Christianity*, 425–26.
152. Ibid., 41.

Stephen Neil comments about the work of the Alliance in Southeast Asia, "Under the French influence, Indo-China had been almost a closed land to Protestants. But just at the end of our period [1858—1914] that great American inter-denominational body, the Christian and Missionary Alliance was able to enter in—Swiss missionaries in Laos, and others in Vietnam and Cambodia in 1911."[153] The goal of Simpson and the early Alliance to reach the unevangelized people of their day still remains as a core focus of the Christian and Missionary Alliance today.

Simpson's original goal was to train Christian workers and missionaries as quickly as possible to bypass the long years of college and seminary training that had been the more traditional training for ministers and missionaries. It was Simpson's aim to nurture and train laypeople to take the gospel to the ends of the earth. Simpson would lovingly refer to the graduates at his school as "irregular regulars." Jacob Klassen comments, "He strove to nurture and train laypeople, 'his irregulars' in order that the Gospel might be preached everywhere. He firmly believed that the higher institutions of learning could not possibly train enough witnesses to accomplish the task of world evangelization."[154] Gerald McGraw remarks that Bible college was a speedier and more action-centered training for the "light infantry" of missionary workers.[155] A number of other Bible and Missionary Training Institutes followed this lead. Klassen, speaking about Simpson's influence on the development of a Bible college movement, wrote, "Simpson, in turn, inspired and encouraged the development of regional institutes where leaders shared his doctrinal and missiological convictions. Soon leaders like D. L. Moody also formed institutes which have trained thousands of missionaries throughout the past century."[156] The Bible college movement was a result of Simpson and the Alliance's burden to see the entire world reached with the gospel.[157]

Tucker emphasizes the impact Simpson made on missions through the innovation of the Bible college. She writes that Simpson's "legacy in the area of Christian education extended far beyond the corridors of one institution. His missionary training school concept launched the Bible institute movement that spread out across North America and became the major

---

153. Neil, *History of Christian Missions*, 346–47.
154. Hartzfeld, and Nienkirchen, *Birth of a Vision*, 252.
155. McGraw, "Legacy of A. B. Simpson," 75.
156. Hartzfeld, and Nienkirchen, *Birth of a Vision*, 255.
157. Goddard et al., *Encyclopedia of Modern Christian Missions*, 134.

recruiting source for independent faith mission societies in the decades that followed."[158] This was not only true in North America, but also wherever Alliance missionaries and other faith missionaries went. Bible colleges and institutes were founded to train indigenous people to minister in their own cultures. The Bible institute would become a worldwide movement stretching to every border. The late missiologist J. Herbert Kane wrote, "The 'lion's share' of evangelical missionaries now on the field has been produced by the Bible College movement," estimating that figure at over 75 percent.[159]

Another important contribution Simpson made to missions was the formation and development of the missionary conventions for churches in North America. Thomas and Draper describe Simpson's innovation when they write,

> In addition, Simpson evidently invented that unique blend of Bible Conference, camp meeting, evangelistic crusade and missionary promotion meeting that came to be known as the missionary convention. Simpson held such conventions across North America, calling hundreds to Christ, to deeper spiritual life and to a commitment and world evangelization.[160]

These conventions became so successful that they soon spread out to many cities in both the United States and Canada.[161] They would host some of the worlds leading speakers and missionaries.[162] A. W. Tozer wrote, "By 1887 they [missionary conventions] had become famous. Thousands flocked to them in the great cities of the North American Continent."[163] These missionary conventions became a chief cornerstone in local churches and branches affiliated with the Alliance. Even today, every Alliance church is required by the local and national constitution to have an annual missionary conference. It was one of the most exciting times of the year in the life of the early Alliance-affiliated churches and branches. It is important to note that these missionary conventions generated tremendous interest from the average churchgoer. Many of the listeners had never been very far from their villages or cities, and a missionary convention brought great

---

158. Tucker, *From Jerusalem to Irian Jaya*, 294.
159. Gangel, "Bible College," 35.
160. Hartzfeld and Nienkirchen, *Birth of a Vision*, 208.
161. Tozer, *Wingspread*, 96.
162. Ibid.
163. Ibid.

excitement to a community. McGraw remarks on those early missionary conventions:

> Annual conventions where Bible teaching abounds and furloughing missionaries reported on their work constituted the very core of the Alliance movement. In addition to national, district, and state conventions, every Alliance branch and affiliated independent churches conducted conventions. The missionary cause raised support by appealing to those in attendance to sign a pledge card to commit themselves to God alone to give to missions in the ensuing year. This dignified method of instilling regular giving remains as the lifeblood of missions support more than a century after the Alliance's inception.[164]

During the first quarter-century of the Alliance's existence, the missionary conventions and the "faith pledge" for missions raised close to four million dollars for the missionary movement. This was an amazing sum of money at that time. Simpson developed and promoted the missionary conventions as a means to promote the interest and vision of missions in North America.

One of the more illustrative contributions Simpson made to worldwide evangelism was his missions magazine. In fact, one of the main reasons Simpson left Louisville and went to New York City was his desire to publish an illustrated missionary periodical. Simpson saw this as a way to present missions to the average churchgoer. He knew and understood the old saying, "A picture is worth a thousand words." He felt an illustrated missionary magazine would awaken the zeal and missionary interest in the average Christian. Simpson began publishing his illustrated missionary periodical *The Gospel in All Lands* in February 1880.[165] Soon after he began publishing the periodical, Simpson's health deteriorated, and so he turned over the responsibility of the magazine to his friend Eugene Smith. Smith, who was a Methodist minister, edited the periodical, which was then taken over by the missionary society of the Methodist Episcopal Church.[166]

In 1882, Simpson began a second missionary periodical similar to his first called *The Word, the Work and the World*. This periodical, like his first, contained interdenominational news and missionary articles. Tozer, would later serve as editor of the same magazine, although its name had changed,

---

164. McGraw, "Legacy of A. B. Simpson," 74.
165. Niklaus et al., *All for Jesus*, 37.
166. Pardington, *Twenty-Five Wonderful Years*, 21.

Simpson's Contributions to Urban and Worldwide Evangelization

comments that "in spite of its name it was undoubtedly one of the finest missionary journals ever published by any religious society anywhere. The sweep and range of it are amazing. Its editor had taken the world for his parish."[167] Tozer felt that one reason Simpson began attracting widespread notice as a missionary leader was because of the missionary periodical.[168] Simpson kept *The Word, the Work and the World* focused on worldwide missions and kept its scope interdenominational, and that is why it was popular.[169]

Simpson's missionary periodical was a forerunner of other missionary periodicals that exist today. Almost all missionary agencies and denominations have illustrated missionary magazines to inform and promote what their missionaries are doing. *The Word, the Work and the World* evolved into the *Alliance Life*, which today is the official magazine of the Christian and Missionary Alliance. It is still popular in evangelical circles and has wide circulation among the members of the Christian and Missionary Alliance. Simpson saw his periodical as a way to disciple Alliance members and help them to grow in faith. He saw the importance of training laypeople to serve Christ in the church. Simpson saw the importance of this training not only in North America, but also on the mission field.

Another of Simpson's contributions was to train national leaders and have them reach their own people. This unique missionary strategy was different than what most mission boards were doing at the time. Many mission societies were reluctant to hand over mission responsibilities to their converts. The objective of Simpson and the early Alliance missionaries was not to establish permanent mission stations but rather to develop native churches. As each church matured, the missionaries would train the local believers to take over their churches. This would allow the missionaries to go to other unreached areas.[170] Klassen comments, "Dr. Simpson was the pioneer in the development of training institutes for national pastors and workers overseas."[171] Thomas and Draper commented that even though Simpson was paternalistic in many ways, he was light-years ahead of his contemporaries on the mission field. They wrote:

167. Tozer, *Wingspread*, 94.
168. Ibid.
169. Ibid., 95.
170. Hartzfeld and Nienkirchen, *Birth of a Vision*, 211.
171. Ibid., 256.

While colonial governors and the majority of Protestant missions hesitated to give any real responsibility to nationals, Simpson insisted that Christians overseas take responsibility for an enterprise that lay close to his heart. Thus Simpson's theological understanding of the need for the world evangelization and his commitment to evangelism as an activity of the entire church ensured that his followers spread the Gospel devoid of many of the cultural accretions that western missionaries tended to include in their presentations.[172]

Simpson and the Alliance made the primary aim and focus of their mission work evangelism and planting churches. This is still the driving force in the Alliance today. This focus was unique among many of the mission boards working at that time. W. R. Hutchinson comments on the Alliance focus by stating, "The Christian and Missionary Alliance was noted for its insistence on the primacy of evangelization and for attempting, like the predominately British China Inland Mission, to avoid all forms of secular cultural imposition."[173] While many missionaries during this period equated bringing civilization to native people with evangelizing, Simpson kept preaching of the gospel as his objective and as that of the early Alliance missionaries. Simpson's goal was to preach the gospel without Western cultural trappings. Paul A. Varg notes, "It is clear that Dennis, Speer, Mott, and other leaders of the missionary movement were advocates of a program whereby conversion of the heathen was gradually becoming a means to an end, namely an improved society."[174] Simpson contributed to the worldwide mission movement with his emphasis on training national leaders and on evangelism in missions work. These remain as important factors in worldwide evangelization.

The burden for missions was a primary focus of Simpson and the early Alliance. This passion for missions would lead to some failures on the mission field. There were two instances in the Alliance during the late nineteenth century when a group of inadequately prepared missionaries were sent out, and both resulted in disaster on the mission field. These groups were not prepared for the harsh realities of missionary life they would face.[175] In 1884, a group of five young graduates of the Missionary

---

172. Ibid., 211.
173. Hutchinson, *Errand to the World*, 128.
174. Marty, *Missions and Ecumenical Expressions*, 13.
175. Niklaus et al., *All for Jesus*, 59.

Training Institute lead by John Condit set sail for the Congo. Condit soon died of fever in the Congo, while three of the remaining missionaries sold their missionary outfits and returned to North America. Only one stayed and continued with a Baptist mission.[176] Later, in 1890, another group went to the Sudan and experienced a similar fate. Although this mission was not officially sponsored by Simpson and the Gospel Tabernacle, they supported this group and their ministry. Four out of the seven died of fever. This group was also not prepared for the harsh rigors of Africa.[177] Both incidents taught Simpson a valuable lesson: the importance of proper preparation. As a result, Simpson and the Alliance started screening their missionary candidates better. They began requiring more education and also home service, by which the candidate would serve in a local church. Missions funds were also collected in the central office.[178] Although the Alliance continued to lose missionaries to death, future missionaries were better prepared and made a greater impact on their respective fields.

Simpson always kept evangelism and starting indigenous churches as his top priorities. He wanted to present the gospel in the simplest and cheapest way possible.[179] Simpson avoided getting involved in building institutions on the mission field because he felt it was not an effective way to evangelize.[180] He felt the best way to evangelize was to identify with those who were being evangelized. Whatever group a given missionary was trying to reach, he or she needed to be seen as one of them. Simpson wrote, "If [we] can better reach China by wearing Chinese dress and living in Chinese houses, [we] give up the customs and comforts that [we] may gain some." Simpson and the Alliance went to areas that were unreached. They were not trying to build on other's efforts. They developed a specific strategy to reach each group. They studied the conditions, customs, and needs of the people and then determined how they would best be evangelized.[181] The goal of the missionary was not to start a missions station but rather to start a native church that would be self-supporting and self-propagating. The goal was then to withdraw the missionaries and let the nationals run the

---

176. Ibid., 60.
177. Ibid., 87–88.
178. Hartzfeld and Nienkirchen, *Birth of a Vision*, 255.
179. Ibid., 210.
180. Ibid.
181. Ibid., 208.

church and plant other churches.[182] The national indigenous churches that the early Alliance began were ultimately one of its greatest successes in its missionary endeavor.

The contribution and impact Simpson made on the church's worldwide outreach at the end of the nineteenth century and the beginning of the twentieth are still being felt in the twenty-first century. McGraw summarized it this way:

> Simpson's contribution to missions has proven to be noteworthy. Besides influencing many other missions and individual missionary statesmen, he fathered a "sending" organization that has demonstrated its viability in pioneering, sacrifice, evangelism, and church growth. Regarded by the Bible college movement as its founder, he instigated a kind of institution that has contributed to the education of some seventy-five percent of current evangelical missionaries. Various churches and missions have learned from his plan of the missionary convention and the missionary pledge. His cooperative spirit and his sense of urgency of the missionary task deserve emulation.[183]

Simpson was one of the great missionary leaders during the Third Great Awakening, and his vision for world evangelism was passed on to the society he founded—the Christian and Missionary Alliance. This is still the denomination's vision and purpose: to reach the world for Christ in this present generation.

Simpson's concern for his own spiritual condition spilled over into his concern for the unreached in the world. This burden became his passion while he was in Louisville. It was in Louisville that he became involved in evangelism on a large scale because of his burden for world missions. In New York City, after he left the Thirteenth Street Presbyterian Church and began the Gospel Tabernacle, this evangelistic outreach blossomed. While in New York City, Simpson and the early Alliance attempted to reach the city with the gospel and also meet the social needs around them. It was here that his burden for world evangelism came to fruition with the birth of the Christian and Missionary Alliance. Simpson became one of the leaders of the missionary movement that played a pivotal role in the Third Great Awakening. Today, Simpson is remembered best for his involvement in the missionary movement that characterized the Awakening.

---

182. Ibid., 211.
183. McGraw, "Legacy of A. B. Simpson," 76.

Simpson's Contributions to Urban and Worldwide Evangelization

Although Simpson died over ninety years ago, his impact and influence is still being felt by the evangelical church. Although he has been largely forgotten in academic circles, his message still resonates in many evangelical churches today. Indeed, his influence and message is still being felt, especially in the Christian and Missionary Alliance, the denomination he founded.

The final chapter of the book will examine Simpson's impact on the church today.

VIII

SIMPSON'S MESSAGE AND ITS RAMIFICATIONS ON THE CHURCH TODAY

In the first chapter, this author attempted to explain how A. B. Simpson has been ignored and neglected by much of modern scholarship in American church history. In many cases, Simpson is simply a footnote at the bottom of a page. Many historians have overlooked or forgotten Simpson and the message of the Fourfold Gospel. They seemed to have missed the key role that Simpson and his message played in the Third Great Awakening, though Simpson's impact was well known by those of his era.

A recent issue of *New Man* magazine, a publication for Christian laymen, featured an article by Simpson in its "spiritual classics" section. The article, entitled "A Larger Christian Life," spoke about what it would take to reach the world for Christ.[1] In his introduction to the article, the editor of the periodical wrote, "A century ago, no one asked, 'Who is Simpson?' He was as well-known as Dwight L. Moody, Andrew Murray or C. I. Scofield—contemporaries who, like him, shaped today's evangelical church."[2]

Simpson and his writings are also finding their way into other types of journals. For instance, Simpson's famous message on sanctification, "Himself," was published under the heading "Thunder in the Pulpit"[3] in *The Fundamentalist Journal*. In *Enrichment*, the Assemblies of God journal,

---

1. Simpson, "Larger Christian Life," 54–55.
2. Ibid., 54–55.
3. Simpson, "Himself—A Timeless Testimony," 44.

author Gary McGee comments on Simpson's impact on the pentecostal movement in the past and present. He writes, "The interest among contemporary pentecostals, charismatics and 'third wavers' in 'power evangelism' can be traced back to Simpson, the Alliance and other radical evangelicals a century ago."[4] McGee concludes that Simpson is still inspiring believers today: "Decades after his death, the ministry of A. B. Simpson still inspires believers to experience the truths in the fourfold gospel and sacrificially devote their time and treasures to God."[5] Simpson's approach in presenting his message is amazing because it attracted Christians from both the fundamentalist and charismatic circles. Both groups lay claim to him, and in fact, his view of sanctification presented in "Himself" is not only accepted but embraced by both groups.

Simpson's popularity is not limited to traditional publications. There are a number of websites that contain articles about Simpson as well as material written by him. One keyword search conducted on April 7, 2003, returned over 3,650 results for "A. B. Simpson." A number of these sites were hosted by local churches ranging from Episcopal churches to independent charismatic fellowships, and they had posted biographical sketches about Simpson and several had even made the full text of Simpson's message "Himself" is available online. There are also a number of book distributors selling Simpson's books in a variety of languages. Many of them have no affiliation with the official publishing arm of the Christian and Missionary Alliance, Christian Publications. It seems that Simpson and the Fourfold Gospel is may be regaining popularity among the younger generation via the Internet.

Why are Simpson's works popular on the Internet? One of the reasons may be that Simpson's works explain in a simple and concise way how one can grow in the Christian life. Simpson relates how one can grow in the "deeper Christian life" and is quite pragmatic in his approach to Christian growth. This is a popular area of interest with both the upcoming generation and Christian reading public, and little has been written on it in recent years.

Simpson's writings also continue to be published as books. His books are helping to spread the Fourfold Gospel. Most of Simpson's books are written in a way that the average Christian can understand, but one way to appeal to a younger reading audience would be to update and modernize

---

4. McGee, "All for Jesus," 85.
5. Ibid., 88.

the language. If Christian Publications would take on this task, it could help spread Simpson's message to a wider Christian audience. Jonathan L. Graf, a former editor for Christian Publications and the current editor for *Pray Magazine*, began this project but never finished.[6] If this project were completed, it would help disseminate the message of the Fourfold Gospel throughout the Christian church. The best place to begin would be with Simpson's book *The Four-Fold Gospel*. Along with an updating of this work, providing a workbook for small groups or Sunday school classes would be helpful in popularizing the message of the Fourfold Gospel and spread Simpson's message to an even larger reading audience.[7]

This message is not only for North America, but also for the mission field. Simpson's burden was always to reach the unreached. Many missionary professors consider Simpson to be one of the foremost missionary leaders of the nineteenth century. Simpson, along with D. L. Moody, A. J. Gordon, and A. J. Pierson, helped generate interest in missions and encouraged Christians to take the gospel to the ends of the earth. They truly believed they could reach their generation with the gospel. This fervor inspired men like John Mott and Robert Speer to lead the Student Volunteer Missionary Movement that helped extend the gospel to unreached people groups. Simpson is remembered for his role in the missionary movement and his founding of a missionary denomination in the Christian and Missionary Alliance.

While Simpson is known for his historical contribution to the missionary movement in the late nineteenth and early twentieth centuries, his contribution to missionary theology, up until recently, has been largely forgotten. The fourth fold in the Fourfold Gospel is Christ as the Coming King. Simpson believed the motivating force for missions was compassion for the lost and the fulfillment of Matt 24:14. This passage states that when the gospel has been preached to all nations, Christ will return. The goal for Simpson and the early Alliance was to take the gospel to all nations. This, they believed, would hasten Christ's return. The rallying cry was to "bring back the King," and this would be done by taking the gospel to the "ends of the earth." This became the great vision and burden for Simpson and the Christian and Missionary Alliance. This theology was taught and embraced in the nineteenth century but lost its appeal in much of the twentieth century. George Reitz, the urban director of the Metropolitan District of the

---

6. Daniel J. Evearitt, interview with the author, February 12, 2003.
7. Daniel J. Evearitt, interview with the author, March 7, 2003.

Christian and Missionary Alliance, refers to the idea of "bringing back the King" as "Closure Theology," saying, "The idea is that we are motivated to put all our effort in missions and bring back Christ the King that will complete the Great Commission."[8]

This vision to "bring back the King" has been adopted recently by some missionary circles. Peter Nanfelt, current president of the Christian and Missionary Alliance, states that a number of mission societies are now picking up the message that Christ's return is tied in with the completion of the Great Commission.[9] This view has also been espoused by some leaders at the US Center of World Missions. In *Mission Frontiers*, the official publication of the US Center of World Missions, Rick Wood and Robert Takenaga published an article entitled "Bring Back the King." The byline under the title reads, "This vision of Dr. A. B. Simpson launched a missionary movement that changed the world. It can change our world too."[10]

The US Center of World Missions has been involved in trying to take the gospel to all unreached people groups of the world. The article spoke of Simpson and his impact on the world for missions as well as his burden to bring back the King. It spoke of his influence then and now. Wood and Takenaga ended their article with this challenge:

> All of us who look at the life of Dr. A. B. Simpson are challenged by his unswerving dedication to the vision of completing the Great Commission and "Bringing Back the King." It is my hope that the worldwide body of Christ along with the Christian and Missionary Alliance will learn from Dr. Simpson's example and dedicate themselves anew to the task of reaching all people with the Gospel. May there be a fresh move of God's Spirit to burn this vision into the hearts of millions of believers all over this world so as to produce the mighty harvest of souls from every tribe, tongue, people, and nation that Jesus asked us for. Let us commit ourselves to this great cause as Dr. Simpson did one hundred years ago with such wonderful results.[11]

Simpson's vision to bring back the King is pertinent for all believers. It should be one of the pillars of missionary theology today, for it is a key incentive for preaching the gospel to the ends of the earth. It may become

---

8. George W. Reitz, interview with the author, February 12, 2003.
9. Peter Nanfelt, interview with the author, December 10, 2002.
10. Wood and Takenaga, "Bring Back the King," 1.
11. Ibid., 5.

the same motivating force it was at the end of the nineteenth century and the beginning of the twentieth. It is still one of the main driving forces in the Christian and Missionary Alliance today. One sees in the passion "to bring back the King" in the focus of the Alliance to reach the unreached people in the world. Wood and Takenaga comment,

> The Christian and Missionary Alliance, however, has not been satisfied to rest on past laurels but is moving forward with new plans to help finish the task of bringing back the King which A. B. Simpson was so dedicated to. One person who has been making a significant heart-felt difference is Harry Boese, a coordinator for the Alliance's own "Adopt-A-People" program, which is called, *Within Our Reach*.[12]

The Alliance currently has a program that has up for adoption a total of 142 unreached groups of people who are within reach of Alliance missions. So far, seventy-six of these groups have been adopted by various congregations of the Christian and Missionary Alliance throughout the United States.[13]

The Alliance is still committed to "bringing back the King."

Simpson's Influence on Contemporary Charismatic and Pentecostal Leaders

Simpson's impact was not only felt in missions, but also in the emerging pentecostal movement. Simpson and the Fourfold Gospel played an integral role in the formulation of the pentecostal movement. Many of the leaders of the pentecostal movement were students from Simpson's Missionary Training Institute. One can see the influence and the stamp of Simpson on these early leaders and their teaching. Simpson is still impacting the charismatic and pentecostal movements today.

Ron Walborn, a professor of pastoral ministries at Nyack College, shared the story of an incident that shows the impact and influence Simpson still has on one charismatic leader. One of the students in Walborn's class was a retired New Jersey state trooper. After he retired from the state police, he decided he would go back to school to become a pastor. He enrolled as a student at Nyack College. To support himself and his family,

---

12. Ibid., 4.
13. Ibid.

he became a bodyguard for Benny Hinn, a well known, if somewhat controversial, charismatic healing evangelist.[14] In 1999, Hinn claimed to have preached to over one million people in evening audiences in the Philippines and Kenya. He reported that over 750,000 people had made first-time decisions for Christ.[15]

One day, this student was working with Hinn as his bodyguard, and Hinn asked him what he did when he was not working for him. The student replied that he was studying to be a pastor and was a student at Nyack College. Hinn became excited and shouted, "A. B. Simpson—that's A. B. Simpson's college!" The student replied, "Yes, it is. I walk by Simpson's grave every time I go to class." Hinn then reached into his briefcase and pulled out two books. One was the Bible, and the other was Simpson's *The Gospel of Healing*. Hinn said he took these two books wherever he went.[16] Hinn has also given out copies of *The Gospel of Healing* to many of his supporters. David Fessenden, one of the editors of Christian Publications, stated that one of the largest orders they ever received for any book was for Simpson's *The Gospel of Healing*. They received an order for 20,000 copies which was ordered by Benny Hinn.[17]

Another charismatic leader greatly influenced by Simpson was John Wimber, the founder of the Association of Vineyard Churches.[18] Wimber was considered a leader in the charismatic movement in the 1980s and 1990s, having written two important works, *Power Evangelism* in 1985 and *Power Healing* in 1987.[19] While Walborn was doing his doctoral work at Fuller Theological Seminary, he had the opportunity to meet and get to know Wimber. One day while Walborn and another pastor were having lunch with John Wimber, Wimber told them one of the primary influences on his life had been Simpson.[20] Wimber had been brought to Christ by a Christian and Missionary Alliance elder in an evangelistic Bible study, and he stated that he had read everything Simpson had ever written.[21] Walborn quoted Wimber as saying, "The Vineyard is simply Christian and Mis-

---

14. Ron C. Walborn, interview with the author, February 15, 2003.
15. Synan, *Century of the Holy Spirit*, 344.
16. Ron C. Walborn, interview with the author, February 15, 2003.
17. David E. Fessenden, interview with the author, April 9, 2003.
18. Synan, *Century of the Holy Spirit*, 407.
19. Ibid., 439.
20. Ron C. Walborn, interview with the author, February 15, 2003.
21. Ibid.

sionary theology."[22] Wimber felt everything he was doing was in line with Simpson and the teaching of the Christian and Missionary Alliance. In fact, Simpson and his Fourfold Gospel message was the basis for the Vineyard movement.

A Unifying Role

Simpson and his message seem to be popular among fundamentalist and evangelical circles as well as among charismatics and pentecostals. They seem to be accepted into each group. In fact, Simpson's message "Himself," which is in tract form, is used by each group. Walborn feels that Simpson and the Christian and Missionary Alliance ministry can act as a bridge to bring those two groups together.[23] The Christian and Missionary Alliance is able to navigate in both groups, and for the most part, is accepted by both. This is an important role that those in the Christian and Missionary Alliance can play; they can help unite both groups to work together to help advance Christ's kingdom.

During the Third Great Awakening, Simpson acted in that role between the fundamentalists and the pentecostals. Many of Simpson's students at the Missionary Training Institute and early leaders of the Alliance were integral to the founding of the Assemblies of God and other pentecostal denominations. Many of the early pentecostals held Simpson in high esteem even though they differed with him on the "evidence doctrine," which held that a believer had to speak in tongues to be filled with the Holy Spirit. The evidence doctrine became a hallmark in many pentecostal denominations. At the same time, C. I. Scofield, a fundamentalist and ardent dispensationalist who was the editor of the Scofield Reference Bible, served on the Christian and Missionary Alliance Board of Managers for twelve years.[24] Simpson and the Fourfold Gospel were accepted by both groups.

Doug Banister has come to the conclusion that congregations need to emphasize both the preaching of the Word and the power of the gospel. Evangelical churches, which would include fundamentalist churches, place most of their emphasis on the preaching of the Word, while pentecostal and charismatic churches place their emphasis on experience. According to Banister, neither group is balanced. Banister's goal at the church he pastors

22. Ibid.
23. Ibid.
24. Daniel J. Evearitt, interview with the author, March 7, 2003.

is to maintain that balance and be a link between these two camps. Banister recognizes that the church needs to have both emphases. He writes, "I saw strengths and weaknesses in both traditions. Both camps hold a piece of the puzzle the other needs."[25]

Both camps have long been isolated from one another and generally do not know what is going on with the other.[26] Banister goes on to say,

> Think of the charismatic and evangelical traditions as two mighty spiritual rivers flowing through our century. Today the two rivers are merging into one mighty flood of spiritual power. God is blending the strengths of both the evangelical and charismatic traditions together in churches across America. I call these "Word and Power Churches."[27]

Banister feels this combining of the evangelical and charismatic emphases into one church is a new phenomenon. He explains that these two groups have gone their separate ways in much of the twentieth century, although there have been exceptions. One of these exceptions is Simpson and the Christian and Missionary Alliance.

The Christian and Missionary Alliance, however, has not always held a balance between these two traditions. In its recent past, it has leaned more toward the evangelical side than the charismatic. The evangelical side was more accepted in traditional Christianity than the pentecostal or charismatic perspective. The Christian and Missionary Alliance, however, seems to be swinging back to this middle role as a church that emphasizes both strong preaching of the Word and also the importance of the Holy Spirit in the Christian life—a role that Simpson illustrated in both his life and ministry.

The author of this book has seen this change in many Alliance churches in the last twenty years. Worship styles have changed to a more contemporary style that places an emphasis on experience. Leadership from the national level down to the district level has begun to emphasize the importance of the Holy Spirit in a Christian's life. Alliance churches have been attracting people with both fundamentalist and charismatic leanings who like the strong priority of the Bible *and* the emphasis on experiencing the Holy Spirit. This change is seen in many of the Alliance churches throughout the United States and Canada.

25. Banister, *Word and Power Church*, 19–20.
26. Ibid., 20.
27. Ibid., 21.

Simpson always kept Christ at the center of his ministry. A. E. Thompson wrote that Simpson's message was "Christ in you, the hope of glory." This became the very heart of Simpson's message.[28] Thompson goes on to say, "No man since the days of Paul has done more to make this vital truth of Christian life real and practical in the church than A. B. Simpson."[29] Although this assessment comes from a close friend and admirer, it shows the practicality of Simpson's ministry and the importance of experience in the Christian life.

The Alliance is presently trying to restore the balance that Simpson once had. Peter Nanfelt, in his presidential report to the Christian and Missionary Alliance General Council in 2002, spoke of this very thing. He said that the Alliance has not always put as much emphasis on its distinctives as it should have. Some of those distinctives have been seen as pentecostal and viewed as extremist. Nanfelt further commented that in the past, the Alliance did not want to be identified with those who were considered "on the fringe," especially in the holiness and healing movements. The Alliance did not stress these doctrines because it did not want to be labeled as pentecostal or charismatic. Nanfelt stressed the need to preach the Fourfold Gospel the way Simpson and the early Alliance had preached it. God would then use this message to change the world.[30] As Peter Nanfelt went on to say,

> The future of the Christian and Missionary Alliance lies in living out the two emphases that gave meaning to the Christian and Missionary Alliance in the first place: the sufficiency of Christ lived out through the power of the Holy Spirit and the whole Bible for the whole world. We are more than a Bible church, and we are more than a Holy Spirit church. We are a church that embraces the Bible as the inerrant Word of God, and we are a church that believes the Holy Spirit applies the Word for holy living and powerful service. This is who we are and if we have drifted personally or corporately from this biblical position, we need to ask God to bring us back to where we need to be.[31]

The Christian and Missionary Alliance can play a vital role as a reconnecting force between the fundamental, evangelical, pentecostal, and charismatic churches. What Banister's church is doing as an individual

---

28. Thompson, *A. B. Simpson*, 176.
29. Ibid.
30. Nanfelt, "Once-In-A-Lifetime Opportunity," 5–6.
31. Ibid., 7.

The Necessity of Holiness

How can the church become a "Word and Power" church? Its members must be characterized by holiness. What is "holiness"? This term is interchangeable with the term "sanctification." Most Christians believe that sanctification includes three things. First of all, the Bible teaches sanctification is in the past, present, and future. Sanctification begins in the past with the separation from sin gained by Christ's redemption. It is in the present because sanctification describes the practice of cultivating a holy life. Sanctification will be complete upon the return of Christ, when the effects of sin will be removed. Secondly, the process of sanctification requires believers to strive to show God's love in their lives. They must devote themselves to Christian discipline daily and each day make choices against evil and choose God's righteousness. Finally, in the process of the struggle against sin in the believer's life, there is victory through the power of the Holy Spirit.[32] To live a holy life is to live in the power of the Holy Spirit and have victory over sin and the world.[33] This is one of the greatest needs in the church today: holiness in the individual believer and the church as a whole. This includes both the clergy and laity. This lack of holiness is seen throughout the church. Christians need to be filled with the Holy Spirit and meet Christ as their Sanctifier. If this is not obvious to Christians, it certainly is obvious to those in the world. They are looking for people filled with the Holy Spirit to confirm that what the Christian has to say is genuine. They are looking for supernatural confirmation of the gospel message. If they do not see its evidence in the life of the believer, they are not going to accept the message.

This is true in evangelical and fundamental churches as well as pentecostal and charismatic churches. The sanctification, or holiness, aspect is sometimes lacking in even pentecostal and charismatic churches. Considering these churches' emphasis on the Holy Spirit, one would not think this would be the case, but it certainly can be. In some pentecostal and

---

32. Gundry, *Five Views on Sanctification*, 7.

33. Stoesz, *Sanctification*, 9. The Alliance perspective of holiness is defined by Simpson when he writes, "Christian holiness is not a slow and painful attainment, but a free gift of God, through Jesus Christ, a glorious and present obtained, received in faith and retained by abiding ever in Him" (ibid.).

charismatic circles, there has long been an emphasis on a certain manifestation of the Holy Spirit rather than one living a holy or sanctified life.[34] This neglect of holiness was portrayed by Jim Bakker and Jimmy Swaggart, two charismatic preachers who claimed to be filled with the Holy Spirit yet fell into immorality.[35]

There is a great need for strong preaching and teaching in churches and seminaries on the importance of being filled with the Holy Spirit. This must begin with leadership and then be taught to the members of our churches. Randall Nelson reports in an interview with H. B. London, the assistant to the president of Focus on the Family, that 35 percent of the calls they receive per month involve moral and sexual failure.[36] Nelson did another interview with one district superintendent in which he stated that an alarming number of pastors in his district were under discipline or had been removed because of moral or sexual failures.[37] If pastors and leaders are not living holy lives, how can one expect the church members to live Spirit-filled lives?

Bruce Wilkerson, speaking on the pursuit of personal holiness in an interview on Focus on the Family, explained that he believes this to be one of the greatest needs of the clergy and laity. Wilkerson produced a workbook and videotape called *Personal Holiness in Times of Temptation* for Promise Keepers. In the first year of publication, over 20,000 video and workbook kits were sold. Over 100,000 more readers have purchased the workbook,[38] and Promise Keepers continues to sell over one thousand kits a month.[39] This shows the interest many Christians have in growing in holiness and living a sanctified life.

Wilkerson stated that he had spoken eighty times over an eight-week period to a total of over 50,000 people, and some of those people were from the largest churches in the nation. Over 80 percent said they had never asked God to fill them with the Holy Spirit.[40] Wilkerson said he preached the message of the necessity of being filled with the Holy Spirit at three pastors' conferences. He preached the need for public repentance and of

---

34. Hartzfeld and Nienkirchen, *Birth of a Vision*, 128–29.
35. Stoesz, *Sanctification*, 5.
36. Nelson, "Examination of the Exodus from Pastoral Ministry," 67.
37. Ibid.
38. See the audiotape of this lecture recorded in Wilkinson, *Pastor to Pastor*.
39. Ibid.
40. Ibid.

believers coming forward to pray to receive the infilling of the Holy Spirit. At those conferences, between 50 and 80 percent of pastors and Christian workers came forward to repent their sins and be filled with the Holy Spirit.[41]

Both clergy and laity need to meet Christ as Sanctifier. They need to be filled with the Holy Spirit. According to Jerry Bridges, "The goal of the pastor-parishioner pilgrimage is to pursue holiness together."[42] The Christian church needs men and women of holiness who are filled with the Holy Spirit. Christians can and do minister without the Holy Spirit, but these efforts will not produce eternal results. Bridges wrote that one way to gauge a ministry is to ask, "If the Holy Spirit were to back out of this effort, would it collapse?"[43] Many, of course, would because they are not based on the Holy Spirit but rather on human efforts.[44] The Christian church today needs Spirit-filled men and women to carry out its work.

Over one hundred years ago, E. M. Bounds wrote,

> The church today needs praying men to execute her solemn and pressing responsibility to meet the fearful crisis which is facing her. The crying need of the times is for men, in increased numbers—God-fearing men, praying men, Holy Ghost men, men who can endure hardness, but count all things but dross for the excellency of the knowledge of Jesus Christ, the Savior.[45]

The message of Christ our Sanctifier needs to be preached to the church and the leaders of the church. It is a biblical message that the church needs to hear. This message can be aided by some of Simpson's writings. Along with his tract "Himself," other Simpson writings that could help spread the message of the Spirit-filled life include *The Four-Fold Gospel, The Holy Spirit, A Larger Christian Life, Wholly Sanctified,* and *When the Comforter Came.* These writings could be distributed not only as books, but also as single chapters that could be used either alone or as part of various websites to help spread the message of holiness throughout the church today. Simpson's works can have a tremendous impact on an individual. Reitz tells of a Haitian pastor who came to Canada to study for the ministry. He began reading some of Simpson's works and then went back to Haiti to

---

41. Ibid.
42. London and Wiseman, *Pastors at Risk*, 188.
43. Ibid., 178–79.
44. Ibid., 179.
45. Bounds, *Best of E. M. Bounds*, 146.

begin planting Christian and Missionary Alliance churches even though he had no financial support from the denomination.[46] The Fourfold Gospel can have a tremendous impact on an individual.

Simpson's message of holiness played an important role in the Third Great Awakening. The message of Christ our Sanctifier can play an important role in the *next* Great Awakening. We will not see another revival until we see pastors and laity broken in repentance, filled with the Holy Spirit, and praying for the church and the world. When we see this, we will see God working in a mighty way, just as he has done in the past.

Conclusion

The purpose of this book has been to show how A. B. Simpson impacted the Third Great Awakening and how his impact still continues to affect the church today. Although Simpson has been forgotten by many church historians and religious scholars, that does not diminish the role he played in the Third Great Awakening. During the time of the Awakening, Simpson was very popular, but as the decades passed his popularity lessened in evangelical circles, except for the Christian and Missionary Alliance. This trend seems to be reversing itself through a resurgence of interest in Simpson and his works within popular Christian literature and the Internet. Simpson's writings speak to people today just as they did over a hundred years ago. His treatises are both biblical and pragmatic, which is always popular with the Christian public. Perhaps Simpson and his work would become even more popular if a new biography of his life were written. The last biography on Simpson was penned by A. W. Tozer over half a century ago.[47]

Simpson's message, the Fourfold Gospel, was not unique during his lifetime. Others preached this same message, but Simpson coined the phrase and helped popularize and spread its message. The most important contribution Simpson made to the church was the society he founded, the Christian and Missionary Alliance. Both the message of the Fourfold Gospel and the method he used to take the gospel to the ends of the earth have been adopted by the Christian and Missionary Alliance, which is still proclaiming the gospel throughout the world today. Simpson's impact and legacy cannot be measured by academicians, but it can be measured by

---

46. George W. Reitz, interview with the author, February 12, 2003.

47. According to an interview with the author conducted February 12, 2003, Daniel Evearitt has been contracted to write a new biography on A. B. Simpson.

what he left behind. He left behind a denomination that is worldwide in scope and has grown to well over one million members. This is the impact that Simpson and his message has made on the Christian church. The Fourfold Gospel is being preached from major cities to tribal villages all over the world by the Christian and Missionary Alliance and those sympathetic to its message.

During the research for this book, one fact that stood out sharply was how little had been written about the Third Great Awakening. An abundance of material has been written on the First and Second Awakenings, but the Third Great Awakening has been largely neglected. Except for information about the Businessman's Prayer Revival in New York City from 1857 to 1859, the period has been largely overlooked.

J. Edwin Orr wrote extensively about the Third Great Awakening, and Kathryn Long wrote *The Revival of 1857–1859* on the Third Great Awakening, focusing solely on her title's three-year period. Almost all scholarly focus to date has been on these three years at the expense of the rest of the period. A full-length comprehensive work has yet to be written on this Awakening. Such a work would be of major importance to American church historians. So much more needs to be presented on important historical figures of the Third Great Awakening such as Phoebe Palmer, D. L. Moody, R. A. Torrey, A. J. Pierson, Charles Cullis, and, of course, Simpson himself. There is sufficient information for such a work, but no one has gathered it together into a thorough treatise.

This author's original research on the divine healing movement revealed little written on that subject either. The only complete work on the divine healing movement at the time was a Drew University dissertation written in 1983; that work was never published. Since then, there has been a number of works on divine healing. One notable work that gives a comprehensive history of divine healing is Nancy A. Hardesty's history of divine healing titled *Faith Cure: Divine Healing in the Holiness and Pentecostal Movements*. There is yet to be a comprehensive work on the divine healing movement and its impact on the third Great Awakening.

Another possible direction for further research and writing includes investigations into the impact of Simpson's missionary theology on the modern missionary movement. Simpson's focus on the imperative of Matt 24:14—to preach the gospel to the ends of the earth so as to hasten Christ's return—should be codified. Although Simpson was not alone in this view, he was its most important spokesperson of his day. A study would be helpful to see how this view of "bringing back the King" propelled the missionary movement forward in the Third Great Awakening and in the early Christian and Missionary Alliance. This line of investigation leads to another question: Why did this view lose popularity in the second half of the twentieth century, except in the Christian and Missionary Alliance?

Another area that needs to be explored is Simpson's relationship with and his influence on other mission boards. Since he was directly involved in the lives of the founders of the Sudan Interior Mission, the African Inland Mission, and the Evangelical Alliance Mission, it would be interesting to compare and contrast these three independent mission boards with the Christian and Missionary Alliance over the last century. It also might be profitable to investigate how Simpson indirectly impacted other mission boards around the world. There are a number of avenues that could be explored concerning Simpson and his involvement in missionary outreach at the end of the nineteenth and the early twentieth centuries.

The center of Simpson's message was Christ, and his goal was to reach the entire world with the gospel. Simpson's message is encapsulated well in the motto of Columbia International University: "To Know Him and Make Him Known." This was Simpson's passion for a lost and dying world. It was satiated by preaching the Fourfold Gospel to the entire world—a legacy that lives on in the denomination he founded.

Even one hundred years later, Simpson's message and method are still burning in the soul of the Christian and Missionary Alliance. Simpson never intended to start a denomination, but his goal was to see the world evangelized. He was not interested in getting any credit for himself; he wanted all the glory to go to God. He wanted to see the kingdom of God advanced. Simpson was not concerned with who gained attention so long as the gospel was preached. As a result, Simpson was well received by other Christian leaders. This was not the case with every leader of the Third Great Awakening or even with church leaders today. This is one of the reasons he saw such success. Simpson seemed to attract people he could work with and who could work with him—no small feat in Christian circles, where many Christian leaders prefer to work alone!

Simpson led by example and by being a servant. No one was too unimportant for Simpson. He was concerned even for the smallest child. Evearitt tells of an interview he had with a man who had grown up in Simpson's Gospel Tabernacle in New York City. The elderly man remembered an incident that happened when he was a small boy no older than seven or eight years old. He recalled that Simpson would enter the pulpit from the back of the church and would walk by in front of the pews before he entered the pulpit. Simpson would come up to where this boy sat at the front pew and kiss him on top of the head. That simple action made an impression on him that lasted over eighty years.[48] No one was insignificant in Simpson's eyes, not even a little boy. All were servants in Christ's kingdom and were worthy of his attention. What an insight for all those who serve the Master!

Simpson wanted to see the gospel preached to the world in his generation. This should be the goal of every generation of Christians. He truly believed the teaching of Matt 24:14 and invested his entire life and all his resources to see it come to pass. He saw it as the highest exercise of love for any Christian.[49] This summarizes Simpson's whole burden and vision for missions. This flame burned in Simpson's heart his whole life, and his goal was to see it passed on from generation to generation.

Simpson's message was Jesus Christ, and he wanted Christians to experience Christ in all his fullness. When this happened, believers would naturally take Christ to their neighbors and to the ends of the earth. This was his goal, and it is still a part of the Christian and Missionary Alliance. Simpson said, "Some people spend their lives trying to get to heaven, other people get there at the start and spend their lives taking others along."[50] What a challenge for all believers: to be involved in God's kingdom and to bring as many people along as possible.

Simpson's message was the message of Christ. It was a biblical message: the simple gospel message found throughout the Scripture. He took the message and preached it faithfully for over a half-century. It is the same message that needs to be preached today. Simpson may have coined the term "the Fourfold Gospel," but the message is straight from the heart of God's Word. Simpson was not a perfect man and had his foibles and weaknesses as all people do, but he was a man who was totally committed to Christ and saw Christ as the central focus of his life. He realized that without Christ, there is no Christianity. Christ was his message, and it was only through the power of Christ that the message could be preached to the entire world. It was only through a surrendered life that the goal of world evangelization could be accomplished. Christ was the answer for a lost world. Simpson wrote,

48. Daniel J. Evearitt, interview with the author, February 12, 2003.
49. Simpson, *Walking in Love*, 111.
50. Ibid., *Christ in the Bible Commentary*, 62.

> The mercy of heaven is big enough to take in all our sinful race. The blood of Christ is rich enough to cover the guilt of every child of Adam. The Gospel is broad enough to save and sanctify and keep the myriads of all of our race, if they will accept it. The heaven that He provides is vast enough for all earths lost generations. And the divine plan is grand enough to take in every kindred and tribe and tongue, all earth's countless inhabitants. There may be limitations in receiving all of God's grace on our part through ignorance, willfulness or indifference of sinful man, but there is no limitation to the sufficiency of Christ's redemption and the universal and all-embracing fullness of the Gospel of salvation.[51]

As the church ministers in the twenty-first century, she must be aware that culture and society has changed in many ways since the Third Great Awakening, but both the gospel message and the need for it have remained. The gospel is as appropriate and valid as it was two thousand years ago, and the message still needs to be taken to the ends of the earth. Simpson saw that the key to everything was in Christ. A hymn he wrote titled "Not I, But Christ" illustrates the centrality of Christ in the message of the Fourfold Gospel. It is because of Christ that the Christian takes the gospel to all who have never heard. This hymn is still sung in Alliance churches throughout the land. It envelopes both the message and its outreach. Simpson wrote,

> Not I but Christ be honored, loved, exalted; not I but Christ be seen, be known, be heard; not I but Christ in every look and action; not I but Christ in every thought and word.
>
> Not I but Christ to gently soothe in sorrow; not I but Christ to wipe the falling tear: Not I but Christ to lift the weary burden; Not I but Christ to hush away all fear.
>
> Christ, only Christ, no idle word e'er falling; Christ only Christ, no needless bustling sound; Christ, only Christ for body and soul, and spirit; Christ, only Christ live then thy life in me.
>
> Christ, only Christ ere long will fill my vision; glory excelling soon, full soon I'll see Christ, only Christ my every wish fulfilling; Christ, only Christ my all and all to be.
>
> REFRAIN:
>
> Oh, to be saved from myself, dear Lord, oh to be loved in thee!

---

51. Ibid., *Cross of Christ*, 77–78.

Simpson's Message and Its Ramifications on the Church Today

Oh, that it might be no more I, but Christ that lives in me![52]

It may be in this generation that the goal of Matt 24:14 will be accomplished; this is the goal of the Christian and Missionary Alliance, which is the proper goal of the entire church. The Christian and Missionary Alliance and many other believers are faithfully preaching the Fourfold Gospel and taking the good news to the ends of the earth. Simpson's message, legacy, and vision to reach the world for Christ is alive and well and is being preached and accomplished in this new millennium.

---

52. Christian and Missionary Alliance Committee on Hymnal Revision, *Hymns of the Christian Life*, 264.

APPENDIX

The Impact of Simpson and His Message on the Christian and Missionary Alliance Today

All organizations, whether secular or religious, go through changes when their founders die. Some groups keep the original vision of their leaders, while others tend to go off into other directions that their leaders never envisioned. In the life of denominations, it is often the case that after the founder dies, the church becomes a religious bureaucracy. It then becomes concerned only with keeping the organization going as it forgets the original guiding vision of the organization. Oswald Chambers comments:

> Look at the history of every vigorous movement born spontaneously of the Holy Spirit: There comes a time when its true spiritual power dies, and it dies in correspondence to the success of the organization. Every denomination or missionary departs from its true spiritual power when it becomes a successful organization, because the advocates of the denomination or the missionary enterprise after a while have to see first of all to the establishment and success of their organization, while the thing that made them what they are has gone like a grain of wheat into the ground and died.[1]

Although this pattern does not hold true in every church or denomination, it is true of a majority of cases. It takes real effort and focus to keep the original vision and passion alive in any denomination or church.

The Christian and Missionary Alliance has struggled with this very issue. There is a concerted effort to return to the original vision and burden that God gave Simpson and the early Christian and Missionary Alliance.

---

1. Chambers, *God's Workmanship and He Shall Glorify Me*, 261.

Appendix

Simpson was compelled to teach and preach the Fourfold Gospel and take the gospel to the unreached masses both at home and abroad. Simpson founded a movement,[2] and those in the Christian and Missionary Alliance want to keep that movement's vision alive within the context of the denomination.

Peter Nanfelt, former president of the Christian and Missionary Alliance, feels that the denomination he leads is gradually becoming more movement-like.[3] Nanfelt wrote to Alliance workers asking them to pray for a fresh infilling of God's Spirit before the General Council convened in May of 2001. He urged prayer for the Christian and Missionary Alliance to again experience a moving of the Holy Spirit similar to what happened in Simpson's day.[4] The theme for that General Council and for the entire Christian and Missionary Alliance in the United States throughout 2001 was "The Wind of God-Empowering the Movement." The leadership saw the necessity of getting back to the original vision and passion Simpson demonstrated.

Nanfelt reminded his constituents that the two distinctives of the Alliance today are the same as they were in Simpson's day. The *message* is the sufficiency of Christ demonstrated in the Fourfold Gospel, and the *mission* is to finish the Great Commission.[5] Donald Wiggins, former vice president for Church Ministries for the Christian and Missionary Alliance, comments that every generation of Alliance leaders has to be captivated by the original vision that God gave Simpson and the early Alliance. He says if there is any glue that binds the Alliance together, it is this vision.[6]

How has Simpson and his message impacted the Alliance today? The Fourfold Gospel is still being preached in Alliance churches throughout the world. Everyone—from the president to local pastors—is still being impacted by the message and the mission. Of the eight leaders in the Alliance that were interviewed for this book, all were deeply and personally impacted by the Fourfold Gospel. The message had changed their lives. They had caught sight of this shared vision of worldwide outreach, and it had become a central focus in their lives. The Alliance has kept the original emphasis

---

2. A movement is focused on outreach and is growing outward to the lost, while a denomination is more inwardly focused and often has a fortress mentality.
3. Nanfelt, "Seeking the Wind of God," 2.
4. Ibid.
5. Nanfelt, "Once-In-A-Lifetime Opportunity," 7.
6. Wiggins, "Captured by God's Vision," 2.

of evangelism that Simpson practiced and preached as a major focus in its work. Its churches still place a great emphasis on Christ as Savior. On any given Sunday in most Alliance churches, one will hear about the necessity of accepting Jesus Christ as Lord and Savior.

Simpson put a great emphasis on the authority and inerrancy of the Scripture, which is also being stressed in Alliance churches today. The Christian and Missionary Alliance did not fall into the trap of the liberal view of higher criticism. Over the course of its history, the Christian and Missionary Alliance has remained true to the authority of the Scripture. Nanfelt writes, "The Christian and Missionary Alliance has done as well as any denomination in holding to the authority of the Scripture. This is a notable achievement."[7] A high view of Scripture is critical when preaching the Fourfold Gospel along with the missionary mandate found in the Great Commission.

Throughout the interviews conducted in the course of researching this book, five aspects of Simpson's message that still impact the Christian and Missionary Alliance today were discovered. Though the impact on the modern-day Christian and Missionary Alliance may not be as it was in Simpson's day, these aspects continue to influence the current Alliance even into the twenty-first century. The Alliance recognizes them and is trying to raise them up to the same level of emphasis Simpson placed on them.

The first of these five aspects is Simpson's passion and vision for not only preaching the Fourfold Gospel, but also *to reach the world for Christ*. This took on the label of Christ our Savior. This is the basis of all Christianity and the Fourfold Gospel. It is the basis of the Christian life.[8] It has to be in the forefront of the message the Alliance preaches. All those interviewed agreed with this notion. The ministry of the Christian and Missionary Alliance is to complete the Great Commission both here and abroad. Nanfelt states the only way this can be done is for the Alliance to become a movement again.[9] Nanfelt states that the Alliance has "to become a movement of churches and Great Commission Christians, who are vibrant, healthy, engaged in evangelism and missions and living the life of Christ."[10] This is not only true of Christ as Savior, but also of the rest of the Fourfold Gospel.[11]

7. Nanfelt, "Once-In-A-Lifetime Opportunity," 6.
8. Daniel J. Evearitt, interview with the author, February 12, 2003.
9. Peter Nanfelt, interview with the author, December 10, 2002.
10. Ibid.
11. Ibid.

Appendix

The second aspect of Simpson's message dealing with individual holiness is Christ our Sanctifier, which Simpson stressed throughout his ministry. Next to salvation, he believed sanctification was the most important experience that could take place in any Christian's life. Sanctification is the key to the individual growth of any Christian and also to reaching the world for Christ. This sanctifying work of the Holy Spirit needs to be demonstrated in the lives of all believers. The Christian and Missionary Alliance believes it cannot carry out God's vision without Spirit-filled clergy and laity. This original vision, as laid out by Simpson, cannot be carried out without experiencing Christ as Sanctifier. This aspect of Simpson's message was likewise understood by all who were interviewed. They all realized the importance of keeping sanctification at the forefront of the Christian and Missionary Alliance's work. All had been changed by meeting Christ as Sanctifier. John Soper, vice president of the Christian and Missionary Alliance, stated, "In the Alliance I found that [filling of the Holy Spirit and holiness of life] were both part of the message of Jesus Christ as my Sanctifier. He gives me power for life and holiness and also for service. It has revolutionized my ministry and my life."[12] The centrality of Christ as Sanctifier is being stressed by the leadership in the Alliance. Nanfelt states that next to his salvation, his experience of sanctification was the most significant event in his life. It was only after this surrender that he felt called into missions.[13] In the January 2004 newsletter to official Alliance workers, *Completing Christ's Commission*, Nanfelt titled his article "Preached a Sermon on Sanctification Lately?" Nanfelt stresses the importance of preaching on sanctification and its key in the believer's life.[14]

The third aspect of Simpson's teaching that continues to impact the Alliance is Christ our Healer. Simpson stressed this aspect the least of any other aspect of his message, but it is healing for which he is best known. This aspect of the Fourfold Gospel is the least stressed in Alliance churches. This may be due to the unbiblical teaching on healing that is being taught in some Christian circles.[15] Some Alliance pastors have shied away from this component of the Fourfold Gospel. There is a fear among some Alliance pastors of appearing to be too pentecostal or charismatic.[16] It is important

---

12. John Soper, interview with the author, September 11, 2002.
13. Peter Nanfelt, interview with the author, December 10, 2002.
14. Nanfelt, "Preached a Sermon on Sanctification Lately?" n.p.
15. Peter Nanfelt, interview with the author, December 10, 2002.
16. Daniel J. Evearitt, interview with the author, February 12, 2003.

Appendix

for all those in leadership to teach this third fold of the Fourfold Gospel. Simpson gave a biblical definition to "divine healing." Because of that biblical definition and the reports of divine healing experienced throughout the world, Simpson's message continues to be well received even today.

The fourth aspect of Simpson's message that continues to influence the Alliance was his burden and vision for missions and his desire to "bring back the King." He labeled this aspect Christ our King. Simpson wanted to see the Great Commission fulfilled in his lifetime. This is still the lifeblood of the Christian and Missionary Alliance today, and in many circles is what the Christian and Missionary Alliance is best known. Simpson taught that every Christian was responsible to preach the gospel and to help "bring back the King." Reitz felt this was the least understood of the four folds—not that Christ is returning, which is understood by all Christians, but the fact that believers can hasten the return of Christ by preaching the good news to the ends of the earth. Many today in Alliance churches do not share the same level of passion, sacrifice, and commitment that Simpson and the early Alliance had to see the gospel preached.[17] Nanfelt also sees a problem in that not all members of Alliance churches today are living with the imminent return of Christ in mind. He feels it is being preached and presented, but whether all Alliance Christians are living with this awareness may be a different question.[18] Again, there is a need to share a vision of God and a commitment to preach the return of Christ. There is also a need to make the sacrifices necessary to complete this task.

The final aspect of Simpson's teaching, which has not been emphasized as much as the first two aspects, is his burden for urban outreach. Although this burden was an important part of his original missionary zeal, Simpson himself ended up putting less stress on this area toward the end of his ministry. Urban outreach is now being rediscovered by those in the Alliance as an aspect that needs to be stressed again as it was in the early days of the Alliance. This burden and vision for urban outreach needs to be rekindled. Even those who have been involved in it get discouraged at times. It has been especially difficult to spread this vision nationally to reach the urban centers. It is often easier to do it locally.[19] The Metropolitan District of the Christian and Missionary Alliance has emphasized urban outreach and has seen much success in the New York City metropolitan

17. George W. Reitz, interview with the author, February 12, 2003.
18. Peter Nanfelt, interview with the author, December 10, 2002.
19. George W. Reitz, interview with the author, February 12, 2003.

Appendix

area. Reitz, the director of urban outreach, often feels like a "voice crying in the wilderness" when trying to generate interest and passion for urban outreach. Yet he continues.[20] Hopefully, the passion and vision Simpson had will once again burn in the souls of the Alliance constituency.

Simpson was one of those set apart as a leader of the Third Great Awakening in the nineteenth and early twentieth century by his exceptional passion and vision for the world. Simpson not only believed in the Fourfold Gospel, he also believed it should be preached to the entire world. He believed that the world could be reached for Christ in his generation. He was convinced that it could be done, and he was going to do it. Simpson attracted like-minded men and women, and soon they were caught up in his burden to reach the world. His fellow early leaders shared this same devotion and goal. It is of key importance that the leadership in the Christian and Missionary Alliance today continue to share this same vision and passion.

Barry Jordan, an Alliance missionary to Indonesia, sees this as one of the greatest problems facing the Alliance church in Indonesia. He feels that too many people do not have the same goal Simpson had: they are too inward-looking and need to concentrate on reaching beyond Indonesia.[21] They need to see the lost the way Christ did. The Indonesian church is surrounded by Muslims, but members have not seen the need to reach them. Jordan felt that translating *Wingspread*, the Simpson biography written by A. W. Tozer, into an Indonesian language might help Indonesian church leaders get an idea of the concern Simpson had for the lost.[22] Simpson modeled this burden and vision in his own life. He was not only burdened for the lost in New York City, but also for the unreached people of the world. Those who worked with him caught this same desire and concern. Simpson's message was a biblical one, and those in the Alliance and the church as a whole need to ask God for this same perspective today. This passion and vision have to be continually kindled; if not, both will be lost.

Walborn, the head of pastoral studies at Nyack College, says one of the goals in teaching students is that they come to have the same concern Simpson felt for the lost. He feels that many of his students are catching this vision and burden that Simpson had.[23] These students will become pastors

20. Ibid.
21. Barry Jordan, interview with the author, November 11, 2002.
22. Ibid.
23. Ron C. Walborn, interview with the author, February 15, 2003.

Appendix

and missionaries who will continue preaching the Fourfold Gospel and reaching the lost for Christ with the same enthusiasm Simpson had.

Daniel Evearitt, professor of theology at Toccoa Falls College, agrees that it is the natural tendency of any movement or church to lose the original vision of its founder. Therefore, this guiding vision needs to be emphasized, taught, and caught by the members. Evearitt tries to do this with his students at Toccoa in a spiritual formation class in which they learn about Simpson's concern and desire to preach the Fourfold Gospel to reach the world.[24] This vision and passion must be instilled in the pastors and missionaries in the Alliance, and they in turn must implant it in their congregations and in the churches that are planted on the mission field. Alliance pastors and missionaries must model Simpson's vision and passion for those who have never heard the name of Christ.

Simpson had a vision of those who had never heard of Christ perishing for eternity. This vision is what drove him. Simpson saw the need around him. Those who are leading congregations and planting churches on the mission field need the same vision and passion. If they have it, members of their congregations will catch it. Larry Zulauf states that Christians need to ask the Holy Spirit to ignite inside them the same burden and passion for the lost Simpson felt. It has to be a work of God in any Christian's life.[25]

Reitz feels the Alliance is still being impacted by that original vision and passion.[26] Reitz reports that he sees this same burden and concern in some of the urban pastors that minister with the Alliance in the metropolitan New York City area.[27] Simpson's dream to reach the world for Christ and to finish the Great Commission was bigger than he was and larger even than the early Alliance. It is greater than the Christian and Missionary Alliance today. It is greater than the church as a whole. It can only be accomplished through the power of Christ. Simpson dreamt big, and the Alliance needs to continue to dream in the same manner. Rick Warren observes, "Some pastors are afraid to ask for big commitment, fearing that they will drive people away. But people do not resent being asked for a great commitment, if there is a great purpose behind it."[28]

---

24. Daniel J. Evearitt, interview with the author, March 7, 2003.
25. Larry Zulauf, interview with the author, February 28, 2003.
26. George W. Reitz, interview with the author, February 12, 2003.
27. Ibid.
28. Warren, *Purpose Driven Church*, 345.

Appendix

Understanding the Fourfold Gospel

Simpson emphasized Christ as Savior as the most important point of the gospel. He stressed Christ as Sanctifier as the second most important part of the Fourfold Gospel. Simpson wrote that "the coming of the Holy Spirit to a human heart is the second great epoch of our spiritual life and marks a crisis just as distinct as conversion itself."[29] Christ as Sanctifier impacts Christ as Healer and Christ as Coming King. One cannot expect to go to God for healing if there is unconfessed sin in one's life. According to James 5:17, to be in that condition, one needs to be filled with the Holy Spirit. It is also necessary to know Christ as Sanctifier if one is going to fulfill the Great Commission. The only way the gospel is going to be taken to the entire world is through Spirit-filled Christians. The gospel cannot be preached to the entire world without the sanctified Christian church. The only way Christians can live a holy life and carry out the service that God has called them to is to know Christ as their Sanctifier. Simpson wrote, "When the Holy Spirit comes, he lifts our minds to new ideals and gives us concepts of things so much in advance of our present experience that we long for higher ground; the saved become sanctified and the sanctified rise to a life of sacrifice and unselfish service."[30] Simpson saw Christ as Sanctifier as the key to Christian life and service. This understanding is still seen as integral among leaders in the Christian and Missionary Alliance.

Although Christ as Sanctifier is central to living a spiritual life, Christ as Sanctifier is not readily understood by all in the Alliance. Of the eight Alliance leaders interviewed, five said it was the least understood aspect of Simpson's folds, and two others also thought it was not readily understood. Walborn states the reason this fold is not understood is because it has been neglected in the teaching of Alliance churches. The Alliance has shied away from it because of the extreme positions of some in the deeper life movement.[31] Walborn continues by saying, "We have raised up a generation of Christians who would feel just at home in a Baptist church as they would be in a Christian and Missionary Alliance church. We have forgotten the deeper life."[32] Nanfelt believes it is not understood because Alliance pastors have been frightened away from preaching this fold due to unbiblical

---

29. Simpson, *When the Comforter Came*, 37.
30. Ibid., 96.
31. Ron C. Walborn, interview with the author, February 15, 2003.
32. Ibid.

teaching on this topic. They have stayed away from preaching on it in the past.[33] He also believes that sanctification is the least understood part of the Fourfold Gospel, and yet, next to salvation, it is the most important.[34]

Evearitt, who served on a committee studying sanctification, found that many pastors who come into the Alliance from non-Alliance schools did not understand the doctrine of sanctification and the filling of the Holy Spirit. Almost 52 percent of these pastors did not understand this aspect of Simpson's vision.[35] This seemed to be confirmed by Mark Haynes, an Alliance pastor on the District Executive Committee in the Northeast District of the Christian and Missionary Alliance. He agreed that sanctification seemed to be the least understood fold of the Fourfold Gospel.[36] John Soper, District Superintendent of the Metropolitan District of the Christian and Missionary Alliance, also found that sanctification was the least understood doctrine among those new pastors.[37]

Soper states there are two main reasons why sanctification is not easily understood. The first is that, in the past, Alliance people did not want to be perceived as pentecostal or charismatic, so they shied away from certain terms that were distinct to pentecostal circles. Secondly, according to Soper, we live in a modern-day Christian culture that does not like to experience sacrifice. In order to be filled with the Holy Spirit, the believer will have to live a sacrificial life. Most people are not willing to make the sacrifice Paul calls for in Rom 12:1 by offering themselves as "living sacrifices."[38]

Jordan, speaking from his experience in the Indonesian Alliance Church, also agrees that the least understood and emphasized aspect of the Fourfold Gospel is Christ our Sanctifier. The deeper Christian life, as the doctrine of sanctification is also known, is poorly understood by the Indonesian church. Jordan continues to preach on Christ as Sanctifier—as well as on the importance of all aspects of the Fourfold Gospel—whenever he gets the opportunity.[39] He feels teaching the centrality of Christ helps to spread Christ as Sanctifier as well as the other folds of the Fourfold

---

33. Peter Nanfelt, interview with the author, December 10, 2002.
34. Ibid.
35. Daniel J. Evearitt, interview with the author, March 7, 2003.
36. Mark Haynes Sr., interview with the author, February 17, 2003.
37. John Soper, interview with the author, September 11, 2002.
38. Ibid.
39. Barry Jordan, interview with the author, November 11, 2003.

Appendix

Gospel.[40] Although translating Simpson's works into an Indonesia language would be helpful, it would be even better if the Indonesian church would write on the Fourfold Gospel in its own cultural context and setting.

Both Walborn and Evearitt emphasize the importance of sanctification in their pastoral training classes. In his "Alliance Distinctives" class, Evearitt spends a majority of the course teaching about sanctification and healing. He feels these are the least understood topics among his students. Between sanctification and healing, he puts the most emphasis on sanctification.[41] Walborn makes an important observation in noting that after the student understands the theology behind sanctification, it is important that they experience Christ as Sanctifier in their own lives.[42] Whereas Walborn highlights the individual's experience, Evearitt stresses the importance of preaching Christ our Sanctifier in a way that the common layperson can understand.[43] This is a challenging idea that should involve all leaders, pastors, missionaries, and others who are serving in the Christian and Missionary Alliance.

Another important distinctive that Simpson taught was Christ as our Healer. Of the four roles of Christ presented in the Fourfold Gospel, Christ as our Healer is probably emphasized the least. Simpson presented divine healing in a simple, biblical way that made it acceptable in many evangelical circles. At the Gospel Tabernacle, Simpson led a healing service every Friday afternoon. Although he may have emphasized divine healing the least among all the aspects of his Fourfold Gospel, Simpson, nonetheless, had strong views on the importance of the message of divine healing. He wrote:

> The true doctrine of healing through the Lord Jesus Christ is most humbling, holy and practical. It exalts no man, it spares no sin, it offers no promise to the disobedient, it gives no strength for selfish indulgence or worldly ends. Rather, it exalts the name of Jesus, glorifies God, inspires the soul with faith and power, summons to a life of self-denial and holy service. It awakens a slumbering church and unbelieving world with the solemn signals of a living God and a risen Christ.[44]

---

40. Ibid.
41. Daniel J. Evearitt, interview with the author, March 7, 2003.
42. Ron C. Walborn, interview with the author, February 15, 2003.
43. Daniel J. Evearitt, interview with the author, March 7, 2003.
44. Simpson, *Gospel of Healing*, 56–57.

Appendix

Simpson believed that healing was given by Christ not only for the benefit of the one being healed, but for future service in his name. The sick person who was healed could take the gospel message to their neighbors and serve their needs. Simpson saw this in his own life. He believed that God had healed him so he could serve the unreached both in New York City and in the whole world. Like sanctification, healing's greater purpose was to advance God's kingdom.

Many Alliance leaders share the belief that healing is poorly understood within in the Alliance. In fact, two of those interviewed said that divine healing was the least understood of the four folds of the Fourfold Gospel. Evearitt stresses that the negative publicity from pentecostal and charismatic groups has caused many in the Alliance to shy away from divine healing.[45] He goes on to say that among his students at Toccoa, many of Alliance members' views on divine healing are not any different from those of non-Alliance students who do not practice divine healing in their churches.[46]

Although divine healing is practiced in a number of Alliance churches in the United States, others know little of the practice. At the Phillipsburg Alliance Church where this author serves, the congregation holds a healing service once every twelve weeks. It is held on Sunday evening, typically with a good number of people in attendance. The author has seen a number of situations where God has touched and healed individuals. All districts have a divine healing service at their annual District Conference. There is also a healing service conducted at General Council, the denomination's nationwide annual meeting.

Divine healing is practiced at every level in the Alliance, yet the number of congregants who have it preached and taught to them is diminishing. Zulauf, an Alliance pastor from the Midwest, believes that divine healing needs more explanation when it is preached and taught. Zulauf feels that many Christians do not understand divine healing, and pastors have to teach their people what Jesus Christ did on the cross for them as well as its effect on their health.[47] It may be that pastors need to offer a series of messages on divine healing so their congregation understands it. Once this aspect of the message is understood, more people will come to God for healing. Evearitt states that at times, divine healing has received less em-

---

45. Daniel J. Evearitt, interview with the author, March 7, 2003.
46. Ibid.
47. Larry Zulauf, interview with the author, February 28, 2003.

phasis than it should have. He shares that as a youth growing up at summer camp meetings, he began to see less emphasis on it in terms of where divine healing programs were placed in the services.[48] He feels divine healing needs to begin with the pastor and his experience with God.[49] If the pastor or Christian worker has had an experience with divine healing, he or she is more likely to have passion and enthusiasm for it. Such leaders are more likely to stress this fold because they have seen how important it is in their life. The author has seen this in the congregation he serves. Divine healing can be an excellent opportunity for Christians to witness to the unsaved. They can share their personal experiences with others and offer to pray for their healing.

While divine healing in the United States might not be emphasized as much as the other distinctives, Jordan writes that in Indonesia, Christ our Healer is greatly stressed. This is due to the fact that most of the members of the Indonesian church do not have access to medical care, so they have no choice but to go to God for healing. They believe in divine healing because for them, it is eminently practical. In turn, one of the reasons that divine healing is not emphasized in the Alliance in the United States is because of the effective medical care available in North America. This level of medical care was not available to many in Simpson's day; hence, they had to rely on God for healing. If Christians would first consult God for healing, then consult their doctor, perhaps we would see divine healings today equal to those of the past.

Louise Rhoads, a ninety-seven-year-old member of the Phillipsburg Alliance Church, stated that when she was a young woman she saw many more healings than she does today. She states two reasons for the number of healings she witnessed when she was a young woman. The first was that people believed God would heal, and he did. They believed in divine healing like they believed in salvation. They had faith that God would save, and he did. They had faith that God would heal, and he did. Those in the past had more faith in Christ and his healing work. Secondly, she felt there was more emphasis on teaching divine healing in the past than there is today. Pastors taught more about divine healing and they also held more healing services—possibly one or two a week. There is not the same emphasis placed on divine healing as there was in the past. It may be helpful to place the same emphasis on divine healing that Simpson did.

48. Daniel J. Evearitt, interview with the author, February 12, 2003.
49. Larry Zulauf, interview with the author, February 28, 2003.

Appendix

When evangelicals think about Simpson and the Christian and Missionary Alliance, the first thing that comes to their minds is missions. Soper states that it is part of our psyche—it is part of who we are. It is part of the "warp and woof" of the Alliance.[50] Is the Alliance today as excited about missions as they were in Simpson's day? The interviews this author conducted revealed mixed responses to this question. Some said that Alliance Christians remain as excited as any in Simpson's day, while others stated that there is no longer the same sacrificial spirit there was at that time. Zulauf stated that the Alliance, as it goes into the twenty-first century, is getting back on the right track with its renewed emphasis on missions. He continued by adding that those in the Alliance are again seeing themselves as a movement instead of just a denomination. This vigor will help the mission emphasis.[51] Haynes comments that the Alliance is trying again to put the same amount of emphasis on missions as it did in Simpson's day.[52] Reitz states he feels there is as much emphasis as in Simpson's day, but there is less passion.[53] Evearitt states that the Alliance is almost as excited about missions as in Simpson's day, although maybe not quite on the same level.[54] Walborn comments that the Alliance is not as excited as it was in Simpson's day. He feels the Alliance became a denomination and ceased to be a movement.[55] Soper feels the average person in the Alliance is not as excited about missions as in Simpson's day, since most members do not have the vision that drove Simpson and the early Alliance.[56] Most felt the Alliance emphasis on missions was just as great but that the commitment within the congregations has diminished over time.

Why has commitment lessened in Alliance congregations? Evearitt states the average member of the congregation does not realize the lostness of humankind or that without Christ they will go to a Christless eternity. Missions and evangelism must not be preached just once a year at the missions conference, but needs to be preached continually.[57] Soper states that members of the Alliance churches must regain the passions their ear-

50. John Soper, interview with the author, September 11, 2002.
51. Larry Zulauf, interview with the author, February 28, 2003.
52. Mark Haynes Sr., interview with the author, February 17, 2003.
53. George W. Reitz, interview with the author, February 12, 2003.
54. Daniel J. Evearitt, interview with the author, February 12, 2003.
55. Ron C. Walborn, interview with the author, February 15, 2003.
56. John Soper, interview with the author, September 11, 2002.
57. Daniel J. Evearitt, interview with the author, February 12, 2003.

lier counterparts had.[58] Missions must again become the lifeblood of the Alliance churches. Zulauf states that the people in the congregation must once again put emphasis on the value of seeing people coming to Christ for salvation.[59] Haynes comments that people must show that same willingness to sacrifice to see the gospel taken to the ends of the earth.[60] It is something that both pastors and missionaries have to model and teach to their congregations. There is still excitement and enthusiasm among the leadership of the Alliance to be involved in "bringing back the King." This passion must be passed on to the congregation. Preachers throughout the Alliance must continue to emphasize that when the gospel has been preached to all nations, then Christ will return.

The believer living a sanctified life should also have an attitude of sacrificial giving. This too may have changed since the early days of Simpson and the Alliance. This type of giving needs to be rekindled. During Simpson's missionary conventions, women would often put jewelry and watches in the offering plate for worldwide mission work. Simpson would later discourage this activity because he did not want to get the reputation of being fanatical.[61] Instead, he encouraged sacrificial giving through the "Faith Promise." This was a mission pledge made by individuals who trusted God to help them supply more for their pledge than they could supply by themselves. This form of giving was much more effective, and it is still practiced in many Alliance churches today as part of their missions conventions.

The Alliance Today

In many ways, the Christian and Missionary Alliance is different today than it was at the end of the nineteenth century and the early twentieth. In the beginning, the Alliance was more of a missions-sending agency loosely affiliated with a group of Bible-believing churches. There was more of a focus on overseas missions and less of a focus on church work at home. What caused the transformation? It was the success and growth of the North American churches. It became necessary to expand the focus of the original vision to reach the unreached of the world to include a church

---

58. John Soper, interview with the author, September 11, 2002.
59. Larry Zulauf, interview with the author, February 28, 2003.
60. Mark Haynes Sr., interview with the author, February 17, 2003.
61. Niklaus et al., *All for Jesus*, 90.

Appendix

organization or denomination.[62] Today, the Christian and Missionary Alliance is a denomination that has churches both at home and abroad. The responsibility of the church has actively expanded since Simpson's day and now has the responsibility of pastoral care as well as outreach. This ever-expanding ministry could be one explanation as to why sacrificial giving per capita has declined.[63] The ministry of the Alliance has expanded, which is not always clear even to those in the Alliance. Most in the Alliance feel that missions is still an integral part of the denomination's makeup, and most would see missions as its top priority. Nanfelt states the Alliance has gone from a missionary organization to a missionary church.[64]

The Alliance needs to continue with its vision and passion for missions. This is vital. The Alliance needs to continue to preach Matt 24:14 as its motivation to "bring back the King." Jesus will only return when the gospel has been preached to all people. This can only be done with Spirit-filled believers who are willing to make the sacrifices necessary to see the task completed. Those in the Alliance recognize this truth, and they realize that this vision has to be passed on to every new generation of young believers as well. Walborn states that he sees a sacrificial attitude in some of his students at Nyack. They are ready to make the commitment to see the Great Commission completed.[65] As this mentality continues to be modeled and taught in the Christian and Missionary Alliance churches throughout the United States, the task that Jesus set before his disciples two thousand years ago can be completed. Simpson wrote, "The great call of the Master today is to the evangelization of the nations and when this has been accomplished, there will be no barrier in the way of His immediate return."[66] This is the mandate not only of the Christian and Missionary Alliance, but of all who call themselves Christ's disciples.

A final aspect of Simpson's message that has historically received less acknowledgement in the Alliance (although this trend has been changing recently) is Simpson's urban outreach. Simpson himself decreased his outreach efforts in New York City later in his ministry. One of the reasons for this reduced emphasis was that his move to Nyack, New York, drew him away from the urban center. Another reason was the change in the

---

62. Peter Nanfelt, interview with the author, December 10, 2002.
63. Ibid.
64. Ibid.
65. Ron C. Walborn, interview with the author, February 15, 2003.
66. Simpson, *Names of Jesus*, 91.

area around the Gospel Tabernacle in New York City. The area immediately around the Tabernacle improved socio-economically, which lessened the need for social outreach near the church.

Another reason for a decrease in the Alliance's "outreach to the masses" was the fundamental-modernist controversy in the 1920s that caused social outreach to become almost solely the domain of the more liberal denominations.[67] Although the Alliance never totally abandoned social outreach and continued to emphasize it overseas, during this time of controversy there was less emphasis on social outreach.

In the early 1970s the Alliance began Christian and Missionary Alliance Services that became known as CAMA Services. It is the relief and social outreach arm of overseas ministries. The ministry of CAMA services expanded until it reached the present-day total of thirty-two full-time CAMA Services workers ministering in eight countries. The projects that CAMA Services are involved in include clean water projects in Asia, medical work in Cambodia, and famine work in Africa.[68] This burden for social outreach and welfare is not only seen overseas—it is also being seen more and more in North America. This increase has been slow, but it is improving.

To this end, the Metropolitan District of the Christian and Missionary Alliance, which includes the New York City area, is concentrating on trying to reach the urban area through church planting. This is the same geographic and social landscape that Simpson tried to reach over one hundred years ago. In many respects, the area is similar to what it was in Simpson's day, as it teems with immigrants from all over the world. The Metropolitan District has planted a host of churches in a number of ethnic and cultural settings throughout New York City. Reitz states that the Alliance needs to place an increased emphasis on cities, just as Simpson did.[69] One of the roadblocks to accomplishing this goal is that many of the Christian and Missionary Alliance churches in North America are located in suburbs and rural areas. This makes it difficult for those churches to partner with churches in the city and to stay involved in outreach together.

This, however, is changing too. Suburban and rural churches are beginning to try to reach out to the urban centers of United States cities as

---

67. Daniel J. Evearitt, interview with the author, February 12, 2003.

68. Andria Glidden, CAMA Services/IFAP Assistant to Michael G. Yount, interview with the author, May 13, 2003.

69. George W. Reitz, interview with the author, February 12, 2003.

Appendix

partners. This attempt is being made in the Metropolitan District, where urban church plants share their ministry with suburban churches to develop a partnership between churches.

Both Nyack College and Alliance Theological Seminary have branch campuses in New York City. One of the goals there is to train students to reach the city for Christ. As a result, a variety of students from different cultures and ethnic groups now attend these campuses, where they can pursue a master of divinity degrees in urban studies. This is one way to reach urban areas for Christ, as Simpson did. Urban areas are once again being seen as a mission field, and the Alliance is trying to reach them.

Many Alliance churches are beginning to see the importance of reaching out in social ministries as well. Randall Corbin calls this type of ministry "transformational evangelism," explaining that the idea is that we are to minister to the whole person.[70] This is what Simpson did at the Gospel Tabernacle in New York City. Corbin writes, "The good news is that many of our Alliance ministries are beginning to see the importance of transformational evangelism as a wholistic approach."[71] This includes reaching the whole person, as Christ did.[72] There are a number of Alliance churches that are doing just this. In York, Pennsylvania, the local Alliance church is trying to reach York's African American population with an after-school mentoring and tutoring program. The Fairlawn Community Alliance Church in Cogan, Pennsylvania, has a community food outreach ministering to the needy. The Allegheny Alliance Church in Pittsburgh, Pennsylvania, has a medical clinic.[73] The Alliance church in Salem, Oregon, has seen a number of people come to Christ through its numerous twelve-step programs.[74] Here we find examples for other Alliance churches to follow in their communities as they preach the gospel. These types of outreaches could be used not only for salvation, but to reach the whole person. This is exactly what Simpson did, and it seems many in the Alliance are catching this vision.

Simpson and his message are still impacting the Alliance today. One cannot look at the Alliance without seeing the message of the Fourfold Gospel. The Alliance has not always stressed the different roles of Christ in the Fourfold Gospel equally, especially Christ as our Sanctifier and as

---

70. Corbin, "Reaching the Lost," 1.
71. Ibid., 2.
72. Ibid.
73. Ibid.
74. Ibid.

Healer, but they have attempted to correct that emphasis. The burden for missions is still at the forefront, and it is a priority and that will continue as long as the Alliance keeps the original vision God gave Simpson. As we saw above, the burden for urban outreach seems to be rekindling. Simpson's vision and passion has to be taught and caught by this generation of Alliance members and then passed on to the next generation of Alliance pastors, missionaries, and laity.

Albert Benjamin Simpson, although less written about than his contemporaries, played an important role in the Third Great Awakening. It is possible that as our present-day Alliance catches the heart of Simpson, they may play an important role in the Awakening yet to come.

BIBLIOGRAPHY

Ahlstrom, Sydney E. *A Religious History of the American People.* New Haven: Yale University Press, 1972.
Anderson, Robert M. *Vision of the Disinherited: The Making of American Pentecostalism.* Peabody: Hendrickson, 1992.
Bailey, Keith M., ed. *The Best of A. B. Simpson.* Camp Hill, PA: Christian, 1987.
———. *The Children's Bread.* Harrisburg, PA: Christian, 1977.
Baker, Robert A. *A Summary of Christian History.* Revised by Robert A. Baker. Nashville, TN: Boardman & Holman, 2002.
Banister, Doug. *The Word and Power Church.* Grand Rapids: Zondervan, 1999.
Barabas, Steven. *So Great Salvation.* London: Marshall, Morgan & Scott, 1952.
Bass, Clarence B. *Backgrounds to Dispensationalism.* Grand Rapids: Eerdmans, 1960.
Bebbington, David W. *The Dominance of Evangelicalism.* Vol. 3 of *A History of Evangelicalism.* Downers Grove, IL: InterVarsity, 2005.
Beers, Mark H., et al., eds. *The Merck Manuel of Medical Information.* 2nd ed. Whitehouse Station, NJ: Merck Research Laboratories, 2003.
Blumhofer, Edith L., and Randall Balmer, eds. *Modern Christian Revivals.* Chicago: University of Illinois Press, 1993.
Blumhofer, Edith L. *The Assemblies of God: A Chapter in the Story of American Pentecostalism, Volume 1 to 1941.* Springfield, MO: Gospel, 1989.
———. *Restoring the Faith: The Assemblies of God, Pentecostalism, and American Culture.* Chicago: University of Illinois Press, 1993.
Bounds, E. M. *The Best of E. M. Bounds.* Grand Rapids: Baker, 1981.
Cairns, Earle E. *Christianity Through the Centuries.* Grand Rapids: Zondervan, 1996.
Carpenter, Joel A. *Revive Us Again.* New York: Oxford University Press, 1997.
Carpenter, Joel A., and Wilbert R. Shenk, eds. *Earthen Vessels.* Grand Rapids: Eerdmans, 1990.
Chambers, Oswald. *Biblical Psychology.* Grand Rapids: Discovery House, 1962.
———. *God's Workmanship and He Shall Glorify Me.* Grand Rapids: Discovery, 1997.
Chappell, Paul G. "The Divine Healing Movement in America." PhD diss., Drew University, 1983.
Choy, Frances Leona. *Powerlines.* Camp Hill, PA: Christian, 1990.
Christian and Missionary Alliance Committee on Hymnal Revision. *Hymns of the Christian Life.* Camp Hill, PA: Christian, 1991.
Clouse, Robert G., ed. *The Meaning of the Millennium.* Downers Grove, IL: InterVarsity, 1977.

Bibliography

Cohen, Daniel. *The Spirit of the Lord: Revivalism in America*. New York: Four Winds, 1975.

Conkin, Paul K. *Cane Ridge: America's Pentecost*. Madison: University of Wisconsin Press, 1990.

Corbin, Randall B. "Reaching the Lost: A Wholistic Approach." *Completing Christ's Commission: Christian and Missionary Alliance Presidential Newsletter*, March 2001.

Cully, Paul C. *The Missionary Enterprise*. Wheaton, IL: Evangelical Teacher Training Association, 1976.

Cunningham, Raymond J. "From Holiness to Healing: The Faith Cure in America 1872–1892." *Church History* 43 (1974) 499–513.

Davis, John Jefferson. *The Victory of Christ's Kingdom*. Moscow, ID: Canon, 1996.

Dayton, Donald W. *Discovering an Evangelical Heritage*. New York: Harper & Row, 1976.

———. *Theological Roots of Pentecostalism*. Studies in Evangelism 5. Metuchan, NJ: Scarecrow, 1987.

Dayton, Donald, and Robert K. Johnson, eds. *The Variety of American Evangelization*. Downers Grove, IL: InterVarsity, 1991.

Dieter, Melvin E. *The Holiness Revival of the Nineteenth Century*. Langhorn, MD: Scarecrow, 1996.

Dorn, Jacob H. "The Social Gospel and Socialism: A Comparison of the Thought of Francis Greenwood Peabody, Washington Gladden, and Walter Raushenbusch." In *Church History* 62 (1993) 82–100.

Dorsett, Lyle W. *Passion for Souls*. Chicago: Moody, 1997.

Duenel, Wesley L. *Revival Fire*. Grand Rapids: Zondervan, 1995

Evearitt, Daniel J. *Body and Soul: Evangelism and the Social Concern of A. B. Simpson*. Camp Hill, PA: Christian, 1994.

———. "Negative Jewish Reaction to Protestant Missions and the Jews from 1880s to Recent Days: Will It Ever End?" *Alliance Academic Review* (2001) 57–81.

———. "The Social Gospel vs. Personal Salvation: A Late Nineteenth-century Case Study—Walter Rauschenbusch and A. B. Simpson." *Alliance Academic Review* (1997) 1–18.

———. Interview with the author by telephone, Phillipsburg, NJ, February 12, 2003.

———. Interview with the author, tape recording, Phillipsburg, NJ, March 7, 2003.

———. Interview with the author, tape recording, Phillipsburg, NJ, November 4, 2003.

Fessenden, David E. "Present Truths: The Historical and Contemporary Distinctives of the Christian and Missionary Alliance." *Alliance Academic Review* (1999) 1–32.

———. Interview with the author by telephone, Phillipsburg, NJ, April 9, 2003.

Figgis, J. B. *Keswick from Within*. New York: Garland, 1985.

Foster, Neil K., and David E. Fessenden, eds. *Essays on Premillennialism*. Camp Hill, PA: Christian, 2002.

Foster, Richard J. *Streams of Living Water*. San Francisco: HarperSanFrancisco, 2001.

Gangel, Kenneth. "The Bible College: Past, Present and Future." *Christianity Today* 24 (1980) 34–36.

Gibson, Scott M. *A. J. Gordon*. New York: University Press of America, 2001.

Gilbertson, Richard. *The Baptism of the Holy Spirit*. Camp Hill, PA: Christian, 1993.

Girolimon, Michael Thomas. "A Real Crisis of Blessing: Part I." *Paraclete* 27 (1993) 17–26.

———. "A Real Crisis of Blessing: Part II." *Paraclete* 27 (1993) 1–6.

Glover, Robert Hall. *The Progress of Worldwide Missions*. Revised by J. Herbert Kane. New York: Harper, 1960.

Bibliography

Goddard, Burton L., et al., eds. *The Encyclopedia of Modern Christian Missions*. Camden, NJ: Nelson, 1967.

Gonzalez, Justo L. *The Story of Christianity: Complete in One Volume*. Peabody: Hendrickson, 2001.

Gordon, A. J. *The Ministry of Healing*. Harrisburg, PA: Christian, n.d.

Gundry, Stanley N., ed. *Five Views on Sanctification*. Grand Rapids: Zondervan, 1987.

Hardesty, Nancy A. *Faith Cure: Divine Healing the Holiness and Pentecostal Movement*. Peabody: Hendrickson, 2002.

Hardman, Keith J. "The Return of the Spirit: The Second Great Awakening." *Christian History* 23 (2010) 24–31.

―――. *Seasons of Refreshing: Evangelism and Revivals in America*. Grand Rapids: Baker, 1994.

―――. *The Spiritual Awakeners*. Chicago: Moody, 1983.

―――. "The Time for Prayer: The Third Great Awakening." *Christian History* 23 (1989) 32–34.

Harrell, David H. *All Things Are Possible*. Bloomington: Indiana University Press, 1975.

Hart, D. G., ed. *Reckoning with the Past*. Grand Rapids: Baker, 1995.

Hartzfeld, David F., and Charles Nienkirchen. *Birth of a Vision*. Camp Hill, PA: Christian, 1986.

Haynes, Mark, Sr. Interview with the author, tape recording, Belvidere, NJ, February 17, 2003.

Hoffman, Fred. *Revival Times in America*. Boston: Wilde, 1956.

Hudson, Winthrop S. *American Protestantism*. Chicago History of American Civilization 3. Chicago: University of Chicago, 1961.

Hutchinson, William R. *Errand to the World: American Protestant Thought and Foreign Missions*. Chicago: University of Chicago Press, 1987.

Ironside, H. A. *Holiness, the False and the True*. New York: Loizeaux, n.d.

Jackson, Jeremy C. *No Other Foundation*. Westchester, IL: Cornerstone, 1980.

Jordan, Barry. Interview with the author, tape recording, Phillipsburg, NJ, November 11, 2003.

Kane, J. Herbert. *A Concise History of Christian World Missions*. Grand Rapids: Baker, 1978.

―――. *Wanted: World Christians*. Grand Rapids: Baker, 1986.

Kaiser, Walter C. *Revive Us Again*. Nashville, TN: Boardman & Holman, 1999.

Kelsey, Morton. *Healing and Christianity*. New York: Harper & Row, 1973.

Kid, A. W. Ronald. *Healing Through the Centuries*. Peabody: Hendrickson, 1998.

King, Paul L. "A. B. Simpson and the Modern Faith Movement." *Alliance Academic Review* (1996) 1–22.

―――. "A Critique of Charles Nienkirchen's Book *A. B. Simpson and the Pentecostal Movement*." *Alliance Academic Review* (2000) 101–114.

Knight, George R. *Millennial Fever and the End of the World: A Study of Millerite Adventism*. Boise, ID: Pacific, 1993.

Kraus, Norman C. *Dispensationalism in America*. Richmond, VA: John Knox, 1958.

Lacy, Benjamin Rice, Jr. *Revivals in the Midst of the Years*. Richmond, VA: John Knox, 1943.

Latourette, Kenneth Scott. *Christianity in a Revolutionary Age*. Vol. 3 of *The Nineteenth Century Outside Europe*. Grand Rapids: Zondervan, 1961.

Bibliography

———. *A History of the Expansion of Christianity*. Vol. 5 of *The Great Century: The Americas, Australasia and Africa*. Grand Rapids: Zondervan, 1943.

———. *A History of the Expansion of Christianity*. Vol. 6 of *The Great Century: North Africa and Asia*. Grand Rapids: Zondervan, 1944.

London, H. B., and Neil B. Wiseman. *Pastors at Risk*. Wheaton, IL: Victor, 1993.

Long, Teresa Kathryn. *The Revival of 1857–1858*. New York: Oxford University Press, 1998.

Magnuson, Norris. *Salvation in the Slums*. Metuchen, NJ: Scarecrow, 1977.

Marsden, George M. *Fundamentalism and American Culture*. New York: Oxford University Press, 1980.

———. *Understanding Fundamentalism and Evangelicalism*. Grand Rapids: Eerdmans, 1991.

Marty, Martin, ed. *Fundamentalism and Evangelicalism*. Modern Protestantism and Its World 10. New York: K. G. Saur, 1993.

———. *Missions and Ecumenical Expressions*. Modern American Protestantism and Its World 13. New York: K. G. Saur, 1993.

———. *New and Intense Movements*. Modern Protestantism and Its World 11. New York: K. G. Saur, 1993.

McGee, Gary B. "All for Jesus: The Revival Legacy of A. B. Simpson." *Enrichment* 4 (1999) 82–88.

McGraw, Gerald E. "A. B. Simpson as a Missions Advocate: His Philosophy and Methodology." *Alliance Academic Review* (1995) 1–26.

———. "The Legacy of A. B. Simpson." *International Bulletin* 16 (1992) 69–77.

McLoughlin, William G. Jr. *Modern Revivalism: Charles Grandison Finney to Billy Graham*. New York: Ronald, 1959.

———. *Revivals, Awakenings and Reform*. Chicago: University of Chicago Press, 1978.

Moberg, David O. *The Church as a Social Institution*. Grand Rapids: Baker, 1962.

———. *The Great Reversal*. New York: Lippincott, 1972.

Muncy, W. L. Jr. *A History of Evangelism in the United States*. Kansas City, KS: Central Seminary, 1945.

Nanfelt, Peter. "A Once-In-A-Lifetime Opportunity: President's Report to General Council." Report to General Council of the Christian and Missionary Alliance, Nashville, TN, May 28, 2002.

———. "Preached a Sermon on Sanctification Lately?" *Completing Christ's Commission: The Christian and Missionary Alliance Presidential Newsletter*, January 2004.

———. "Seeking the Wind of God." *Completing Christ's Commission: The Christian and Missionary Alliance Presidential Newsletter*, February 2001.

———. Interview with the author, tape recording, Phillipsburg, NJ, December 10, 2002.

Neil, Stephen. *A History of Christian Missions*. A Pelican History of the Church 6. New York: Penguin, 1964.

Nelson, Randall W. "An Examination of the Exodus from Pastoral Ministry." DMin diss., Gordon-Conwell Seminary, 2003.

Nettleton, Asahel. "Did You Know?" *Christian History* 8 (1988) 30.

Nienkirchen, Charles W. *A. B. Simpson and the Pentecostal Movement*. Peabody: Hendrickson, 1992.

Niklaus, Robert L., et al. *All for Jesus: God at Work in the Christian and Missionary Alliance over One Hundred Years*. Camp Hill, PA: Christian, 1986.

Bibliography

Noll, Mark A. *A History of Christianity in the United States and Canada.* Grand Rapids: Eerdmans, 1992.

Noll, Mark, et al., eds. *Eerdman's Handbook to Christianity in America.* Grand Rapids: Eerdmans, 1983.

Nutt, Rick. "G. Sherwood Eddy and the Attitudes of Protestants in the United States toward Global Mission." *Church History* 66 (1997) 502–21.

Orr, J. Edwin. *The Fervent Prayer.* Chicago: Moody, 1974.

———. *The Light of the Nations.* Devon, UK: Paternoster, 1965.

———. *The Second Evangelical Awakening.* London: Marshall, Morgan & Scott, 1964.

Outler, Albert C., ed. *John Wesley.* New York: Oxford University Press, 1964.

Pardington, G. P. *Twenty-Five Wonderful Years 1889–1914: A Popular Sketch of the Christian and Missionary Alliance.* New York: Garland, 1984.

Pollack, John C. *D. L. Moody: Moody without Sankey.* Ross-Shire, UK: Christian Focus, 1997.

———. *The Keswick Story.* London: Hodder & Stoughton, 1964.

Prosser, Peter E. *Dispensationalist Eschatology and Its Influence on American and British Religious Movements.* Texts and Studies in Religion 82. Lewiston, NY: Edwin Miller, 1999.

Reiter, Richard R., et al. *The Rapture: Pre-, Mid-, or Post-Tribulational.* Grand Rapids: Zondervan, 1984.

Reitz, George W. "A. B. Simpson, Urban Evangelist." *Urban Mission* 8 (1991) 19–26.

———. Interview with the author, tape recording, Phillipsburg, NJ, February 12, 2003.

Rewluk, George, and Mark A. Noll, eds. *Amazing Grace.* Buffalo: McGill-Queens University Press, 1994.

Riss, Richard M. *A Survey of Twentieth-century Revival Movement in North America.* Peabody: Hendrickson, 1988.

Roberts, Liardon. *God's Generals—Why They Succeeded and Why Some Failed.* Tulsa, OK: Albury, 1996.

Sandeen, Ernest R. *The Roots of Fundamentalism.* Chicago: University of Chicago Press, 1970.

Salter, Darius. *American Evangelism: Its Theology and Practice.* Grand Rapids: Baker, 1996.

Scharpff, Paulus. *History of Evangelism.* Translated by Helga Bender Henry. Grand Rapids: Eerdmans, 1966.

Schneider, A. Gregory. "A Conflict of Associations: The National Camp Meeting Association for the Promotion of Holiness Versus the Methodist Episcopal Church." *Church History* 66 (1997) 268–83.

Shattuck, Gardiner H., Jr. "Revivals in the Camp." *Christian History* 33 (1992) 28–31.

Shelly, Bruce L. *Church History in Plain Language.* Nashville, TN: Nelson, 1995.

Simpson, A. B. *A Larger Christian Life.* New York: Christian Alliance Publishing, 1890.

———. "A Larger Christian Life." *New Man* 8 (July-August 2001) 54–55.

———. *Christ in You.* Camp Hill, PA: Christian, 1997.

———. *The Christ in the Bible Commentary: The Kings and Prophets, Psalms, Isaiah.* Vol. 3 of *Christ in the Bible.* Camp Hill, PA: Christian, 1993.

———. *The Cross of Christ.* Harrisburg, PA: Christian, 1969.

———. *The Four-Fold Gospel.* Harrisburg, PA: Christian, n.d.

———. *The Gospel of Healing.* Camp Hill, PA: Christian, 1994.

———. "Himself—A Timeless Testimony." *Fundamentalist Journal* 4 (1985) 44–46.

———. *The Holy Spirit.* 2 vols. Harrisburg, PA: Christian, n.d.

———. "How I Was Led to Believe in Premilennialism." *Communicate* 10 (2000) 6.
———. *In Step with the Spirit*. Camp Hill, PA: Christian, 1998.
———. *The Life of Prayer*. Harrisburg, PA: Christian, 1979.
———. *The Lord of the Body*. Camp Hill, PA: Christian, 1996.
———. *Missionary Messages*. Camp Hill, PA: Christian, 2001.
———. *The Names of Jesus*. Harrisburg, PA: Christian, 1967.
———. *Serving the King: Doing Ministry in Partnership with God*. Camp Hill, PA: Christian, 1995.
———. *Walking in Love*. Camp Hill, PA: Christian, 1995.
———. *When the Comforter Came*. Camp Hill, PA: Christian, 1991.
———. *Wholly Sanctified*. Harrisburg, PA: Christian, 1982.
Sizer, Sandra S. *Gospel Hymns and Social Religion*. Philadelphia: Temple University Press, 1978.
———. "Politics and a Political Religion: The Great Urban Revivals of the Late Nineteenth Century." *Church History* 48 (1979) 81–98.
Smith, Timothy L. *Revivalism and Social Reform*. Baltimore: John Hopkins University Press, 1980.
Soper, John. Interview with the author, tape recording, Ocean Grove, NJ, September 11, 2002.
Steer, Roger. "Pushing Inward." *Christian History* 52 (1996) 10–18.
Stoesz, Samuel J. *Sanctification: An Alliance Distinctive*. Camp Hill, PA: Christian, 1992.
———. *Understanding My Church*. Camp Hill, PA: Christian, 1983.
Sweet, William Warren. *Revivalism in America*. New York: Scribner, 1945.
Synan, Vinson. *The Century of the Holy Spirit*. Nashville, TN: Nelson, 2001.
———. *In the Latter Days*. Ann Arbor, MI: Servant, 1984.
———. *The Holiness-Pentecostal Movement in the United States*. Grand Rapids: Eerdmans, 1971.
———. *The Holiness-Pentecostal Tradition: Charismatic Movements in the 20th Century*. Grand Rapids: Eerdmans, 1997.
Tait, Edwin W. "The Cleansing Wave." *Christian History and Biography* 82 (2004) 22–25.
Taylor, William D., ed. *Global Missiology for the 21st Century*. Grand Rapids: Baker Academic, 2000.
Terry, John M. *Evangelism: A Concise History*. Nashville, TN: Boardman & Holman, 1994.
Towns, Elmer, and Douglas Porter. *The Ten Greatest Revivals Ever*. Ann Arbor, MI: Servant, 2000.
Thompson, A. E. *A. B. Simpson: His Life and Work*. Harrisburg, PA: Christian, 1960.
Tozer, A. W. *Wingspread*. Camp Hill, PA: Christian, 1943.
Travis, Drake. *Christ Our Healer Today*. Camp Hill, PA: Christian, 1996.
Tucker, Ruth A. *From Jerusalem to Irian Jaya*. Grand Rapids: Zondervan, 1983.
Van Hoogen, Joel. "Premillennialism and the Alliance Distinctives." *Alliance Academic Review* (1998) 41–70.
Wacker, Grant. *Heaven Below*. Cambridge: Harvard University Press, 2001.
———. "The Holy Spirit and the Spirit of the Age in American Protestantism, 1880–1910." *The Journal of American History* 72 (1985) 45–62.
Wagner, C. Peter. *On the Crest of the Wave*. Ventura, CA: Regal, 1983.
Walborn, Ron C. Interview with the author, tape recording, Belvidere, NJ, February 15, 2003.

Bibliography

Walls, Andrew F. *The Missionary Movement in Christianity History*. Maryknoll, NY: Orbis, 1996.

Warren, Rick. *The Purpose Driven Church*. Grand Rapids: Zondervan, 1995.

Weber, Timothy P. *Living in the Shadow of the Second Coming*. Grand Rapids: Zondervan, 1983.

Weisberger, Bernard A. *They Gathered at the River*. Chicago: Quadrangle, 1958.

Wesley, John. *The Letters of John Wesley*. Edited by John Telford. Vol. 7. London: Epworth, 1931.

———. *The Works of John Wesley*. Edited by Thomas Jackson. Vol. 12. Grand Rapids: Zondervan, 1959.

White, Charles E. "Holiness Fire-Starter." *Christian History and Biography* 82 (2004) 16–21.

Wiggins, Donald A. "Captured by God's Vision." *Completing Christ's Commission: The Christian and Missionary Alliance Presidential Newsletter*, July 2002.

Wilkinson, Bruce. *Pastor to Pastor*. Vol. 39. Audiotape of lectures by Jerry Bridges, R. C. Sproul, Vernon Grounds, and Bruce Wilkinson with H. B. London. Colorado Springs, CO: Focus on the Family, 1999.

Winehouse, Irwin. *The Assemblies of God: A Popular Survey*. New York: Vantage, 1959.

Wood, Rick, and Robert Takenaga. "Bring Back the King." *Mission Frontier*, July 1, 1994. http://www.missionfrontiers.org/issue/article/bring-back-the-king.

Zulauf, Larry. Interview with the author, tape recording, Phillipsburg, NJ, February 28, 2003.

INDEX

A.B. Simpson: His Life and Work
  (Thompson), xiii
Adopt-A-People program, 158
Adventist movement, 109–10n17
Africa Inland Mission, 10, 143, 168
Africa, missionary outreach to, 2
African Americans
  in Christian and Missionary Alliance, 137
  Simpson involvement with, 136–37
Ahlstrom, Sydney E., *A Religious History of the American People*, 27
Alexander, Charles M., 26–27, 61
Allegheny Alliance Church (Pittsburgh, Pennsylvania), 189
Alliance Life, 149
Alliance Theological Seminary, 189
Alliance Weekly, 136
altar theology, 12
American Board of Commissioners for Foreign Missions, 8
amillennialism, 107
  and Constantine, 108
  Simpson objection to, 115
Anderson, Robert, 68, 72–73
"anxious seat," 5
Apostolic Faith (revival newspaper), 84
Argentina, Alliance missionaries in, 145
Asbury, Francis, 2
  on sanctification, 67–68
Asia, missionary outreach to, 2
Assemblies of God, 87, 90
  missionaries, 89–90
Association of Vineyard Churches, 159

Augustine, 108
authority of Bible, 175
Azusa Street Revival, 84–85

Bailey, Keith, 93–94
Bakker, Jim, 164
Balfour Declaration, 116
Banister, Doug, 160–61
Baptism of the Holy Spirit, 13, 70, 81
  gift of tongues and, 86
  and Moody, 14
Baptist church
  Board of Missions, 8–9
  sanctification in, 13
Barnett, Amelia, 134
Baur, F.C., 2
Bebbington, David, 19
Beecher, Lyman, 4
belief in Jesus Christ, 44
"The Believers' Meetings for Bible Study," 113
Berachah Home for Healing, 38, 102, 134
Berachah Orphanage, 134
Bethel Bible College, 83
Bible
  19th century conflict over, 2, 15
  authority and inerrancy, 175
  challenges by scholars, 16–17
  as literal and historically accurate, 113
  miracles in, 21
  as primary for Simpson, 41
  Isaiah 53:4–5, 96, 105
  Matthew 8:17, 96, 105

Index

Bible *(continued)*
  Matthew 24:14, 100, 116, 117, 119, 156, 167, 169, 187
  Matthew 28:19-20, 51
  Luke 4:18, 37
  Acts 1:8, 51, 129
  Romans 8:11, 101-2
  Romans 12:1, 181
  James 5:14-15, 94-95, 105
  James 5:14-16, 100
  James 5:17, 180
  1 John 3:3, 116
  1 John 3:12, 118
Bible college movement, 14, 146-47
Bible Institute of Los Angeles, Torrey as Dean, 61
Bingham, Roland, 143
Blackstone, W.E., *Jesus Is Coming*, 113
Bliss, Phillip P., 36, 46, 122
Blumhardt, Johann, 93, 102
Blumhofer, Edith, 78, 82-83
  views on pentecostal revival, 89
Boardman, William, 70, 82, 92
  The Great Physician, 95
  in healing movement, 92
  The Higher Christian Life, 13, 45, 69
Boese, Harry, 158
Booth, Evangeline, 18
Booth, William, 3, 18
  In Darkest England and the Way Out, 18
Bosworth, F.F., 87
Bounds, E.M., 165
Boxer Rebellion, 145
Boyer, Paul, on dispensationalism, 112-13
Brainerd, David, 7
Breeze, Phineas F., 15
Bridges, Jerry, 165
Broadway Tabernacle Church, 5
Brooklyn, Moody campaign in, 59
Brooks, James H., 113, 114
Brooks, J.H., 112
Brumback, Carl, 90
Buckley, James, criticism of divine healing, 99-100
Bundy, David, 78
Burma, 8

Businessman's Prayer Revival, 167

Cairns, Earle, 7
Caledonia Hall (New York), 38
CAMA Services, 188
Cane Ridge meetinghouse (Kentucky), 23
Carey, William, 2
  An Enquiry into the Obligation of Christians . . ., 7
  in India, 8
Carpenter, Joel, 31, 55, 63
Century Magazine, 99
Chalmers, Thomas, 19
Chambers, Oswald, 173
  on pentecostal movement, 89
Chapman, Walter, and premillennialism, 108
Chapman, Wilbur, 26, 28, 60, 74, 131
  Moody's impact on, 62
Chappell, Paul, 92, 97, 103, 106
  on Simpson's healing message, 104
charismatic leaders, Simpson's influence on, 158-60
Chestnut Hill Presbyterian Church, 54
Chestnut Street Presbyterian Church, ix, 36, 44-45, 121, 126
Chile, Alliance missionaries in, 145
China
  Alliance missionaries in, 145
  Taylor in, 2
China Inland Mission, 9, 143
Chinese Evangelization Society, 9
Christ, 169
  as Coming King, 50-51, 114-19, 156-58, 177, 180
  faith in, 76
  as Healer, 46-49, 96, 97, 104, 176-77, 180, 182-83
  Moody on personal relationship, 57
  roles in believer's life, 40-41
  as Sanctifier, 74, 79, 163, 165, 176, 180-82
  as Savior, 55, 175, 180
  surrendering control to, 45
Christian Alliance, 38-39
Christian and Missionary Alliance, xiii, 10, 14, 27, 64, 141-42, 166, 188

Index

in 21st century, 186–90
African Americans in, 137
beginnings, 38–40, 131
charismatic vs. evangelical perspectives, 161–62
and divine healing, 105
evangelization as priority, 150–51
and gift of tongues, 87–88
impact of Simpson, 173–90
incorporation papers, 30–31
Margaret Simpson as financial secretary, 128
message, 174
Metropolitan District, 137, 177–78
church planting, 188
pentecostal movement impact, 85–86
primary message of, 55
as unifier, 160–61
The Christian and Missionary Alliance Weekly, 133
Christian Catholic Church, 97
Christian millennialism, 107
Christian perfection, 11
Christianity
19th century conflict over Bible, 2
Moody on, 57
Christianity and Social Crisis (Rauschenbusch), 21
Christianity, the Social Order (Rauschbusch), 21
Christians in Great Britain, concern for poor, 17–18
The Christian's Secret of a Happy Life (Whitehall), 13
chronic fatigue syndrome, 96n19
church
early church fathers as premillennial, 108
growth 1800 to 1914, 1
intellectual threats, 15–17
missionary development of self-supporting, 151–52
Simpson on, x
Church of God, 15
Church of the Nazarene, 15
church planting, 188
circuit riders, Methodist, 2

City of Refuge, 132–33
Civil War in U.S., revival impact on armies, 25
Clouse, Robert, 108
Cohen, Daniel, 27–28
The Spirit of the Lord; Revivalism in America, 28
college students, as foreign missionaries, 10
colonies, missionaries in, 8–9
Columbia Bible College, 14
Columbia International University, 168
Columbian Exposition, evangelical outreach, 60
Commodianus, 108
Completing Christ's Commission, 176
Condit, John, 151
Congo, 145, 151
Congregational church, sanctification in, 13
Conkin, Paul K., 23
Constantine, and amillennialsm, 108
contemporary church
inspiration of Simpson, 155
missions in, 185
necessity of holiness, 163–66
need for preaching on Holy Spirit, 164–65
Simpson's writings and, 154–55
conventions
Gospel Tabernacle, 80
International Convention on Holiness and Divine Healing, 42–43, 75, 95
Keswick Convention (Great Britain, 1875), 71
missionary, 144–45
in North America, 147–48
Simpson and, 79–81
Summer Faith Convention, 95
Tozer on, 104
conversion, 14
joy of, 7
Methodist Church and, 12
struggle over, 54
Corbin, Randall, 189
Council of Ephesus, 108
Cravett, Joshua, 101

Index

Creation, vs. evolution, 16
Cullis, Charles, 48, 92, 94, 95, 102, 106, 167
Culpepper, J.B., 78
Cunningham, Ray, 92, 94, 101

Dabney, Robert L., 109
Dahms, John, 133
Dallas Theological Seminary, 14
Darby, John Nelson, 111, 112
Darwin, Charles, *On the Origin of the Species*, 2–3, 15
Davis, John Jefferson, 109
Dayton, Donald, 130–31
deeper life message, 72, 180, 181
Dieter, Melvin, 67, 69, 71–72
dispensationalism, 111–12, 114
divine healing, 91, 96, 167, 177. *See also* healing movement
   decline in emphasis, 184
   Simpson and, 47, 48–50, 98, 100
Dixon, A.C., 55–56, 60
Door of Hope ministries, 132, 135
Dorsett, Lyle, 63–64, 101, 112
Dowie, John Alexander, 83, 97–98
Dowkonut, George, 134–35
Draper, Ken, 64, 122–23, 147, 149–50
Dwight, Timothy, 23

Earle, A.B., 70
East India Company, 8
Ecce Venit: Behold He Cometh (Gordon), 51
Ecuador, Alliance missionaries in, 145
Eddy, Sherwood, 11
Edwards, Jonathan, 7, 24, 109
Eleventh Street Mission, 134
An Enquiry into the Obligation of Christians. . . (Carey), 7
Enrichment (periodical), 154–55
Erdman, W.J., 51
Evangelical Alliance, 35
The Evangelical Alliance Mission (TEAM), 10, 143, 168
evangelical groups
  public invitation at meetings, 5
  Simpson's popularity, 160
  social outreach, 130–31

Evangelical Missionary Alliance, 39
evangelism
  before Christ's return, 117
  development, 26
  with European immigrants in NY, 135
  Simpson and, 54–65
  transformational, 189
evangelists, 3–7
Evearitt, Daniel, 95, 131, 134, 139, 168, 179, 182, 183
  on mission emphasis, 185
evidence doctrine, 160
  Simpson opposition to, 86–87
evolution theory, 3, 15–16
experience, 42

Fairlawn Community Alliance Church (Cogan, Pennsylvania), 189
Faith Cure (Haresty), 167
faith, in Jesus Christ, 76
"Faith Missions," 9–10
Faith Promise, 186
Faith Rest Cottage (Buffalo), 132
Female Missionary Society of the Western District, 4
filling by Holy Spirit, 181
  Moody, Dwight Lyman (D.L.), 58, 121
financial panic (1857), 25
Finney, Charles, 1, 3–7, 12, 66
  on sanctification, 68
  in Second Great Awakening, 24
First Great Awakening
  in Great Britain, 2
  missions movement and, 7
Focus on the Family, 164
For God and the People: Prayers of the Social Awakening (Rauschenbusch), 21
The Four-Fold Gospel (Simpson), xiii, 30–31, 74, 114, 156, 165
Fourfold Gospel, 52, 55, 166, 174
  basics, 180–86
  Christian Alliance and, 39
  Nanfelt on need to preach, 162
  pentecostal leaders' adoption, 89
  Simpson and, 40–43, 178

Index

Franson, William, 143
Frost, Henry, 40
fundamental-modernist controversy (1920s), 188
The Fundamentalist Journal, 154–55
fundamentalists, Simpson's popularity with, 160
The Fundamentals, 17
Funk, Albert, 135

Geddie, John, 32, 124
Gee, Donald, 89
German theologians, 16
Gilbertson, Richard, 81
Gladden, Washington, 3
Gladstone, William, 20
  Moody meeting with, 6
Glover, Robert, 133, 145
God, as Creator, 16
Goforth, Jonathan, 30
Gordon, A.J., 7, 13, 55–56, 60, 74, 80, 104, 112, 114, 117, 131, 141, 156
  contribution to Simpson's periodicals, 82
  Ecce Venit: Behold He Cometh, 51
  in healing movement, 92
  and higher life, 70
  The Ministry of Healing, 102
  and premillennialism, 108
Gordon College, 14
Gordon-Conwell Theological Seminary, xiii–xiv
The Gospel in All Lands (periodical), 148–49
The Gospel Mystery of Sanctification (Marshall), 34, 44
The Gospel of Healing (Simpson), 96, 102, 159
Gospel Tabernacle (New York), ix, 38, 54, 128, 129, 140
  conventions, 80
  evangelistic outreach from, 152
  Friday afternoon healing, 100–101, 182
  leaders, 132
  rescue missions, 133–34
  urban evangellism, 118
grace, second work of, 11–12

Graf, Jonathan I., 156
Graham, Billly, 1, 56
Gray, James M., 80, 116
Great Awakening. *See* First Great Awakening; Second Great Awakening; Third Great Awakening
Great Britain
  Christians in, concern for poor, 17–18
  industrialization, 17
  revival, 2
"Great Century of the Church," 1
  chronology of, xix
Great Commission, 117, 157, 177, 187
  correlation with Christ's second coming, 51
The Great Physician (Boardman), 95
Guiness, Mrs. H. Grantham, 99
Guinness, H. Grattan, ix

Hadley, S.H., 131
Hardman, Keith, xiv, 24, 68
Haresty, Nancy A., *Faith Cure*, 167
Hatch, Nathan, 56
Havner, Vance, 61–62
Haynes, Mark, 181, 185, 186
healing home, 93
healing movement
  Simpson's influence, 92–106
  in Third Great Awakening, 92
Hell's Kitchen, Second German Baptist Church, 129
heroes, ix
"Higher Christian Life," 14
The Higher Christian Life (Boardman), 13, 45, 69
higher life, 70
"Himself" (sermon by Simpson), 75–77, 154
Hinn, Benny, 159
Hippolytus, 108
Hodge, A.A., 109
Hodge, Charles, 109
Hoffman, Fred, 59, 60
holiness
  necessity in contemporary church, 163–66
  pastor-parishioner pursuit of, 165

Index

holiness *(continued)*
  Simpson's promotion of, 79–82
  Wesleys and, 2
holiness movement, 11–15, 18, 66–91
  and healing, 92
  and Methodist Church, 14–15, 66–68
  missions link to, 81
  Simpson and, 77
  and social reform, 19
  Taylor and, 10
  in Third Great Awakening, 91
Holiness, the False and the True (Ironside), 88–89
Holy Ghost and Us Church, 83
Holy Spirit, 46, 58, 71. *See also* Baptism of the Holy Spirit
  Moody's filling by, 58, 121
  outpouring of, 55
  role in Awakening, 73
  surrendering control to, 13
  Third Great Awakening and, 73
The Holy Spirit (Simpson), 42, 165
The Holy Spirit: The New Testament (Simpson), 79
The Holy Spirit: The Old Testament (Simpson), 79
Hutchinson, W.R., 150
Huxley, Thomas, 16

immigrants, Thirteenth Street church refusal to welcome, 127
immigration, to U.S., 3
In His Steps (Sheldon), 20, 21
India
  Alliance missionaries in, 134
  Carey in, 2
  famines, 135
Indochina, Alliance missionaries in, 145–46
Indonesia, 178
  Christ the Healer in, 184
industrial missions, 135
Industrial Revolution, 3
Industrial School for Girls (Buffalo, NY), 135
inerrancy of Bible, 175
Inland South American Mission, 10

innate sin, 13
Inskeep, John, 15
International Convention on Holiness and Divine Healing, 42–43, 75, 95
International Missionary Alliance, 39
Internet, Simpson's popularity on, 155
Inwood, Charles, 80
Irenaeus, 108
Ironside, Harry, *Holiness, the False and the True*, 88–89

Jerusalem, 116
  Alliance church in, 145
Jesus. *See* Christ
Jesus Is Coming (Blackstone), 113
Jones, Sam, 62
Jordan, Barry, 178, 181
Judd, Carrie, 104
Judd-Montgomery, Carrie, 132
  Triumphs of Truth, 133
Judson, Adoniram, 8–9
Judson, Ann, 8–9
justice, 20
Justin Martyr, 108

Kaiser, Walter, xiv
Kane, J. Herbert, 141
Kansas Mission to the Soudan (Sudan), 99
Kerr, D.W., 87
Keswick Convention (Great Britain, 1875), 71
Keswick movement, 13, 14, 71–72
  Wesleyan-Holiness movement argument against, 78
Kimball, Edward, 57
King, Louis L., on Alliance's missionary work, 144
Klassen, Jacob, 146, 149
Knight, George, *Millennial Fever and the End of the World*, 109–10n17
Knox College (Toronto), ix, 34
Knox Presbyterian Church, ix
  Simpson at, 121
Ku Klux Klan, Parham and, 85

labor rights, 20
Lactertius, 108

Index

Lanphier, Jeremiah, 25
A Larger Christian Life (Simpson), xiii, 79, 165
Latourette, Kenneth Scott, 1, 6, 145
Layman's Movement, 140
laypersons
  in Faith Missions, 9
  as missionaries, 146
liberalism
  negative impact, 10
  opposition to, 113
The Life of Prayer (Simpson), 30
Livingston, David, 8
Lockyear, Herbert, 99
London, H.B., 164
Long, Kathryn, *The Revival of 1857–1859*, 167
lost, Simpson's burden for reaching, 54, 143
Louisville, Kentucky
  division after Civil War, 36
  impact of conversions, 46
Love-Joy Missions Institute, 136
Luther, Martin, 44, 93

MacArthur, William, 41
Magdalene Home for Girls, 132
Magnuson, Norris, 98, 103, 130, 131
  on Simpson's involvement in temperance movement, 138
Mahan, Asa, 11–12, 66
  on sanctification, 68
Marsden, George M., 78, 113
Marshall, Walter, *The Gospel Mystery of Sanctification*, 34, 44
Martyn, Henry, 7, 8
Maurice, F.D., 19
McGee, Gary, 155
McGraw, Gerald, 126, 146, 148, 152
McLoughlin, William, 23
  Modern Revivalism, 27
  Revivals, Awakenings and Religion, 27
McNabb Street Wesleyan Methodist Church (Hamilton, Ontario), 25
medical care, 184
medical establishment, Dowie attack on, 97

Merritt, Stephen, 82
Methodist Church
  founding, 2
  and holiness movement, 14–15, 66–68
  and sanctification, 11, 12
Methodius, 108
Meyer, F.B., 7, 29, 72, 77, 80, 131
  and higher life, 70
midtribulationists, 111
Millennial Fever and the End of the World (Knight), 109–10n17
Miller, William, 109–10n17
The Ministry of Healing (Gordon), 102–3
Mission Frontiers, 157
missionaries
  in the Congo, 151
  deaths, 144, 145
  training local, 149–50
  westernization by, 150
missionary conventions, 144–45
  in North America, 147–48
missionary journal, by Simpson, 125, 126
Missionary Messages (Simpson), 51–52, 144
missionary movement, in U.S., 140
missionary outreach, 2
  Simpson on, 117
missionary responsibility, and second coming of Christ, 51
Missionary Training Institute, 118, 139, 142
missions
  in contemporary church, 185
  Simpson link to holiness, 81
  Simpson's interest in, 124–26
Mitchell, J.M., 34
Moberg, David, 138
Modern Revivalism (McLoughlin), 27
modernism, 17
  negative impact, 10
Moffat, Robert, in South Africa, 8
Monod, Theodore, 72
Moody Bible Institute, 61

Index

Moody, Dwight Lyman (D.L.), 1–2, 3, 24, 26, 72, 73–74, 80, 131, 141, 156, 167
   and Baptism of the Holy Spirit, 14
   conversion, 57
   and dispensationalism in U.S., 112
   evangelistic meetings in New York City, 63
   filling by Holy Spirit, 58
   in Great Britain, 58
   in healing movement, 92
   and higher life, 70
   influence, and Third Great Awakening, 28
   as layman, 5
   lieutenants, 60–63
   Northfield Bible Conferences, 80
   and premillennialsm, 108
   Second Coming of Christ, 112
   theology of three Rs, 57–58
   in U.S., 6–7
Moody Evangelistic Association, Christian Worker's Conference, 45
Moravian Church, 141–42
Morgan, G. Cambell, 88
Morrison, Robert, in China, 8
Mott, John, 10, 156
Moule, Handley, 72
Mount Kearsarge, Simpson hike, 49
Mueller, George, 112
Muncy, W.L. Jr., 61
Murray, Andrew, 72, 80, 104, 131
   in healing movement, 92

Nanfelt, Peter, 157, 162, 174, 175, 177, 187
Nardi, Michele, 136
National Camp-Meeting Association for the Promotion of Christian Holiness, 15
National Camp Meeting Association for the Promotion of Holiness, 73
Neil, Stephen, 146
Nelson, Randall, 164
nervous breakdown, of Simpson, 44
Nettleton, Asahel, 1, 3
   constrained approach, 4
New Man (periodical), 152
"New Methods," Finney introduction of, 4–5
New York City
   evangelism with European immigrants, 135
   evangelistic meetings, 63
   health ministries, 134
   Simpson in, 64, 133
New York Gospel Tabernacle, ix, 38
New York Missionary Training College, 38
New York Stock Market, crash in 1857, 25
New York Times, on Simpson's missionary impact, 141
Niagara Bible Conference, 113–14
Niebuhr, Reinhold, 11
Nienkirchen, Charles, 86, 89, 90
Noll, Mark, 19, 140
North Dutch Reformed Church (New York City), 25
Northfield Bible Conferences, 7, 10
"Not I, But Christ" (hymn), 170–71
Nyack College, 14, 38, 178, 189
Nyack, New York, Missionary Training Institute, 89–90, 139

Oberlin College
   Finney at, 5
   and holiness movement, 66
Ohio, Alliance work in, 136–37
Old Orchard, Maine
   Simpson vacation in, 47–48
   summer conferences, 80, 95
On the Origin of the Species (Darwin), 2–3, 15
Orr, J. Edwin, 24, 25–26, 28, 55, 69, 142, 167
   on Christian and Missionary Alliance, 31
outcasts in NY, Simpson's concern for, 129–30
overpopulation, in urban areas, 3
Ozman, Agnes N., 83–84

Page, Kirby, 11
Palestine, return of Jews, 116
Palmer, Phoebe, 12, 24, 66, 77, 80, 167

Index

Palmer, Walter, 24, 66
Papias, 108
Pardington, George, 55, 64, 115–16, 122, 123, 130
Parham, Charles Fox, 83
  and Ku Klux Klan, 85
pastor-parishioner pursuit of holiness, 165
Pennsylvania, Alliance work in, 136–37
pentecostal movement, 13, 105
  evangelist leader views, 88
  leaders vs. Simpson, 86
  Simpson's influence, 82–91, 158–60
perfectionism, 66. *See also* holiness movement
Personal Holiness in Times of Temptation, 164
Phillipsburg Alliance Church, 183
Pierson, A.J., 55–56
Pierson, Arthur T., 13, 29, 51, 72, 80, 82, 89, 104, 116, 117, 131, 141, 156, 167
  in healing movement, 92
  and premillennialsm, 108
Pilgrim Holiness Church, 15
Plymouth Brethren movement, 111
poor, British Christians concern for, 17–18
Porter, Douglas, 5
postmillennialism, 107
  in early 19c., 109
  Simpson objection to, 115
  view of Christ's second coming, 50–51
  Whitley introduction of, 109
posttribulationists, 111
Power Evangelism (Wimber), 159
Power Healing (Wimber), 159
Pray Magazine, 156
prayer meetings, 5
preaching gospel, before Christ's return, 117–18
premillennialism, 50–51, 107–19
  division over, 114
  growth, 108
Presbyterian Church
  in Canada, ix
  in London, Ontario, 34

sanctification in, 13
pretribulationists, 111
Promise Keepers, 164
Protestant churches
  changes in NY, 129
  missionary movement, 7
Pullis, Joseph, 138
Pyles, Franklin, 117

racial separation, and pentecostal churches, 85
Rader, Paul, 62
rapture, 111
  Simpson's belief in, 116
Rauschenbusch, Walter, 3, 20, 21
  A Theology for a Social Gospel, 129
Reiter, Richard, 114
Reitz, George, 128, 129, 136, 139, 156–57, 165, 177, 178, 179, 188
  on mission emphasis, 185
A Religious History of the American People (Ahlstrom), 27
religious knowledge, Simpson on, 43
Rescue Day, 132
Revell, Fleming, 112
The Revival of 1857–1859 (Long), 167
revivals, xiv
  and holiness, 68
  in Louisville, Kentucky, 122
  in Second Great Awakening, 24
Revivals, Awakenings and Religion (McLoughlin), 27
Rhoads, Louise, 184
Richards, E.J., 128
Riss, Richard, 67, 85
Ritsel, Albrecht, 19
Robert, Dana, 117
Roberts, Evan, 26
Rochester Seminary, 21
Roman Catholic Church
  amillennialism in, 108
  missions emphasis, 7
The Roots of Fundamentalism (Sandeen), 28

Salem, Oregon, Alliance church in, 189
Salvation Army, 3, 18
  in U.S., 18

Index

sanctification, 7, 163, 176
  Boardman interpretation of, 69
  Christ as Coming King and, 52
  differences in views, 77–78
  and Methodist Church, 12
  non-Wesleyan view, 13
  return of Christ and, 116
  Wesleyan-Holiness view of, 73
  Wesleyan-Holiness view vs. higher life, 70
  Wesleys and, 2, 11
Sandeen, Ernest, 113
  The Roots of Fundamentalism, 28
Sanford, Frank, Holy Ghost and Us Church, 83
Sankey, Ira, 1–2, 72
  in Great Britain, 6, 58
Saratoga Springs, music, 47
Sawin, John, 39–40, 51, 75, 101, 105, 125
Scandinavian Alliance Mission, 10
Scharpff, Paulus, 59
Scharpft, Paulus, 24
Schneider, Gregory, 11
Scofield, C.I., 29, 80, 111, 113, 116, 160
  Scofield Reference Bible, 73
Scott, Peter Cameron, 143
Scripture. *See* Bible
Seaman's Christian Association, 132
Second Berachah Mission, 134
second coming of Christ, 50–51, 107, 177
  and Great Commission, 51
  historical events before, 116
  Simpson on, 117
Second Coming of Christ (Moody), 112
Second German Baptist Church, 129
Second Great Awakening, 3, 23
  societies founded, 8
"second work of grace," 11–12, 14
Senft, Frederic, 42
Seymour, William J., 84, 87
Shaw, Edward, 29–30
Shedd, W.G.T., 109
Sheldon, Charles, *In His Steps*, 20, 21
Shelly, Bruce, 16, 20
Simpson, Albert Benjamin (A.B.), ix, 7, 10, 13, 60, 74, 117, 141

belief in pretribulation rapture, 116
birth, ix
chronology of life and ministry, xv–xvii
concern for souls, 130
conflict with church leaders, 37, 54, 123–24
conversion, 44
crises, 43–53
  nervous breakdown, 44
criticism of, 99
decline in social conerns, 139–40
Dowie and, 98
evangelism, 63–65
and Fourfold Gospel, 40–43
healing, 46, 95–96
and higher life, 70
"Himself" (sermon), 75–77
on Holy Spirit, 180
illness in teen years, 34
impact, 166–71
  on charismatic and pentecostal leaders, 158–60
  on Christian and Missionary Alliance, 173–90
Knox College graduation, 35
life, 32–37
Missionary Messages, 144
on need for mission to "regions beyond," 143–44
neglect of, 27–29
reason for, 31–32
in New York City, 63–64
passion and vision, 175
  for missions, 150–51
pentecostal adoption of Simpson hymns, 90
vs. pentecostal leaders, 86
permission to pursue ministry, 33
popularity of, 29–31
prayer requests to, 101
as premillenialist, 115
religious family of, 33
and sanctification, 13, 36, 74
on Torrey, 74
vision of lost of world, 124–25
Simpson, Albert Benjamin (A.B.), writings

208

Index

A Cloud of Witnesses, 103
   continued publication, 155–56
The Discovery of Divine Healing, 103
The Four-Fold Gospel, xiii, 30–31, 52, 74, 96, 114, 156, 165
Friday Meeting Talks, 103
The Gospel of Healing, 96, 102, 103, 159
   on holiness, 81
The Holy Spirit, 42, 165
The Holy Spirit: The New Testament, 79
The Holy Spirit: The Old Testament, 79
Inquiries and Answers Concerning Divine Healing, 103
A Larger Christian Life, xiii, 79, 165
The Life of Prayer, 30
Missionary Messages, 51–52
When the Comforter Came, 165
Wholly Sanctified, 75, 79, 165
The Word, the Work, and the World, 30, 38, 100, 102
Simpson, Howard, 34
Simpson, Margaret, 125, 127
   diphtheria when 3-year-old, 49
sin, innate, 13
slums, suffering in, 130
Smith, Eugene, 148
Smith, Hannah Whitehall, 71
Smith, Robert Pearsall, 71
Smith, Timothy, 66, 69–70
Social Gospel, 3
Social Gospel movement, 17–22
   liberal views of, 19
social ministries, 189
social outreach, 188
social reform, 19
Soper, John, 176, 181, 185
souls, Simpson's concern for, 120–26, 130
South America, Alliance missionaries in, 145
speaking in tongues, 13, 83, 86, 160
Speer, Robert, 10, 131, 156
Spencer, Herbert, 16
The Spirit of the Lord; Revivalism in America (Cohen), 28

Stewart, Lyman and Matthew, 17
Stock, Eugene, 72
Stockmayer, Otto, 80, 93, 104
Stoesz, Samuel, 45, 76, 115
street evangelism, 37
Strong, A.H., 109
Student Volunteer Missionary Movement, 2, 7, 10–11, 156
   motto, 140
Sudan Interior Mission, 10, 143, 168
summer conferences
   divine healing message in, 103–4
   Simpson and, 79–81
Summer Faith Convention, 95
Sunday, Billy, 28, 60, 62
Sunday School Times, 141
Swaggart, Jimmy, 164
Synan, Vinson, 68, 87

tabernacle evangelism, 62–63
tabernacle-type building. *See also* Gospel Tabernacle
   Broadway Tabernacle Church, 5
   Simpson's plan for, 123
Takenaga, Robert, 157
Talmage, T. Dewitt, 29
Taylor, Hudson, 2, 9, 72, 80, 143
temperance movement, 137–38
Tertullian, 108
A Theology for the Social Gospel (Rauschenbusch), 21, 129
They Gathered at the River (Weisberger), 27
Third Great Awakening, 3, 23–27, 167
   beginnings, 24–25
   in NYC, 5
   counter-attack on critical view of Scriptures, 17
   evangelism in, 56
   holiness movement in, 91
   and Holy Spirit, 73
   impact of, 52
   Methodists and, 68
   Moody's impact on, 56–60
   Orr's phases, 25–26
   Palmer and, 12
   phases, 55

Index

Thirteenth Street Presbyterian Church, ix, 36–37, 126
  Simpson's resignation, 136
  Simpson's vision of evangelism vs. church leaders, 37, 54
Thomas, Griffith, 99
Thomas, T.V., 64, 122–23, 147, 149–50
Thompson, A.E., 36, 80–81, 162
  A.B. Simpson: His Life and Work, xiii
  on Moody and Simpson, 29
  on Simpson's rearly conception of evangelism, 121
Toccoa Falls College, 179
tongues, speaking in, 13, 83, 86, 160
Torrey, R.A., 13, 26, 28, 60–61, 74, 80, 88, 104, 116, 131, 167
  contribution to Simpson's periodicals, 82
  evangelistic world tour, 61
  in healing movement, 92
  and higher life, 70
  and premillennialsm, 108
  Simpson on, 74
Towns, Elmer, 5
Townsend, Charles, 80
Tozer, A.W., 28, 44, 86, 98, 147, 148–49, 166
  on conventions, 104
  on Simpson's first week at Knox church, 35
  Wingspread, xiii, 178
training, of national leaders, 149
transformational evangelism, 189
Travis, Drake, 104
Triumphs of Truth (Judd-Montgomery), 133
Trudel, Dorothea, 93, 102
  Cullis visit to healing home, 94
True Peace (medieval treatise), 42
Tucker, Ruth, 141
Turnbull, Walter, 42, 51, 79

United States Center of World Missions, 157
United States, Moody return to, 59
universalism, 10
urban areas
  overpopulation in, 3
  Simpson's concern for, 126
urban evangelism, 177, 187–89
  Finney and, 5
  Simpson and, 31, 120

Varg, Paul A., 150
vision, 179
  of Alliance, 187
  of Simpson, 124–25, 175
  for missions, 150–51
von Zinzendorf, Nicolaus Ludwig, 141

Wacker, Grant, 13–14, 15, 70, 84, 87
Walborn, Ron, 158–59, 160, 178, 180, 182, 185, 187
Wardrobe, Dr., 121
Warfield, Benjamin B., 109
Warren, Rick, 179
Watkins Glen, New York, Believer's Conference, 124
W.C.T.U. (Women's Christian Temperance Union), 138
Weber, Timothy, 107, 111–12, 119
websites, with Simpson writings, 155
Weisberger, Bernard, *They Gathered at the River*, 27
Wellhausen, Julius, 2
Welsh Revival, 26, 55
Wesley, Charles, 2, 7
Wesley, John, 2, 7
  on individual salvation, 11
  on sanctification, 66–67
Wesleyan-Holiness movement, 72–73, 77
westernization, by missionaries, 150
Westminster Shorter Catechism, 43
"What would Jesus do?" (WWJD), 21
When the Comforter Came (Simpson), 165
White, Charles, 12
Whitehall, Hannah, *The Christian's Secret of a Happy Life*, 13
Whitfield, George, 7
Whitley, Daniel, 109
Whittle, Daniel, 36, 46, 51, 63, 80, 122
Wholly Sanctified (Simpson), 75, 79, 165
Wiggins, Donald, 174

210

Index

Wilkerson, Bruce, 164–65
Williard, Francis, 131
   letter in *The Alliance Weekly*, 138
Williard Tract Repository, 94
Wilson, Henry, 86, 132, 138
Wimber, John, 159–60
Wingspread (Tozer), xiii, 178
Within Our Reach, 158
Wittemore, Emma W., 132
Woman's Industrial Center, 135
Women's Christian Temperance Union,
   Evangelistic Training School,
   137–38
Wood, Rick, 157
Word of God, Bible as, 19

The Word, the Work, and the World
   (Simpson), 30, 100, 102, 148–49
world evangelism
   Simpson on necessity, 120
   Simpson's burden for, 124
   Simpson's impact on, 140–53
World War I, and end of Third Great
   Awakening, 62

Yale University, 23
YMCA, 11

Zionist movement, 116
Zulauf, Larry, 179, 183, 185
   on mission emphasis, 186

www.ingramcontent.com/pod-product-compliance
Lightning Source LLC
Chambersburg PA
CBHW052339230426
43664CB00041B/2488